The Planctus Mariae *in the Dramatic Tradition*
of the Middle Ages

SANDRO STICCA

THE

PLANCTUS MARIAE

IN THE DRAMATIC TRADITION

OF THE MIDDLE AGES

TRANSLATED BY

JOSEPH R. BERRIGAN

THE UNIVERSITY OF GEORGIA PRESS

ATHENS AND LONDON

© 1988 by the University of Georgia Press
Athens, Georgia 30602
All rights reserved
Set in Linotron Janson
The paper in this book meets the guidelines for permanence and
durability of the Committee on Production Guidelines for
Book Longevity of the Council on Library Resources.

Printed in the United States of America
92 91 90 89 88   5 4 3 2 1

Library of Congress Cataloging in Publication Data

Sticca, Sandro, 1931–
[Planctus Mariae nella tradizione drammatica del Medio Evo. English]
The Planctus Mariae in the dramatic tradition of the Middle Ages / Sandro
Sticca; translated by Joseph R. Berrigan.
p.   cm.
Translation of: Il Planctus Mariae nella tradizione drammatica
del Medio Evo.
Bibliography: p.
Includes index.
ISBN 0-8203-0983-4 (alk. paper)
1. Planctus Mariae.   2. Mary, Blessed Virgin, Saint, in fiction, drama,
poetry, etc.   3. Liturgical drama.   4. Passion-plays—History and
criticism.   5. Christian drama, Latin (Medieval and modern)—History and
criticism.   6. Drama, Medieval—History and criticism.   7. Theater—
History—Medieval, 500–1500.   I. Title.
PA8405.P57E5 1988
809.2'02—dc19
87-12537
CIP

British Library Cataloging in Publication Data available

O Maria, mater Christi,
Quem dolorem habuisti,
Cum in cruce conspexisti
Contemplando filium! . . .

Stabas, virgo, cum dolore
Iuxta crucem cum maerore,
Quasi virga sine flore
Et amittens lilium,
Nec a cruce recedebas
Et in corde perferebas . . .

Intus eras cruciata
Et in mente vulnerata,
Tota quoque denigrata
Perdens vultum roseum,
Duras plagas Iesu Christi
Sola corde pertulisti,
Vere martyr tu fuisti
Per doloris gladium.

De compassione Beatae Mariae Virginis,
Codex Vallicellanus

CONTENTS

FOREWORD

THE great medieval Passion plays stem from the *Ludus Passionis*, from the Latin dramatization of the judgment and Crucifixion of Jesus Christ. This is a point that Sandro Sticca's earlier work has persuasively demonstrated. In the beginnings of *Ludus Passionis*, there was no doubt a representation of the Resurrection framed by the liturgical dialogues between the blessed women and the angel; these were sung in the ninth-century Church and have been called the *Quem quaeritis* after their *incipit*. But there was also the lamentation of Mary at the foot of the Cross, that moving Latin poetry of pathos which leads into a splendid, uninterrupted lyricism that extends from the eleventh century through the *Stabat Mater* of Jacopone da Todi in the thirteenth century and reaches the end of the Middle Ages.

It is that *Planctus Mariae* which Sticca studies here, not just with erudition but with the intellect and feeling which have made his research so valuable. To shed light on this difficult question, it is not enough to be a formidable specialist in the history of theater (and Sticca's eminence in this domain is incontestable). The question requires someone who is also in some sense a man of the field—that is, someone who knows the cult devoted to Mary through lived experience; someone who knows the Mediterranean faith, which is especially constant in the veneration of the Virgin. Not that Sticca depends here on some religious experience that is unrelated to rigorous scholarship. I shall go so far as to say that I do not want to know whether Sticca is a believer or an agnostic. What is vital is that he has seen Italian fervor at work here and has understood what the cult of Our Lady and its basic motivating force have meant for the faithful, whether medieval or modern.

Sticca is a man at the crossroads of cultures, just as the land he came from is at the crossroads of civilizations. Central Italy, in the Middle Ages, enjoyed a privileged location where Byzantium met the West. Byzantium worshipped the *Theotókos*. solemn Mother of the Pantocrator. Herself a Virgin Empress and Mother of an Emperor, she remained fixed in an eternal hieraticism and, in her glory, ignored the suffering of her life on earth. In the West, Mary was given a different face, more touching and fraternal in spite of the majesty of the personage. Sandro Sticca is in an exceptionally good position to understand this metamorphosis, because he himself belongs to two cultures: that of his homeland and that of young America, where he teaches. Through his own individuality, he lives out the enrichment that the contact between these two modes of thinking provides. He knows what the harmonious synthesis between tradition and modernity is, and since he is attached to no one particular school, he has not been taken in by fashionable ideas.

It would no longer seem expedient to return to history and perform a genetic study. Several years ago, in *Cercle magique* (which I do not disparage and which I continue to consider a good book), Henri Rey-Flaud pronounced the death of all evolutionism in medieval theater, where, between liturgical drama and mystery, it should be necessary to establish a solution of radical continuity. Indifferent to Henri Rey-Flaud's interdiction on all evolutionary research, Sandro Sticca has preferred to readdress the problem from zero, as Elie Konigson had done previously in his *Espace théâtral médiéval*. The scope of Sticca's research, however, is different altogether, because he ventures into a field dreaded by the Romanists: that of theology and liturgy.

Still, before considering the cult of Mary, or while defining the modalities of this cult, we must not lose sight of another aspect of the matter, an aspect that interests both the theater historian and the poet. By this I mean the affective, even touching, impact the *Planctus Mariae* had on the medieval mind. Medieval art and literature in the West are readily brought to the expression of paroxysm, a paroxysm discerned in the discourse and gestures of the character suffering. The *Planctus Mariae* partakes of the *planh*, the great funereal lament (which I designate with a noble Occitan word because the troubadours so conspicuously used this moving genre). The death of the hero in the chanson de geste and the romance, or the death of the prince who patronized the poet, is in itself already in lyrical poetry an absolute scandal against which the art of the invective and sorrow dolorously protests. But what can we say when a mother (and what a mother!) grieves over the torture the Son of God has just suffered! Now the striking thing about these lamentations is their relative restraint, their understated discourse, which retains its controlled tone until Mary recalls the Jews' cruelty. Then her words (and I do not hesitate to say "Alas!") yield to the temptation of violence—but have we the right to judge? This is an instance of anti-Judaism more than anti-Semitism, because the issue is not racism, but rather an indignation which is both maternal and religious and which expresses the agitation of the Christian conscience before the revolting condemnation of the Just among just. Is it a coincidence that precisely in these texts is introduced, in the middle of a declamation in Latin, a formulation in the vernacular first almost accidental and fragmented, then better organized, with whole sentences? As early as the twelfth century, in the *Sponsus* by Limouse and the *Jeu de Daniel* by Beauvais, the vernacular had made its appearance in moments of extreme tension. With the *Planctus Mariae*, the presence of the vernacular reinforces the depth of communion between the listeners and the man or woman reciting. The rhetoric, which includes anaphora and plays on words, coincides both with the lyricism and with the dramatic intensity. Did not the most beautiful religious canticles of the Latin liturgy (which, alas, disappeared with Vatican II) spring from this meditation on Our Virgin of Sorrows? I have in mind the *Stabat Mater*, so magnificently orchestrated by the greatest musicians, even before Monteverdi.

The *Planctus Mariae* thus became like a sublime bridge between the two cultures, the Latin and the vernacular, while at the same time it assembled the Mariology of the theologians and the popular devotion of Our Lady in a shared cult of the Woman among all women, who reconciled virginal innocence with the suffering of motherhood. The veneration of Mary expanded in the late eleventh century, after Fulbert de Chartres, and especially in the early twelfth century with Bernard of Clairvaux and, toward 1150, with Eadmer, disciple of Saint Anselm, who contributed to the definition of the Immaculate Conception.

Eva-Ave. To the Eve of perdition, responsible for the fall, is opposed the new Eve, hailed by angels, who was chosen by the Father, was made fruitful by the Holy Spirit, and gave birth to the Redeemer. The *Ordo representacionis adae*, improperly called the *Jeu* or *Mystère d'Adam*, makes full use of this opposition. The early Eve easily falls prey to the Devil's rhetoric, but the succession of the prophets, which makes up the third part of the text (and the most important from a theological point of view) never ceases to highlight the hope for Redemption, of which Mary will be the instrument. In this sequence the poet expands upon the serious pun on *verge* (the rod wielded by Jesse to save suffering humanity) and *Verge* (the Anglo-Norman spelling of *Vierge*, "Virgin"). Gautier de Coinci in turn takes up the development of this rhetoric on *Ave*, anagram of *Eva* (Eve). But he goes even further: for the lady of courtly poets, he substitutes Notre Dame. He writes admirable love songs whose music and lyrics are like those of the most sensitive *trouvères*. The beginning of his songs appears as an enigma: the most perfect woman must be praised; but Gautier informs us very quickly that she whom he glorifies has no court in this world, doesn't deceive her devotees like an earthly woman, is well above all human love affairs, and will intercede for us on Judgment Day by pleading our cause to her divine Son. From Gautier there exist spoken, not sung, contemplations on Mary, written in an anaphoric style whose eloquence foreshadows the art of Charles Peguy. I do not believe this to be fortuitous, inasmuch as the adoration of Mary is, to use a current but very poor expression, extraordinarily "text generating," according to the variations of a style that spontaneously draws inspiration from the litany, with its repertory of refrains, hyperboles, metaphors, and deliberate repetitions.

If it appears that these remarks are quite unrelated to the *Planctus Mariae*, do not be misled. The impetus for this form is inscribed within a greater context. First the twelfth century, and then the thirteenth, saw the West cover itself with cathedrals, most of them dedicated to Our Lady. Innumerable are the portals recounting the life of the Virgin, and the stained-glass windows devoted to Mary. Indeed, the scene that unquestionably dominates these portals and stained-glass windows is that of the heavenly coronation. In iconography, the glorious mystery prevails over the sorrowful mysteries, at least until, in sculpture and painting, there appear the realistic scenes of the apostles' mourning of Mary's death, and the *Pietà* where the *Mater dolorosa* holds the tortured body of Christ on her lap. In the interim Franciscan preaching became widespread. More sensitive to suffering and pathos, because it was more attentive to the humanity of the Savior and his Mother, this preaching did not proceed from a vacuum. It used pre-existing elements as its impetus. The devotion to Mary needed concrete representations. Some of these representations relied on the canonic Gospels for all that concerns the birth and infancy of Jesus; others are based on the Apocrypha for all that concerns the engagement and marriage of Mary and Joseph. Finally, others are the daughters of prayer, of that mystical meditation on the Crucifixion which nurtures religious contemplation, and I will gladly say that the *Planctus Mariae* finds its true origins here, in the inspired and fervent communion of the suppliant with the Madonna of suffering.

Mary is Woman among women, Mother among mothers, but she is also and above all at the foot of the cross, the image of absolute affliction, and her tears fall with the weight of universal evil. Psychoanalysts, whose authority and competence I do not question, can elaborate as much as they like on the people of the Middle Ages who lived in a paternal civilization while cultivating a sort of nostalgic idolatry of maternity. The fact remains that the faith in Our Lady cannot be reduced to this; it expresses something else, which is not only the precious comfort of an indulgent intercession in time of danger, but which can also become a violent discourse when faced with that crime of crimes which is the death (deicide!) of the Just among just. The *Planctus Mariae*, in this perspective, is the channel through which indignation and rage break loose in a controlled manner. Can one not go so far as to say that the *Mater dolorosa* is in some sense spokeswoman for the humble, the mute, all those overwhelmed in the presence of power and injustice? The order of the world is God's: it is not to be questioned. But there are moments when humanity needs to stir, even cry out, and Mary in turn, through submission and restraint, takes on this basic need.

The "mystère" is about to be born, and it will be revealed as a genuinely popular theater type, bringing together around its tumults the entire urban community in a gathering that is both turbulent and unanimous. The *Planctus Mariae* is a sort of obligatory passage point in the unfolding of the performance. It constitutes a "scène à faire" particularly anticipated by the public and which the "fatist" has no right to overlook.

FOREWORD

The *Planctus Mariae* is generally a learned work of art, and its declamation, which was long and slow, demanded of the actor endurance and of the audience its prolonged attention. Through it, we discover an art of speaking, and even an art of living. Sandro Sticca has understood this. He has seen in these lyrics the basis for a great book, and I wish this book an audience comparable to that of the great medieval texts—that is, an audience with leisure, fervor, and wonder, not rushed and thus imprisoned by time, but which on the contrary might, through reading, be raised to a certain contemplation.

JEAN CHARLES PAYEN
Université de Caen
TRANSLATED BY MICHÈLE M. HEALY

PREFACE

N the Western theatrical tradition, the *Planctus Mariae* constitutes a lyrical-dramatic motif of remarkable importance not only as a literary form but, in particular, as an essential and fruitful manifestation of the Marian exegetical thought of the Middle Ages. In the history of the medieval theater, the *Planctus Mariae* did not assume a prominent role in the commemoration of the most salient and dramatic events in Christ's Passion until the beginning of the twelfth century. Its genesis and evolution must be found, however, in the confluence of the Eastern and Western cultural and spiritual traditions. With the authority and speculative vigor of their exegesis of the behavior of the Virgin at the foot of the cross, these traditions wove a liturgical and theological fabric upon which were grafted the lyrical and dramatic dimensions of the character of the Mother in the Passion plays.

Born, as a thematic-liturgical motif, within the confines of the ecclesiastical culture of the Eastern world, the *Planctus Mariae* was the expression of a liturgical heritage that inserted in the concrete reality of the divine drama of the Son the consideration of the anguish of the human drama of the Mother. In the sacred and solemn mystery of the Redemption of the world, Eastern theological thought dwelled on the illumination of the most intimate maternal aspects of Mary, who, by manifesting at the foot of the cross her sorrowful humaneness, in her inner tragedy participated in the bloody physical martyrdom of her Son.

A chronological study of the sources reveals that in the twelfth century in particular, the dramatization of Christ's Passion was marked by a more intimate, vibrant, and pervasive participation of the Virgin in her Son's redemptive sacrifice. This was accomplished through the creation of a new and intensely powerful iconography of the Passion in which a highly sensitive dramatic language heightened the tragic character of the divine sacrifice. This sacrifice in turn was reflected and detailed with incisive and tortured etching in the Mother's heart.

The origins of the forces that endowed the sorrowful symphony of the maternal anguish and torment at the foot of the cross with expressive vitality and sensitivity are to be found, however, at the dawn of the Eastern theological tradition. In illustrating the dogma of the human redemption, the early Eastern tradition exhibited the initial character and the vital theological trends that led toward the actual historical development of the doctrine of the compassion of the Virgin Mary. Beginning in the second century, with the earliest biblical exegeses and the direct testimonies of the first Church fathers, and extending through the tenth, the motif of the *Mater dolorosa* was expressed in tableaux of daring dramatization and tender spiritual sensitivity. Thus the suffering Virgin communicated the ontological and theological meaning of the Passion and Resurrection of her Son.

During the early years of the patristic era, the Western church elaborated an atemporal and rigid vision of the Virgin at the foot of the cross, a Virgin completely abstract and dogmatic in her expression of a composed inner plaint. At the beginning of the eleventh and especially during the twelfth century, the vision moved from the confines of this hieratic and iconic representation of the Virgin to express—in vibrant emotional effusions, with psychological subtlety, and in scorching dramatic language—all the extreme agony carved in the face and in the heart of the grieving Mother as she contemplated the intense torment and suffering of her Son.

In the exploration of the earliest historical phases and of the most ancient manifestations of the *Planctus Mariae* and, later, in the description of the rich blossoming of *Planctus* that occurred in successive centuries, I have tried to reproduce a considerable number of *Planctus*, often in their entirety. The inclusion of these selections, which range from the most ancient compositions to the most recent texts (at times not easily found) not only strengthens our research but offers the opportunity for a reading of those texts that constitute a tangible and illustrative manifestation of the genesis and elaboration of the *Planctus Mariae* throughout the centuries.

The fundamental purpose of this work is twofold. First, I shall attempt to illustrate, chronologically, the delineation of the spiritual attitudes and the theological motifs and trends that determined the origin and development of the motif of the Virgin's compassion within the tradition of the Eastern, and later the Western, church. Second, we shall examine the articulation of the motif—its vitality and its characteristics in the medieval Latin dramatic tradition, and particularly its extraordinary fortune in the Latin Passion plays of the twelfth and thirteenth centuries. To illumine and nourish the study of the various phases in the evolution of the *Planctus Mariae*, we shall consider, in the context of the ecclesiastical culture of the Middle Ages, the cultural and ritual patrimony of the Catholic liturgy. The *Planctus Mariae* draws its essential character from the liturgy, and within the liturgy it expresses its tendencies and its theatrical elaborations. The volume will also study the vernacular Passion dramas of the later Middle Ages by employing a comparative method of inquiry to address the difficult problem of influence and affinities and of transmission and convergence between national traditions, together with the question of the relation of later to earlier *Planctus*. We shall also consider the nature of dramatic *inventio*, the function of literary bilingualism, and the influence exercised on the late medieval drama by the uninterrupted liturgical tradition.

SANDRO STICCA
Vestal, New York—Tocco Casauria, 1988

The Planctus Mariae *in the Dramatic Tradition*
of the Middle Ages

CHAPTER I

THE CRITICAL CONTEXT

OVER the years students of medieval sacred drama have conducted deep and systematic researches on its origins, its forms, and its diffusion. These researches have been marked by the remarkable amount of space they have assigned to the investigation and explanation of the role of the Virgin in medieval drama. In the traditional context of the penetrating studies dedicated to commenting on and interpreting the dramatic texts of the liturgy of Holy Week, especially those that recall the central events of the Passion, death, and Resurrection of Christ, there have been some studies devoted to illuminating the theme of the dramatic tension in the heart of the Virgin, who shares in the sorrows and suffering of her Son.

The dramatic presentation of the redemptive sacrifice of the God-Man was formed and presented within the stylistic structure of the symbolic language and of the traditional ceremonies associated with the liturgy. Within the limits set by the learned and austere rituals of the Church, medieval dramatists were able to express in detail through passionate dramatic movements the emotional intensity evoked by the Mother's pathos projected upon the central background of her Son's Passion. The traditional exegesis of the New Testament had established a deep and vital bond between the Mother and the Son. This bond was theologically consecrated and nurtured by the mystery of the incarnation, which proclaimed her *Theotókos*, Mother of God. It had been vivified by her acceptance of her Son's sorrowful mission, by her conformity to his Passion, and by her sharing in his sufferings upon the cross. As a mystical and human relationship, it was deeply engraved upon the mind of medieval man. And it is precisely on the human motherhood of Mary, in whose heart are stamped the suffering and the death of her Son, that the medieval dramatist dwells with delight, to interpret and to represent theatrically her profound inner anguish.

Medieval authors in their dramatic presentation of the Passion of Christ thus assigned a pre-eminent and enormous role to the Virgin; this role transcends the eschatological and spiritual character of her divine motherhood and finds expression in the representation and evocation of a mother's tenderness. It comes to full voice in independent lyrical compositions, the *Planctus Mariae*, which emphasize the image of the sorrowful Virgin at the foot of the cross and in perfect communion with the sufferings of her Son. As such, they symbolize and embody the sorrow and the compassion of her human motherhood. The consideration of the abundant production and dissemination of these *Planctus Mariae* and their presence in the most ancient dramas of the Passion have led some scholars to regard the lament of the Virgin as the kernel of the drama of the Passion.

The majority of the early students of medieval religious drama considered the *Planctus Mariae* as the most important factor and stimulus in determining the origin of the drama of the Passion. Already in 1893 Wechssler declared, in his *Die Romanischen Marienklagen*, that the High Middle Ages did not know any dramatic representation of the Passion apart from the *Planctus Mariae*.[1] The same theory was held by the French scholar De Julleville and the German Creizenach.[2]

A more cautious opinion was expressed by George Coffin Taylor, one of the first English scholars to interest himself in the study of the *Planctus*. Although he realized that the theory that considers the *Planctus* as the kernel of the drama of the Passion was not applicable to such late dramatic compositions as the English representations of the fourteenth century, he still held that it could be applied to the most ancient or primitive period of medieval drama.[3] A few years later, Karl Young, one of the most noted specialists in medieval religious theater, concluded, after presenting a splendid examination of the *Planctus*, that "so far as we can tell, the composition of the *Planctus Mariae* was the first step taken towards the dramatization of the Passion."[4] Young was following in the footsteps of Chambers, who had already in 1903 categorically affirmed that the *Planctus* had to be considered the starting point of a drama of the Passion.[5]

This theory had already been suggested by Sepet in 1901. After indicating that the semidramatic chanting of the Passion in the Roman liturgy of Holy Week was the first step toward the redaction of a drama of the Passion, he said that "les lamentations dialoguées du vendredi saint fournirent un des moyens de développement de ces premiers drames de la Passion."[6] The conclusions reached by Young derive from his theory, shared by other contemporary students of medieval drama, that the custom of using the *Planctus Mariae* in the drama may have been suggested to ecclesiastical poets by more ancient laments, such as those uttered by the three Marys, and by such diverse laments of the Virgin of the twelfth century as the *Planctus ante nescia* of Geoffrey of Breteuil and the intensely dramatic *Planctus* of the thirteenth century, which begins "Flete, fideles anime."[7]

In more recent times, Richard Kienast, in his essay "Die deutschsprachige Lyrik des Mittelalters," has contributed to this polarization of ideas by asserting that the laments of Mary are a lyrical subspecies of ecclesiastical Latin poetry which later developed in dramatic form. These laments, which according to Lipphardt[8] and Kienast[9] were originally sung in the liturgical office of Good Friday, were sometimes transformed into semidramatic representations. Cremaschi has traced their passage from lyric to dramatic form.

In the beginning their form was lyric; but soon the dialogue kernels developed. And with the delineation of the action, from the hymn one passed into drama, which gave shape to the representation of the attitudes of the *Virgo dolens* and of the Marys present with her at the foot of the Cross, with a realistic development and an elaborate amplification of the scene hardly alluded to in the Gospel.[10]

The deeply dramatic *Planctus* of the fourteenth century preserved at Cividale,[11] for example, which was recited *in die Parasceven* and which includes numerous precious rubrics prescribing imitative gestures for the actors, contains about nine stanzas identical with those we find, in large measure, in the lyrical *Planctus* "Flete, fideles animae."[12] We shall provide only a couple of stanzas to give an idea of the textual identity of the two *Planctus*.

Cividale *Planctus*	"Flete, fideles animae" *Planctus*
Flete, fideles anime,	1a. Flete, fideles animae,
flete, sorores optime,	flete, sorores optime,
ut sint multiplices	ut sint multiplices
doloris indices,	doloris indices
planctus et lacrime	planctus et lacrime.
Fleant materna viscera	1b. Fleant materna viscera
Marie [matris] vulnera	Marie matris vulnera
materne doleo	materne doleo
que dici soleo	que dici soleo
felix puerpera.	felix puerpera.

To intensify the dramatic moment, the writers of subsequent *Planctus* usually would indiscriminately incorporate in their laments stanzas taken from earlier laments; they were much less concerned with thematic unity than with the creation of pathos. One of the two Latin *Planctus* of the fourteenth century, recently discovered in the Biblioteca Civica of Bergamo,[13] includes four stanzas also found in the "Flete, fideles animae" and two in a *Planctus* of uncertain date which begins "Qui per viam pergitis."[14] A third *Planctus* of the fourteenth century, contained in the *Ordinarium ecclesiae Patavinae*,[15] has about twelve stanzas that are also found in the *Planctus* "Flete, fideles animae" of the thirteenth century. This *Planctus*, discovered by Billanovich, is the very same text made known by the bishop of Padua, Dondi Orologi, in his *Dissertation upon the Rites, Discipline, and Customs of the Church of Padua to the Fourteenth Century* (1816). This *Planctus*, which constitutes a text similar to the lament "Flete, fideles animae" published by Young, is exactly the text the American scholar sought in vain to discover.[16]

The *Ordinarium ecclesiae Patavinae* acquires a very high importance in the history of the medieval religious theater, not only because its two processionals include rites of an earlier period but also because the *Planctus Mariae*, *Offitium sepulchri*, and *Planctus Magdalenae* contained in them constitute, as Billanovich declares, "a summary drama of the Passion."[17] The procession of Holy Saturday, which is described in the second *Processional*,

C 56, is palpably dramatic in its liturgical language as well as in some of its gestures, which are decidedly imitative.

In general terms, the theories expressed by Young and Kienast are conceptually identical with that of Creizenach, who had asserted that the amplifications of dialogue in the sequence *Planctus ante nescia* were used in a period in which there were no authentic dramas of the Passion and that the authors of the dramas of the Passion used them later for their own purposes or dramatic intentions.[18] Creizenach admits the possibility that the contrary could have happened, that is, that the authors of the dramas of Good Friday could have derived their material from extensive texts of the Passion.

Although different theories have been offered to show the derivation of the drama of the Passion from the *Planctus*, no substantial evidence has so far been presented to prove the origin of a drama of the Passion from a *Planctus*. Even the laments from Cividale, Bergamo, and Padua, though they are full of realistic expressions and actions which approach a true dramatic action, do not represent the events that precede and follow the Crucifixion itself.

Possibly, as some scholars have suggested, one could consider the *Planctus* as one of the elements of development, though not as the formative starting point, of the drama of the Passion.[19] In this regard, we are in agreement with the theatrical critic Hardin Craig, who has wisely observed that "although these *Planctus* are always found in Passion plays, they are not in essence dramatic and are not the seed from which the Passion grew."[20] We are in agreement with him but not for the reason given. In an article entitled "The Origin of the Passion Play: Matters of Theory as Well as Fact," Craig observes that, for a work to be dramatic, it must possess action, personification, and dialogue, the *sine qua non* of a drama; he adds that the *Planctus* are not dramatic because they lack action.[21]

One can affirm, to the contrary, that a *Planctus* included in a drama can be rendered dramatic by the addition of movement and through the lyrical intensification of the dramatic moment. A fundamental confirmation of our assertion is found in the dramatic Latin Passion of Montecassino, composed in the first half of the twelfth century. This Passion concludes with a brief *Planctus* or lament of the Virgin which contains precisely the three elements that Craig considers essential for a drama: action, personification, and dialogue. In this Passion, in fact, the Virgin is described as weeping with imitative gestures at the foot of the cross, while she recites a lament of three verses in the vernacular.

> . . . te portai nillu meu ventre
> Quando te beio [mo] ro presente
> Nillu teu regnu agi me a mmente.[22]

But we must return to the theory of Young to determine both its validity and the problems it raises. The fundamental argument upon which he and his successors have based the theory of the origin of the drama of the Passion from the *Planctus* is that some laments of the Virgin are dramatic and that the *Planctus ante nescia*, which appears in many dramas of the thirteenth century, actually goes back to the twelfth.[23] It is the same argument recently repeated by Grano, who declares along the same lines as Young that the "*Planctus ante nescia*, composed during the twelfth century, is especially important for the dramatic intensity of the laments of the Virgin; some of the stanzas of this poem in fact will be subsequently taken up again and included in dialogue *Planctus* of successive epochs."[24]

Whatever value we might attribute to this temporal succession contemplated by Young and the scholars who share his theory, even in as weak a form as a *post hoc, ergo propter hoc* argument, we can now decisively reject it altogether, because the drama of Montecassino presents a Passion of the twelfth century more intensely dramatic and more ample than any extant formal laments, whether of the twelfth or thirteenth century. Further, at its conclusion it contains a brief *Planctus*, which is as old as the ample and lyrical *Planctus ante nescia* and probably even older. The theory, then, that the *Planctus* is the germinal point of the dramas of the Passion loses all its value and must be rejected. Since we now possess a text of the Passion older than or contemporary with the *Planctus*, the latter loses its importance as the creative element of the Passion.

Furthermore, there does not appear to be any theoretical reason to make us suppose that the *Planctus* should be considered older than the representation of the Passion itself, since, after all, the most important liturgical event that the faithful had to recall during Lent was not the lament or the plaint of Mary but the Passion of Christ. The lament of the Virgin constituted a secondary, accessory element in the Passion and not the other way around. As Emile Mâle, the brilliant critic of art, observes with intellectual lucidity, the Passion of Christ constituted the most stirring, incessant, total, and universal speculative interest of the Middle Ages; in fact, "la Passion fut, à vrai dire, l'unique étude du moyen âge."[25]

The Church emphasized the paschal liturgy because the consecration and sanctification of Christ, realized in his Resurrection, had an effect upon all men, and the definitive grade of Christian perfection was reached with one's corporeal resurrection in Christ. "Pascha nostrum immolatus est Christus. . . . Qui mortem nostram moriendo destruxit, et vitam resurgendo reparavit."[26] And naturally, as several scholars have declared, the history of the liturgy, especially the knowledge of the history of the liturgy of Holy Week and of the dramatic character that distinguishes it, is fundamental for our understanding of how the *Planctus* was inserted in the events therein described.[27]

Although it is true, as Young declares, that the meditations upon the sufferings of Mary appear early in the Western church, it is just as true that these meditations always appear in connection with the Passion of Christ. Even in such tracts on the sufferings of Mary, as the *Dialogus Mariae et Anselmi de Passione Domini* of Anselm (1033–1109)[28] and the *Liber de Passione* of Bernard (1091–1153)[29] of the twelfth century, the *Meditationes vitae Christi* of Pseudo-Bonaventure (1221–74)[30] and the *Stabat Mater* of Jacopone da Todi (1230–1306)[31] of the thirteenth century, the *Arbor vitae crucifixae Jesu* of Ubertino da Casale (1259–1329)[32] and the *Vita Christi* of Ludolph of Saxony (d. 1377)[33] of the fourteenth century, and the *Sermo LVI: De sanctissima Passione et mysteriis crucis* of Bernardine of Siena (1380–1444)[34] of the fifteenth century, the Passion of Christ always occupies the central and preponderant part. In the *Liber de Passione* of Bernard, for example, we are struck by the sentiments and emotions given to Mary.

> Aspiciebat et ipse benignissimo vultu me matrem plorantem, et me verbis paucis consolari voluit. Sed ipsis consolari non poteram, sed flebam dicendo, et dicebam plorando: Fili mi, quis mihi dabit, ut ego moriar pro te? Moritur

filius, cur nec secum misera moritur mater ejus? Amor unice, fili me, fili me dulcissime, noli me derelinquere post te, trade me ad te ipsum, ut ipsa moriar tecum.[35]

But in his *Meditatio in Passionem et Resurrectionem Domini*, in his *Lamentatio in Passionem Christi*, in his *Sermo de vita et Passione Domini*,[36] it is to the Passion of Christ that he gives pre-eminence. And in his *Rhythmica oratio ad unum quodlibet membrorum Christi patientis et cruce pendentis* he sings a hymn to the sufferings of Christ which is regarded as one of the noblest raptures of compassion ever expressed by the human heart.

AD PEDES

Clavos pedum, plagas duras,
Et tam graves impressuras
Circumplector cum affectu,
Tuo pavens in aspectu,
Tuorum memor vulneratum . . .

Plagas tuas rubicundas,
Et fixuras tam profundas,
Cordi meo fac inscribi,
Te modi amans omnibus . . .

AD GENUA

O quam pauper! o quam nudus!
Qualis est in cruce ludus
Derisorum totus factus,
Sponte tamen, non coactus,
Attritus membris omnibus! . . .

In hac cruce te cruentum,
Te contemptum et distentum,
Ut requiram, me impelle,
Et hoc imple meum velle,
Facturus quod desidero . . .

AD MANUS

Manus clavis perforatas,
Et cruore purpuratas,
Corde primo prae amore,
Sitibundo bibens ore,
Cruoris stillicidium . . .

In hac cruce sic intensus,
In te meos trahe sensus,
Meum posse, velle, scire,
Cruci tuae fac servire,
Me tuis apta brachiis . . .

AD LATUS

Salve, latus Salvatoris
In quo latet mel dulcoris,
In quo patet vis amoris
Ex quo scatet fons cruoris,
Qui corda lavat sordida . . .

Plaga rubens, aperire,
Fac cor meum te sentire,
Sine me in te transire,
Vellem totus introire;
pulsanti pande pauperi . . .

AD PECTUS

Pectus mihi confer mundum,
Ardens, pium, gemebundum,
Voluntatem abnegatam,
Tibi semper conformatam,
Juncta virtutum copia . . .

Dulcis Jesu Christi pectus,
Tuo fiam dono rectus,
Absolutus a peccatis,
Ardens igne caritatis
Ut semper te recogitem . . .

THE PLANCTUS MARIAE

AD COR

O mors illa quam amara,
Quam immitis, quam avara;
Quae per cellam introivit,
In qua mundi vita vivit.
Te mordens, cor dulcissimum . . .

O cor dulce praedilectum,
Munda cor meum illectum,
Et in vanis induratum;
Pium fac et timoratum,
Repulso tetro frigore . . .

Viva cordis voce clamo,
Dulce cor; te namque amo:
Ad cor meum inclinare,
Ut se possit applicare,
Devoto tibi pectore . . .

AD FACIEM

Salve, caput cruentatum,
Totum spinis coronatum,
Conquassatum, vulneratum,
Arundine verberatum,
Facie sputie illita . . .

In hac tua passione,
Me agnosce, Pastor bone,
Cujus sumpsi mel ex ore,
Haustum lactis cum dulcore,
prae omnibus deliciis.

Non me reum asperneris,
Nec indignum dedigneris,
Morte tibi jam vicina,
Tuum caput hic inclina,
In meis pausa brachiis.

> Tuae sanctae passioni
> Me gauderem interponi,
> In hac cruce tecum mori;
> Praesta crucis amatori
> Sub tua cruce moriar.[37]

The devotion to the Passion of Christ, nurtured by the exquisite sensibility of Saint Anselm, finds its greatest expression in the intense pathos accorded to it by Saint Bernard. An inexhaustible love for Christ crucified was the central point of the life of Saint Bernard and the guide for his feelings and his emotions: "Haec mea sublimior interim philosophia, scire Jesum, et hunc crucifixum."[38] The contemplation and the elaboration, on the part of Saint Bernard, of the sufferings of Christ initiated a new stream of spirituality, because, as Pourrat observes, his mystical writings "des le XIIᵉ siècle, orientèrent les coeurs vers les mystères de la vie terrestre, en particulier vers ceux de sa naissance et de sa passion."[39]

Even in the thirteenth century, the fundamental mystical activity of Saint Bonaventure is centered on considerations of the life and Passion of Jesus in the *Lignum vitae*, in the *Officium de Passione*, in the *Vitis mystica*, and in other writings of his. In the *De perfectione vitae* he writes, for example, "Quoniam devotionis fervor per frequentem Christi passionis memoriam nutritur et conservatur in homine, ideo necesse est, ut frequenter, ut semper oculis cordis sui Christum in cruce tamquam morientem videat qui devotionem in se vult inextinguibilem conservare."[40]

This dwelling upon the Passion of Christ was a duty of the Christian and especially of the Franciscan, for whom the entirety of his religious experience was summarized in the motto of the order, "Mihi absit gloriari nisi in cruce Domini."[41] This participation in the Passion of Christ was a cherished and sought-after ideal for Saint Francis.[42] In fact, the sufferings of the Redeemer upon the cross constitute for Saint Bonaventure, as for every Franciscan, "the center of all man's hope of salvation, his only consolation, his sorrow and his delight."[43] In his splendid volume *Letteratura religiosa dal Due al Novecento*, Getto emphasizes the Christocentric spirituality of Saint Francis by asserting that to the theme of the wounds of the crucified Christ outlined by Saint Bernard, Saint Francis contributed "a decisive impetus, so that under the banner of Franciscan spirituality there . . . develop[ed] the typical devotions of the creche and of the way of the cross." He further asserts that together with the devotion to the humanity of Christ, "the theme of the Passion of Christ forms an essential motif of the saint's biography."[44]

The centrality of the human nature of Christ, experienced so dramatically and expressed so realistically by Saint Francis, was emphasized more incisively and elaborated more spaciously in successive centuries by such illustrious Franciscan theologians and exegetes as Alexander of Hales, Robert Grosseteste, Richard of Middleton, Scotus, Berthold of Regensburg, William Melton, and Nicholas Phillip. Both the constant contemplation of the sufferings of Christ and the absolute devotion to his Passion remained the fundamental pivots of Franciscan spirituality, since they were regarded as essential in achieving conformity with the Person of Christ.[45]

Since the physical and human reality of the sufferings of Christ during his Passion is founded upon, as we shall see later, the authority of Holy Scripture and constitutes a fundamental truth of theology, we could almost affirm with Etienne Gilson, although in the context of our investigation this may seem paradoxical, that "les Franciscains n'ont jamais considéré la dévotion à la Passion comme une dévotion nouvelle, mais ils ont vécu ce drame avec une intensité jamais égalée jusqu'à saint François, le mettant au centre de tout."[46] Especially during the thirteenth century, this new Christocentric spirituality, in the footsteps of the inheritance passed down by Saint Francis, was structured in systematic forms of Christocentric spirituality focused upon devotion to Christ and to his Passion.[47]

Of particular importance in our context is the flowering, in the Abruzzi, of Christocentric sequences, especially those composed by Thomas of Celano, which begin respectively "Fregit victor virtualis" and "Sanctitatis nova signa." Thomas displays the dynamic influence of Franciscan Christocentric inspiration—in fact, he was a member of the order—when he recalls with a power both emotional and realistic, in the sequence "Fregit victor virtualis," the importance that the sufferings of Christ crucified had for Saint Francis:

> Dicas nobis, O Francisce,
> cur affixus sis in cruce?
> —Quia mundi abdicator
> atque crucis imitator,
> vitae Christi baiulus
>
> Dicas nobis, o Francisce,
> cur affixus sis in cruce?
> —Amor Iesu me incendens,
> atque dulcor cor absorbens,
> auxit desideria . . .
>
> Dic, Francisce, quid vidisti
> contemplando plagas Christi?
> —Mentem mire inflammari,
> ac Dilecti transformari
> in fulgidam speciem.
>
> Dic, Francisce, quid vidisti
> contemplando plagas Christi?
> —Manus, pedes conclavari,
> dextrum latus lanceari,
> Christi servum immutari
> in Suam effigiem . . .[48]

The expressive and realistic intensity of this Franciscan Christocentric spirituality manifested itself during the thirteenth century, in Europe, in popular religious poetry. Its most exalted impulse, both lyrical and dramatic, was offered in Italy by the Passion-centered mysticism of Jacopone da Todi.[49] Formed in the cultural context of a spirituality blended of Benedictine and Franciscan elements,[50] "he assimilated and developed the grand themes of primitive Franciscanism and of the Spirituals."[51] He exploded in a poetic experience founded upon penitential asceticism, which gushed forth violently and dramatically from an exuberant and dramatic Christocentrism and from the "firm conviction of human incapacity to compensate for the sacrifice of Christ."[52]

The novelty and the emotional content of Franciscan spirituality, so far removed from sacramental traditions and theological symbolism, was widely propagated and diffused by means of the spread of the Franciscans in the Western world. Of particular significance is the contribution of Franciscan spirituality to the development of medieval theater in England. The first group of Franciscans reached England in 1224. Within five years of their arrival they had established a dozen communities of friars, and by 1240 there were already thirty-four communities of the Friars Minor. Even more extraordinary is the fact that by 1282 or so the Franciscan order possessed 1,583 communities in Europe.

The first contact of the Franciscans with the English theater took place by order of Bishop Grosseteste of London, himself a Franciscan. Concerned about the irreverent character of contemporary religious dramas, he encouraged the Franciscans to take charge of them. Franciscan spirituality, as both Jeffrey and Pasch have declared, made a fundamental contribution to the aesthetics of medieval England of the thirteenth and fourteenth centuries, especially in the fields of art, lyric, and drama. It opened a new chapter in English art and literature, which now transcended the absolute, abstract, and doctrinaire values of tradition and emphasized the devotional and popular aspects of its several forms of cultural activity.[53] It seems now to be a matter of historical certainty that as long as the religious dramas were presented in church or on church grounds, first the Franciscans and later the other friars and secular clergy were directly responsible for the presentation of these dramas.[54]

In one study of elevated sensibility, both critical and interpretative, entitled "Franciscan Spirituality and the Rise of Early English Drama," a study of inestimable value for an understanding of the full influence of Franciscan spirituality upon the theater of medieval England, Jeffrey points out that the two oldest theatrical representations which made an original contribution to the spread of the dramatic tradition in the vernacular in the Middle Ages are the Anglo-Norman *Jeu d'Adam*,[55] composed between 1140 and 1175, and the drama of the Nativity of Saint Francis, which was probably presented for the first time around 1223.[56] The value of the drama of the Nativity of Saint Francis consists in its being the prototype, in the evangelical program of the Franciscans, of a dramatic tradition based on biblical themes, on the use of lyrics in the vernacular, and on the participation of confraternities in theatrical representations. These initial cultural activities of the Franciscans were distinctive precisely for their profoundly popular character and their use of the vernacular.

No less important are those studies which have attempted to weigh the contribution of the dramatic qualities of the homily or sermon of Dominican and Franciscan preachers to the development of the theater in medieval England. These qualities influenced the transition of medieval English theater from liturgical to conspicuously indigenous and popular forms.[57] According to Jeffrey, one of the principal aspects of Franciscan religious pedagogy in England was the semidramatic structure of its sermons, especially those passages intended to accentuate the spectacular elements of biblical episodes in preaching.[58] Jeffrey establishes a direct relationship between the dramatic sermon of England and the Italian *sermone semidrammatico*, a semitheatrical form originally introduced into their sermons by Franciscans in Italy. De Bartholomaeis ascribes the origin and development of the semidramatic sermon exclusively to the Franciscans of the Abruzzi.[59] The influence of Franciscan spirituality and aesthetics is reflected not only in the English sermon of the thirteenth and fourteenth centuries, but especially in the dramatic productions of England in that time. MS Cotton Vespasianus D. VIII, for example, the manuscript which contains the dramatic cycle of the city of Coventry, indicates the role of the Franciscans in the representation of these plays: "Videntur olim coram populo sive ad instruendum sive ad placendum a Fratribus Mendicantibus representata." And on the flyleaf, in a later hand, one can read: "Elenchus contentorum in hoc codice: Contenta Novi Testamenti scenice expressa et actitata olim per monachos sive fratres mendicantes vulgu dicitur hic Liber Ludus Coventriae sive Ludus Corporis Christi."[60]

The active role of Franciscans in the staging of religious dramas in the city of York and the influence of their spirituality upon the dramatic structure of the morality play *The Castle of Perseverance* (first part of the fifteenth century) and of the processional drama *The Conversion of Saint Paul* have already been established.[61] Other studies have evaluated the available material and have studied in detail the verse satire *On the Minorite Friars*, of

Wycliffite origin, which deals explicitly with the Franciscans and their activities in the field of religious theater.[62] They have thus provided the proper frame and perspective for the Franciscans' contribution to early English drama. The present state of research indicates that, in its totality and complexity, the early religious dramatic activity in England developed in large measure within the orbit of Franciscan spirituality, upon the background of the spirit of joy, song, and drama inherited from the sainted founder of the order.[63]

The profound interest in the sufferings of Christ and the pathos which meditations upon them provoked can be better seen in some stanzas from the *Laudismus de sanctae crucis*[64] of Bonaventure with whom "le Crucifix vint occuper la place centrale dans la plus haute synthèse qu'ait jamais élaborée la théologie contemplative."[65] In this hymn the faithful are invited to recall the Passion of Christ, to meditate upon it and to take delight in it:

> Recordare sanctae crucis
> Qui perfectam vitam ducis,
>   Delectare iugiter;
> Sanctae crucis recordare,
> Et in ipsa meditare
>   Insatiabiliter.

And as if this were not enough, the faithful are exhorted to live in the light of the cross and to grow under its banner with all the yearning of their heart. This is an ascetic program of inner experience, which is translated into an ardent and rigorous contemplation of the *Christus patiens*. It involves the whole existence of the faithful in a tension toward the realization of the finest and most exquisite participation in the *mysterium Passionis*.

> Stes in cruce Christo duce,
> Donec vivas in hac luce
>   Moto procul taedio,
> Non quiescas nec tepescas,
> In hoc crescas et calescas
>   Cordis desiderio.

> Ama crucem, mundi lucem,
> Et habebis Christum ducem
>   Per aeterna saecula;
> Cruce corpus circumcinge,
> Hanc constringe, manu pinge
>   Consignando singula . . .
>
> Crux in corde, crux in ore
> Quodam intimo sapore
>   Det tibi dulcedinem,
> Crux in membris dominetur
> Et ubique situetur
>   Intra totum hominem.

The faithful are invited to contemplate the physical results of the bloody Passion of Christ, to understand its mystical and theological intensity and value:

> Quaere crucem, quaere clavos,
> Quaere manus, pedes cavos,
>   Quaere fossam lateris;
> Ibi plaude, ibi gaude
> Sine fraude summa laude,
>   Quantumcunque poteris.

And finally, after an intense meditation and elaboration of the stupendous theological and symbolical significance of the cross, the final mystical sublimation is achieved by a direct luminous relationship between the faithful and the cross:

> Circa crucem exercere
> Mentem debes, huic placere
>   Et hanc semper gerere;
> Hoc est opus salutare
> Circa crucem laborare
>   Corde, ore, opere . . .

Bone frater, quidquid agas
Crucifixi vide plagas
Et sibi compatere,
Omni tempore sint tibi
Quasi spiritales cibi,
His gaudenter fruere.[66]

It seems obvious, therefore, in the light of this devotional emotionalism and of the speculative vigor of medieval Christocentric concentration upon the Passion, that the meditations on the Passion of Christ of the twelfth and thirteenth centuries are contemporaneous with the meditations upon the sufferings of Mary.

CHAPTER II

MARY AS CO-REDEMPTRIX

THE temporal coexistence of this Christian and Marian piety can be explained more fully and simply in relation to the *Zeitgeist* of the twelfth century, which made possible their parallel development. The mystical concentration upon the human suffering of Christ and upon the compassion of Mary for her Son are in fact felt most intensely in that century. And just as the impulse toward a representation of a drama of the Passion was supplied by a consideration of the human nature of Christ in the act of redemption, so too it is possible to discover the antecedents of the *Planctus Mariae* in the light of theological discussions concerning the role of Mary in the redemption of the human race.

Nowhere in the Bible are any expressions of sorrow attributed to Mary. Of the four evangelists only John notes her presence at the Crucifixion; and yet this episode was to receive special attention from medieval dramatists. They were fascinated by the dramatic possibilities inherent in the behavior of Mary at the foot of the cross, and invariably they emphasized her maternal sorrow at the sight of her suffering Son. On this subject they preferred to follow the authority of tradition. The early fathers and theologians of the Church, while they recognized that the Virgin suffered on Calvary, debated at great length the question of her behavior. On the basis of the biblical account of John, "Stabant autem iuxta crucem Iesu mater eius, et soror matris eius, Maria Cleophae, et Maria Magdalene,"[1] Saint Ambrose conjured up the vision of a firm and stalwart Virgin on Golgotha, in his *Letter LXIII* to the church of Vercelli. "Fugientibus apostolis, ante crucem stabat, et piis spectabat oculis vulnera, quia expectabat non pignoris mortem, sed mundi salutem";[2] in his *De institutione Virginis*, "Stabat ante crucem mater, et fugientibus viris, stabat intrepida. . . . Stabat non degeneri spectaculo,

19

quae non metuebat preremptorem. Pendebat in cruce Filius, Mater se persecutoribus offerebat";[3] and even more explicitly in his *De obitu Valentiniani consolatio*, "Stabat sancta Maria juxta crucem Filii, et spectabat Virgo sui unigeniti passionem. Stantem illam lego, flentem non lego."[4]

The vision of an austere and ascetic Virgin seems to have been prevalent in the early years of the Christian era. Her constancy and her strength during the Crucifixion are commented upon, for example, in an Ambrosian *Missale* in the preface to the feast of the seven sorrows of Mary.

> Per Christum Dominum nostrum. Cuius sacratissima Humanitas ligno crucis suspensa, astante Virgine Matre, Adae posteros, vetitae arboris attactu iustae morte addictos, ad aeternam vitam misericorder revocavit. Vulnera, quae Iudaeorum perfidia castissimis Iesu Christi membris infligebat, fortis dilectio in dulcissimae Matris corde revocabat. Christus ad delenda hominum peccata mortem subire non timuit: Maria proprium pectus, morientis Filii doloris aemulum, immolavit.[5]

In theological terms the doctrinal problem that presented itself to the medieval exegetical tradition was this: to determine if in her participation in the act of Redemption on Golgotha the Virgin experienced more joy than sorrow or, to express the concept with a different terminology, if her sorrow was so intense that it eliminated every trace of joy or if the latter was so complete that it prevailed over every expression of sorrow. Richard of St. Victor (d. 1173), for instance, affirms that the Virgin was utterly prepared to endure every torment with dignity: "De nullo enim sanctorum rectius creditur quam de ipsa, quod parata fuerit semper quantum in ipsa fuit, ad omnia tormentorum genera pro Christi nomine sustinenda."[6] Alan of Lille (c. 1128–c. 1202) exalts the faith and the strength of the Virgin during the Passion of Christ and observes that "cum passionis tempore discipuli defecerunt a fide, Virgine a statu fidei non deficiente . . . et tanta virtute Christum dilexit ut ad titulum suae laudis sufficiat, quod . . . fugientibus discipulis oblita sexus fragilis, ipsa cum lacrymis astans cruci et condolens morienti, animam suam pro filio suo, et si minime, posuit patiendo, tamen exposuit compatiendo."[7]

The strength, the impassivity, and the stoicism of the Virgin at the time of the Passion of Christ were especially exalted by Christian authors of the patristic age, even if they did not attribute to this testimonial and testamentary presence of the Virgin any co-redemptive merit in the redemptive sacrifice, but only acquiescent participation. As we have already seen, in his commentary on the biblical phrase "stabat iuxta crucem mater," Saint Ambrose, even though admiring the resolution of the Virgin, eliminated the possibility of interpreting her action as active cooperation in the Redemption, when he affirmed, "Ante crucem stabat et piis spectabat oculis filii vulnera, quia expectabat non pignoris mortem, sed mundi salutem: aut fortasse quia cognoverat per filii mortem redemptionem aula regalis, etiam sua morte putabat se aliquid publico additurum muneri. Sed Jesus non egebat adjutore ad redemptionem omnium, qui omnes sine adjutore servavit. Unde et dicit: 'factus sum sicut homo sine adjutore inter mortuos liber (Psalm 87:5, 6).' "[8]

The question of the thought of Holy Scripture and the fathers of the early Christian church on the Co-Redemption of Mary has been debated by different scholars. Roschini, for instance, after examining the allegorical passages of the Old and New Testament that prefigured the Co-Redemption of Mary, affirms that "Beata Virgo, igitur, singulari suo consensu, ad opus redemptionis generis humani *directe* et *immediate* cooperata est."[9] He holds further that the Virgin as the *Mater Victimae*, standing near the cross, abdicated her maternal rights in favor of the Victim and "pro aeterna salute generis humani, Filium suum, quantum ad se pertinebat, immolabat, et consequenter generis humani Corredemptrix fiebat."[10] Roschini arrives at the same conclusion after examining the writings of the early fathers of the Christian church, which he cites as proof of the existence even from that period of the doctrine of the Co-Redemption of Mary. "Nil mirum igitur si Patres, sicut *immediate* tribuerunt ruinam Adae et reparationem nostram Christo, ita pariter *immediate* tribuerunt ipsam ruinam nostram Evae et ipsam reparationem nostram, cum omnibus suis effectibus, Mariae."[11]

Carol expresses a different opinion. He declares that, although it can be affirmed, on the testimony of the early fathers of the Church, that the Virgin had participated in the redemption of the human race *scienter* and *volenter*, that is, "per positivum et deliberatum actum voluntatis, obedientiae et submissionis ergo voluntatem divinam,"[12] it cannot be asserted on this basis that the fathers of the Church held the doctrine of the Co-Redemption of Mary. Carol holds that an examination of the testimonies left us by the fathers of that epoch is not sufficient "ad solidam demonstrationem doctrinae de *immediata* Virginis Beatissimae cooperatione ad obiectivum Redemptionis nostrae opus."[13] What the fathers of the Church generally affirm, continues Carol, is that the Virgin can be considered "mundi redemptrix" in virtue of having borne the Redeemer of mankind: "quatenus Redemptorem hominibus genuit."[14]

The first, if not yet clear, testimonies of the Co-Redemption of the Virgin appear in the ninth century and reach their most luxuriant flowering in the twelfth and thirteenth centuries under the strong influence of the exegetical spirituality of that time. In a sequence of the *Mariale* of Joseph the Hymnographer (d. 883), for instance, there is outlined the concept of the participation of the Virgin in the *reparatio* of the sin of Adam through her consent to the Incarnation. "Ecce, o Virgo immaculatissima, in utero tuo concepisti Verbum Patri coaeternum, et incarnatum peperisti, a quo universis ex Adam natis iam collapsis donatur reparatio."[15] But the earliest indisputable affirmation of the Co-Redemption of the Virgin is formulated within the Eastern church, precisely at the end of the tenth century, by the Byzantine monk John the Geometer,[16] who declares that the Virgin had been set up as "the second mediatrix next to the first mediator": "νῦν δευτέρα μεσῖτις πρὸς τὸν πρῶτον μεσίτην."[17]

Even though this concept, as expressed by John the Geometer, does not yet contain the notions of sacrifice, satisfaction, and merit as they will be elaborated by Anselm in the West, the Byzantine monk remains the first to have enunciated in theological terms the cooperation of the Virgin in the redemption of the world. He pointed out, as Galot observes, "la source de sa cooperation à l'activité rédemptrice du Christ" not in Mary's divine motherhood, but in her "collaboration active à la Passion."[18] In his *Laus in Dormitionem B. M. Virginis*, for instance, written in Greek like all his works, John the Geometer proclaims the principle of the Co-Redemption of Mary; he rests his case particularly on the concrete participation of the Virgin in the suffering and death of her Son and upon her contribution in obtaining the grace of salvation for the human race. We here reproduce the significant passages in a French translation made by Wenger.

Comment a-t-elle pu supporter . . . en la passion une telle douleur, et comment n'en est-elle pas morte, si ce n'est pas là dire une chose nouvelle! . . . Elle versait de larmes . . . Elle voyait à découvert le corps de son Fils jadis maltraité, outragé, meurtri. . . . Nous te rendons graces d'avoir souffert pour nous de si grans maux et d'avoir voulu que ta Mère souffrît de si grans maux, pour toi et pour nous, afin que non seulement l'honneur de partager tes souffrances lui valût la communauté de gloire, mais encore afin que le souvenir des souffrances endurées pour nous lui fasse operer notre salut et qu'elle nous garde son amour non seulement à cause de la nature mais encore à cause du souvenir de tout ce qu'elle a fait pour nous au cours du toute sa vie.

Nous te rendons grâces parce que tu t'es donné comme rançon pour nous et parce que, après toi, tu donnes ta mère comme rançon à chaque instant afin que toi tu meures une fois pour nous, et qu'elle meure des milliers de fois dans sa volonté, brulée dans ses entrailles, tout comme pour toi, pour ceux pour qui, tout comme le Père, elle a donné son Fils tout in le sachant livré à la mort.[19]

In the West, Arnauld Bonnaevallis or Carnotensis (d. 1160), as he is variously known, seems to have been the first to articulate in precise terms the Co-Redemption of Mary; Carol considers him "corredemptionis marialis primus adsertor."[20] Arnauld's judgment on this subject acquires a certain doctrinal validity, since he explains theologically the particular cooperation of the Virgin in the mystery of Redemption. In his small work "De septem verbis Domini in cruce,"[21] in which he offers an exegetical interpretation of the seven last words of Christ *ex illa cathedra crucis*, Arnauld comments on the association of the Virgin with the sacrifice of the cross:

Nimirum in tabernaculo illo duo videres altaria, aliud in pectore Mariae, aliud in corpore Christi. Christus carnem, Maria immolabat animam. Optabat quidem ipsa, ad sanguinem animae et carnis suae addere sanguinem, et elevatis in cruce manibus cum filio sacrificium vespertinum, et cum Domino Jesu corporali morte redemptionis nostrae consummare mysterium; sed hoc solius summi sacerdotis privilegium erat, ut de sanguine munus intra sancta inferret; nec poterat ei consors haec esse cum aliquo dignitas, et in reparatione hominis nulli angelo, nulli homini cum eo fuit, aut esse potuit communis auctoritas. *Cooperabatur tamen plurimum secundum modum suum ad propitian-*

dum Deum ille matris affectus, cum tam propria quam matris vota charitas Christi
perferret ad Patrem, cum quod mater peteret, Filius approbaret, Pater donaret.[22]

The justification and the doctrinal force of the Co-Redemption of Mary,
as elaborated by Arnauld, is nourished by the consciousness that the Virgin participated in the Redemption, not simply by virtue of having given
birth to the Redeemer but also by having shared on Calvary with the
Redeemer in the work of reconciliation, as she sacrificed herself along with
her son and along with him offered to the Father a unique holocaust and
sacrifice. On this subject Arnauld expresses himself in a theoretically absolute and precise manner in his treatise *De laudibus Beatae Mariae Virginis:*

Maria Christo se spiritu immolat et pro mundi salute obsecrat, Filius impe-
trat, Pater condonat. Magnum quidem est quod latroni conceditur venia; sed
et hoc stupendum quod consummata dispensatione incarnationis, ex-
spiraturus Jesus matrem tanto affectu honorat, victor suppliciorum, et quasi
sui immemor, ad matrem de cruce convertitur, et colloquitur intimans quanti
apud eum meriti esset et gratiae, quam solam in illo puncto respiceret, cum
jam capite vulnerato, fossis manibus et pedibus, in ultimis esset. *Movebat enim*
eum Matris affectio, et omnino tunc erat una Christi et Mariae voluntas, unumque
holocaustum ambo pariter offerebant Deo: haec in sanguine cordis, hic in sanguine
carnis.[23]

Arnauld's conception of the Virgin as *coadiutrix* in the work of redemption will soon be integrated in the consciousness of the monastic spirituality of the contemporary West. During the following centuries, especially the thirteenth and fourteenth, it will dominate the medieval
attitude to Marian studies. But while the formulation of the concept of the
Co-Redemption of Mary is based in general, until the time of Arnauld,
upon the stoic and impassive cooperation of the Virgin toward the goal of
redemption, contemporary exegetical tradition and that of the following
centuries adds to the traditional arguments of the Co-Redemption of Mary
discussions of the theological value of her compassion at the moment of
the sacrifice on Calvary, discussions which will propose, with Albert the
Great, an understanding of the Virgin, *coadiutrix et socia*, not only because

she *sola sub cruce perstitit*, but also because *vulnera quae Christus corpore, ipsa corde suscepit.*[24]

With Albert the Great (1193–1280), however, we see the development of a speculative attitude toward the presence of the Virgin on Calvary, an attitude which prefigures a dual position on her behavior at the foot of the cross. This position proposes and affirms an inner moral equilibrium between the Virgin's participation in the sacrifice of the cross on the one hand and the offering of her suffering on the other, and those of her divine Son for the redemption of mankind. In deeply affected tones, suffused with contemplative spirituality, Albert employs a descriptive intuition, which seems to derive from figurative art, to illustrate the Virgin's bloody internal suffering, which approximates the concrete reality of the bloody physical suffering of Christ on the cross. "Tunc vero . . . facta est ut sanguis, quando assistens cruci vidit filii caput spinis laceratum et dorsum et omne corpus sanguine cruentatum. Cum etiam vidit manus et pedes clavis perforari et postremo latus ejus crudeli lancea transfigi, quis sufficienter explicare poterit quantos dolores tunc sustinuit Virgo Maria?"[25]

Grasping the metaphorical image inlaid in the prophecy of the old Simeon, "et tuam ipsius animam pertransibit gladius,"[26] Albert restricts its emblematic transcendence and makes it more realistically concrete, more actually visible in its existential reality, as deeply experienced by the Virgin. "Vulnera quae Christus corpore, ipsa corde suscepit: unde et gladius ipsius animam pertransibit."[27] Albert establishes a moral proportionality between the tormented anguish of the Virgin and the agonizing sufferings of Christ. "Et tuam ipsius animam pertransibit gladius. Passionem enim quam Filius in corpore pertulit, intus in anima sustinuit mater, dum in cruciatu corporis Filii maternus affectus contorquetur." And in an incomparable and extraordinarily unified image he displays the convergence of the sorrow of the mother and of her Son into a single indissoluble unity: "cuius animam gladius doloris Filii sui pertransibit."[28]

But although Albert is even moved to declare that, in the strictly temporal frame of the Passion, the Virgin suffered more than Christ— "Omnes amaritudines passionis, quas Filius Dei bibit, bibit et ipsa et quodammodo plus ipsa. Lancea quippe, quae perforavit latus Salvatoris, dolorem non fecit Filio sed matri. Quod etiam post mortem 'seductor' appellatur dolorem Filii non aggravat sed genitricis ipsius"[29]—he does, however, assert that the proximate and immediate participation of the Virgin in the sufferings of Christ in the act of Redemption would have been useless if this participation had not been united with her solidarity and her faith, as well as with all the intentions and purposes of her Son in the redemptive sacrifice. The sorrow of Mary would have been, in fact, "douleur suprême mais douleur inutile, douleur vaine, douleur perdue, si elle n'avait pas eu à son principe une foi inébranlable. Car à elles seules, les souffrances endurées avec Jésus ne suffisent pas à constituer ce privilège qu'est la communion au Christ souffrant, la 'communicatio passionis.' "[30]

The maternal compassion of Mary and her participation in the sorrows of Christ, prophesied by old Simeon, and her faith and her solidarity with the redemptive work of her Son constitute the requisite elements of the "communicatio passionis," to such a great extent that she can be said to have been crucified with him: "Sola beatissima Virgo tunc fidem habuit et compassionem crucifixi Dei et hominis et per se passionem ex compassione patientis. Et sic sola fuit cui datum est hoc privilegium scilicet communicatio passionis."[31] And it is precisely through the double realization in her mother's heart, of compassion and passion, as Albert affirms in a famous passage, that the Virgin experienced a natural *sorrow* in her participation in the sufferings of her Son and at the same time a supernatural *joy* in her complete fidelity to the immolation of Christ for the redemption of the world.

> Sicut Dominus omnium simul habuit summum gaudium et summum dolorem, sic Domina nostra simul habuit summam compassionem et summam congratulationem, compassione existente in natura simul et *in ratione ut natura*, congratulatione autem *in ratione ut ratione*. Et intelligantur haec verba sicut in materia Dominicae passionis. Vel dicatur quod summum tristabile in tali genere est dupliciter accipere: uno modo ut summe contrarium appetitui, et sic summum infert dolorem; alio modo prout est via et medium ad summum delectabile, et sic infert summum gaudium. Et sic anima beatissimae Virginis apprehendit mortem Filii sui ut summe contrariam appetitui, et sic summum intulit ei dolorem; et ut medium in redemptionem humani generis, et sic causavit in ea summam delectationem.[32]

The doctrine of the coexistence in the heart of the Virgin of *dolor* and of *gaudium* at the most awful moments of the Passion of Christ was held by a contemporary of Albert, Peter Olivi (d. 1298), one of the most brilliant theologians of his time. He had demonstrated his exegetical gifts as reader in theology at the universities of Paris (1279), Montepellier (1285), and Florence (1288), among others. In terms of doctrinal rigor, the participation of Mary in the redemptive sacrifice of Christ is based, according to Olivi, upon the consent of the Virgin to the Incarnation, since by accepting the physical motherhood of Christ, the Virgin consented internally and externally to the work of Redemption, even to embracing the Crucifixion of her Son: "Quando consensit, sensit se per suum consensum dedicari et iungi praefatis humilitatibus et humilibus officiis Redemptoris. . . . Quando magis Virgo cum Christo crucifixa est in hora conceptionis."[33] And upon the premises of this doctrine of the consent of Mary to the Incarnation, Olivi affirms the proximate and active participation of the Virgin in Redemption, by means of her compassion and her faith, which allowed her to experience both sorrow and joy at the sacrifice of Calvary.

> Licet Virgo perfectissima voluntate et caritate voluerit Christum pati, secundum quod ipsa passio erat a Deo et Christo homine volita, non tamen creditur de Filii passione tunc gavissa fuisse, immo summe doluisse. . . . Christi enim passio instar acutissimi gladii cor Virginis penetravit et transverberavit; sic quod non creditur tunc aliquod gaudium habuisse, saltem tantum ac tale quod esset sensibile cordi eius . . . contrarium esset indecens.[34]

Some years later the coexistence of *dolor* and *gaudium* in the soul of Mary at the moment of the act of redemption was held by another Franciscan theologian, the Catalonian Raymund Lull (c. 1231–1315), who has left us fundamental studies on the spiritual motherhood of Mary, especially the one devoted to that theme in his *Arbor scientiae*, even if his ecumenical and missionary activity, as a Franciscan tertiary, was generally conducted in the vernacular in his writings. Lull asserts that the Co-Redemption of Mary is affirmed and realized in two distinct moments: in the Incarnation, in which she participated materially and formally by her consent to her motherhood, and on Calvary, by means of her compassion, which allowed her to share in the sorrow of her Son and in the joy of the redemption of the world.

> E fora morta nostra Dona per la gran passió e dolor que sentía, si no fos lo plaer que sentía e havía quant son Fill moria; car nostra Dona sabía que son Fill havía plaer de morir, car si no volgués morir no morira; ma volía morir per honrar la deytat qui tan havía honrada la humanitat, e encara, per recrear l'uma linatge. E car nostra Dona covenía que hagués plaer do tot ço que son Fill havía plaer, li covenía haver plaer de la mort de son Fill per ço car recreava l'uma linatge, la qual recreació era agradable a nostra Dona per ço car es piadosa.[35]

But if in this passage Lull appears a traditional and doctrinal theologian in presenting to us a Virgin who cooperates in the redemptive sacrifice of her Son with maternal piety and dignity, in his lyrical composition *Plant de la Verge* (Plaint of the Virgin), composed around 1275, Lull expresses himself in terms which are clearly Franciscan, as he presents in deeply human terms the authenticity and intensity of the maternal compassion and sorrow of the Virgin. In it the Virgin comments on the most notable events of the Passion of Christ, from the betrayal and kiss of Judas, through the mockery, flagellation, crucifixion, and death, to the piercing by Longinus, the taking down from the cross, and the burial:

XII. DE LA PENA QUE SENTIA
NOSTRA DONA

Sentia nostra Dona per son fil grans dolors,
tant que tota estava in sospirs e en plors,
e en axí tremblava com fembra per paors.
Lo seu cors verge tot era en gran sudors,
e lo cor se departia per forsa de langors.
Tan gran dolor avia que anc no fo majors:
Les sues mans torsia, e cridava: "Seynors!
volentera morria, car li gran desonors
e la pena que dats a mon fil, qui amors
lo fan morir en la creu per tuyt li pecadors,
mi constreynen tan fort mon cor ab amargors,
que tot se deslassa e.s bayna en dolors.[36]

XXIII. COM NOSTRA DONA PREGAVA
A LOS ANGELS QUE AJUDASSEN
A SON FIL

Levava nostra Dona les mans e.ls uyls al cel,
e.n altes vots cridaba a l'àngel sent Miquel,
Serafí, Cherubí, Gabriel e sen Rafael:
"Avallats e vejats est mort tan cruel,
la qual fan a mon fil li malvat infeel,
sens que el no ha colpa, ans ha estat feel
al Payre qu.l tramés en mi per Gabriel.
Ve.us e com mor de set, e donen-li de fel
ab suja e vinagre, pus contraris a mel
que no es foc ardent a aygua ni a gel.
A, senyors! ajudats; car anc Caim d'Abel
no ac mays de crueltat com an cest infidel."[37]

The decidedly lyrical character of these two stanzas and of the entire
Plant is underscored not only by the exquisiteness of the maternal emotion
and the lyrical expressiveness of the language but also by the consideration
that this *Plant*—which Lull terms a *xant* (chant) in the last stanza—was
probably sung before a presentation of the paschal drama *Quem quaeritis.*[38]

Clearly inspired by a lyric-dramatic intensity intended to recall, with
stirring and tragic emotion, the loving solicitude and maternal anguish of
Mary during the tragedy of Golgotha, is a *Pianto* from the Abruzzi. Composed some years after the *Plant* of Lull but probably before 1296, the
Lamentatio Beate Marie de Filio is today preserved in the Museo of Sacred
Art in the city of Aquila. It is found in a manuscript which seems to have
belonged to Pietro del Morrone, Pope Celestine V.[39] In this *Lamentatio*
from the Abruzzi the lyric-dramatic agitation of its thirty strophes is completely directed to the exaltation and transfiguration of the inner distress
of the Virgin. Detached from the hieratic and static quality of the principal episodes of the Passion of Christ, summarized in five stanzas (II–VI),
the Virgin becomes the true protagonist of the drama. The co-participation of the Virgin in the Passion of her Son and, on the level of ritual and

culture, the *participatio* of the faithful are brought to full reality, especially in the seventh and eighth strophes, at the moment of the Crucifixion:

> VII. Sancta Maria cum Christo stava,
> Quando na Croce se clavellava;
> Scì grand dolore de lui menava
> Ke spexamente scì nde angossava.

> VIII. Audite, gente, gran pietate.
> Dice la mamma: "Christo me date
> Oi me con issu crucifigate.
> Set issu more, me non lassate."

It happens again later, at the Deposition and the Burial. Sorrowing, the Virgin yearns to be buried with her Son:

> XXVII. "Or me favella, dolce meu amore,
> Maritu et filiu et patre e siniore.
> Or so feruta scì nde lu core
> Ke sempre moro de lu dolore."

> XXVIII. Poy fu portatu a ssepelire,
> Sancta Maria volea morire;
> Diceali: "Filiu et dolce meu sire,
> Da te me n'voglio iammay partire."[40]

This *Lamentatio* of the Abruzzi constitutes, as we shall show, a document of fundamental importance in the evaluation of the lyrical associations and the literary circumstances which led in Italy to the substitution of the vernacular *Pianto* for the Latin *Planctus* and, consequently, to a discussion of the more general problem of sources and the passage, in the field of the lyric, from Latin to the vernacular. The *Lamentatio* still remains, in the fullness of its lyrical and theological proportions, a mighty explosion of the human spirit. It exploits to the fullest the expressive possibilities of the Virgin. Upon the stock of the historical and eschatological mission of the sacrifice of the Son it engrafts the temporal reality of the Mother's love, a love which in its suffering unites humanity to the bloody and sorrowful divine sacrifice for the salvation of the world.

CHAPTER III

THE PLANCTUS MARIAE

AND THE

EASTERN TRADITION

UR preliminary investigation of the behavior of the Virgin on Calvary has shown a dualistic attitude on the part of the Western exegetical tradition in the Middle Ages. On the one hand, there is the image of an ascetic, formal, and austere Virgin at the foot of the cross, an image in agreement with the doctrinal assertion of a Virgin conscious of the salvific value of her co-participation in the redemptive act through her voluntary offering of her divine Son for the redemption of the world. On the other, there is the vision of a Virgin who, although she participated consciously and firmly in the objective Redemption of the world, did not fail to show externally the sorrows and the sufferings which internally savaged her maternal piety as she assisted at the harsh Passion of her Son. An objective and comprehensive judgment of the problem seems to indicate that the early Middle Ages in general demonstrated a disdainful aversion to any evocation or presentation of the Virgin on Calvary which, rejecting the majestic rigidity of an icon and the stylized formality of the liturgy, emphasized the emotional qualities of the Mother, her sorrowful or pathetic expressions. The vision of a motionless and austere Virgin at the foot of the cross, as though hewn in the immovability of an icon without external indication of emotional or pathetic feelings—even if the full tidings of her torment and sorrow were recorded within herself—seems to have been, in the early Middle Ages, not only emblematic of her fundamental assent to the supreme sacrifice of her Son but also symbolic of that quality of moral resoluteness necessary to bear with dignity, albeit with grief, the sorrow of the loss of a dear one. On this subject Lipphardt observes that "dem ganzen frühen Mittelalter galt Maria under dem Kreuz als das Vorbild für alle, die einem lieben toten zu betrauern hatten. Wie sie durch Christus gestärkt worden war, so sollten sich alle christen nach ihrem Beispiele verhalten und in der Trauer standhaft bleiben."[1] The fathers of the Church, in particular, suggest that Mary was aware of the mystery of the Redemption and consequently bore the death of her Son for the salvation of mankind. This is the reason that in the West, during the first ten centuries of the Christian era, there are no lengthy meditations on the sufferings of the Virgin.

A different tradition, however, especially in the Eastern church, emphasizes the maternal feelings and tears of Mary. A full understanding of this tradition requires a careful documentation and a scrupulous analysis of texts. As a result of the dynamic development of the Eastern tradition across the centuries, around the eleventh and twelfth centuries there occurred in the Western church a dramatic and fundamental intermeshing of the two traditions on the subject of the compassion of the Virgin on Calvary.

The actual historical development of the doctrine of the compassion of the Virgin Mary can be set in two distinct temporal periods. The first of these, extending until the twelfth century, is divided in turn into two phases: the period that comprises the patristic age and the early Middle Ages, and a second period extending from the thirteenth century to our own days.[2]

Before beginning an exposition of patristic commentaries on and interpretations of the Virgin's compassion, we must observe how sporadic and infrequent are the testimonials of the early Church fathers on the Virgin Mary, in general, and on her compassion, in particular: "Qui priorum saeculorum scripta percurrat, non poterit non mirari quam raro Patres Ecclesiae de B. Maria Virgine verba faciant. . . . Hoc maxime locum habet in doctrina de B. Mariae Virginis Compassione."[3]

The first mention of the compassion of the Virgin in the fathers of the Eastern church is that of Origen (185–254) in his confused interpretation of the prophecy of the old Simeon which foresaw the presence of Mary at the foot of the cross: "Et tuam ipsius animam pertransibit gladius."[4] In his commentary on this passage Origen says:

> Deinde Simeon ait: *Et tuam ipsius animam pertransibit gladius.* Quis est iste gladius, qui non aliorum tantum, sed etiam Mariae cor pertransit? Aperte scribitur, quod in tempore passionis omnes sint apostoli scandalizati, ipso quoque Domino dicente: *Omnes vos scandalizamini in nocte hac.* Ergo scandalizati sunt universi. . . . Quid? putamus quod, scandalizatis apostolis, Mater Domini a scandalo fuerit immunis? Si scandalum in Domini passione non passa est, non est mortuus Jesus pro peccatis . . . utique et Maria illo tempore scandalizata est. Et hoc est quod nunc Simeon prophetat, dicens: *Et tuam ipsius animam,* quae scis absque viro peperisse te Virginem . . . *pertransibit* infidelitatis *gladius,* et ambiguitatis mucrone ferieris, et cogitationes tuae te in diversa lacerabunt, cum videris illum, quem Filium Dei audieras, et sciebas absque semine viri esse generatum, crucifigi et mori.[5]

In his erroneous exegesis Origen interprets the metaphor of the sword that shall pierce the soul of the Virgin not as a prophecy that unites the compassion of the Mother with the Passion of the Son but as one of a doubt or uncertainty of the Virgin concerning the divinity of the Savior: a sword of doubt which would particularly torment her at the moment of the Passion of her Son. Even if his terms are not precise, Origen remains, all the same, the first to have expressed the concept of the mirroring of the Passion of Christ in the soul of Mary: "Cogitationes tuae in diversa lacerabunt cum videris illum quem Filium Dei audieras . . . crucifigi et mori."[6]

The most ancient authentic plaint or lament of the Virgin as a liturgical motif is found in the apocryphal Greek gospel *Acta Pilati B,* composed at the beginning the the fourth century, at the time of the persecutions of Maximinian or, in any case, no later than the end of that century.[7] Here we read that the Virgin fainted on the way to Golgotha and wept uncontrollably at the foot of the cross. After the apostle John had told her that they had condemned her Son to be crucified, the Virgin waited on the road that led to Calvary and at the sight of her Son exclaimed, "My Son, my Son, what evil have you committed to be led away to be crucified?"[8] But it is particularly at the foot of the cross that the Virgin, abandoned and sorrowful, with tormented tenderness and human emotion, dissolves in a lament dominated by the metaphorical and liturgical image of her Son, as a meek and innocent Lamb, hung on the cross in all its bloody and brutal reality:

O you men, make room for me, so that I may embrace the shoulders of my lamb; make room for me so that I may bewail my dearest Son, the lamb of my soul.[9]

Δότε μοι, ἄνδρες, ὁδὸν περιπατῆσαι καὶ περιπλακῆναι τῷ τραχήλω τοῦ ἀρνίου μου δότε μοι, ἄνδρες, τόπον ὅπως κλαύσω τὸν παμφίλτατον υἱόν μου, τὸ ἀρνίον τῆς ψυχῆς μοῦ

Alas, alas! O my sweet Son, the light of my eyes, the king of the universe. Alas, alas! How can I bear to see you hanging on the cross? Alas, alas! Where now are the glad tidings of Gabriel? Come here, all of you, and bewail my soul, brutally wounded by sorrow, since I see my sweet Son, my only Son led like an innocent lamb to the Cross and like a condemned man his hands are bound.[10]

Οἴμοι οἴμοι γλυκύτατε υἱέ, φῶς τῶν ἐμῶν οφθαλμῶν, παμβασιλεῦ. οἴμοι οἴμοι, πῶς ὑπομενῶ θεωρῶν σε ἐν σταυρῷ κρεμάμενον; οἴμοι οἴμοι, ποῦ μοι τοῦ Γαβριὴλ τὰ εὐαγγέλια; δεῦτε πάντες κλαύσατε τὴν τετραυματισμένην μου ψυχήν, ὅτι τὸν μονογενῆ μου υἱὸν καὶ γλυκύτατον βλέπω ἀπαγόμενον ὡς ἀρνίον ἄκακον ἐπὶ σταυροῦ καὶ ὡς χατάδικον ταῖς χερσὶ δεδεμένον.

She uttered a great shout and said, "My Lord, my Son, What has happened to the beauty of your body? How can I bear seeing you suffer so much?" And with these words she tore her face with her fingernails and beat her breast.[11]

ἐβόησε φωνῇ μεγάλη λέγουσα· κύριέ μου, υἱέ μου, ποῦ τὸ κάλλος ἔδυ τῆς μορφῆς σου; πῶς ὑπομενῶ θεωρεῖν σε τοιαῦτα πάσχοντα; καὶ ταῦτα λέγουσα κατέξαινε μετὰ τῶν ὀνύχων τὸ πρόσωπον αὐτῆς καὶ ἔτυπτε τὸ στῆθος.

And when Jesus presented John to the Virgin as her son and the Virgin to John as his Mother, she contemplated the cross and exclaimed:

Lean down to me, O cross, so that I may receive my Son, so that I may kiss my Son, whom I have nourished on this breast of mine, though of my own will I have known no man.[12]

Κλῖνον, σταυρέ, ἵνα περιλαβοῦσα τὸν ἐμόν, υἱὸν, ὅν ἐν τοῖς μασθοῖς τούτοις ξενοτρόπως ὡς μὴ ἄνσρα γνῶσα ἐθήλασα.

The dramatic, tormented, personally lived, and anguished spirit of this plaint tends to make sensible and to elaborate with imaginative daring and a keen lyrical sense the slashing pathos of the Virgin. It is far removed from the formal and schematic rigidity of the Virgin at the foot of the cross as shaped and elaborated by the exegetical tradition of the West in the early Middle Ages.

One of the earliest laments of the Virgin, still within the orbit of the Eastern church, is that of Ephraim the Syriac, a doctor of the Church and one of the greatest authors and elegant poets of Syriac literature. He was born at Nisibis in Mesopotamia and early in his life became a disciple of Bishop James (303–38); around the year 363 he moved to Odessa, where he died in 373. In the Eastern tradition Ephraim acquired great renown thanks to his exegetical and theological work—it is held that he is the first father of the Church to teach the doctrine of the Immaculate Conception—and thanks to his immense production of metrical homilies and hymns on every type of theological subject.[13] He is especially famous for the originality of his Marian thought.

The lament of the Virgin composed by Ephraim the Syriac is entitled *Threni; id est, Lamentationes gloriosissimae Virginis Mariae super Passione Domini*.[14] It is a harrowing image of the irreversible and tortured final drama of her Son: "Ecce gladium: ecce vulnus, mi fili, et Deus meus. Mors tua, cor meum subiit: disrupta sunt mea viscera: lumen meum obscuratum est; pectusque meum dirus gladius pertransiit."[15] Ephraim the Syriac presents an image of the Virgin "stans juxta crucem" which transcends the bounds of any language of liturgical and traditional symbolism with its rigidity and intellectuality. Instead, the Virgin is portrayed in powerful glimpses of expressive realism without any precedent. By this means the dramatic tragedy of the Virgin is described with overwhelming intensity and multiplicity of detail. The dramatic agitation that governs the Virgin on Calvary is underscored from the very beginning of the lament, as she considers "*magno cum planctu*" her Son crucified and mentions individually and altogether the precise instruments of his bloody Passion:

Stans juxta Crucem pura et immaculata virgo, Salvatoremque in ea suspensum cernens, dirissimas plagas perpendens, et clavos, querimonias, alapas,

flagellaque prospiciens, magno cum planctu, lamentisque dolore plenis ex-
clamabat, dicens: Mi fili dulcissime, fili mi carissime, quo modo Crucem
istam portas? Mi fili, et mi Deus, quo pacto sputa, clavos, et lanceam suffers?
quo pacto colaphos, irrisiones, injurias, ac contumelias pateris? quo pacto
coronam spineam, vestemque purpuream, spongiam, arundinem, fel et
acetum sustines? Quomodo in ligno pendens mortuus, ac denudatus, fili, qui
coelum nubibus tegis? . . . Quid fecisti: aut in quo Hebraeorum gentem, fili
mi, offendere potuisti? Et cur scelerati simul atque ingrati illi, te in ligno
Crucis suspenderunt? . . . At tu quomodo jam occideris, mi fili dulcissime,
idemque magnanime Deus? Deficit mihi animus, dum te Cruci suffixum intueor, conclavatumque ac plagis plenum, amantissime fili. . . . Et quomodo
in Cruce jam exstinctus es, fili mi, et Deus meus?[16]

In great distress, the Virgin then turns to the archangel Gabriel and
asks him rhetorically what has happened to that happy *Ave* which had
announced happiness and blessedness to her and had proclaimed her
blessed among women. The joy foreshadowed at the moment of the Incarnation is now obscured in the face of the present sorrow prophesied by the
old Simeon as, abandoned and childless, she contemplates the dire Passion
of her Son:

O Simeon admirande: ecce jam gladius, quo cor meum trajiciendum praedix-
isti. Ecce gladium: ecce vulnus, mi fili, et Deus meus. Mors tua, cor meum
subiit; disrupta sunt mea viscera: lumen meum obscuratum est; pectusque
meum dirus gladius pertransiit. Tremendum tuam passionem intueor, fili mi,
et Deus meus. . . . Miserere jam desolatae, atque orbatae matris, mi fili.
Miserere dejectae ac derelictae Mariae, o dulcissime. . . . Respice, mi fili,
lacrymas meas: attende suspiria mea ac gemitus, et os tuum aperi. Solatium
mihi praebe, mi fili. . . . Tu mihi es pater, tu frater, tu filius.[17]

Until now she has presented, in a most visible manner, the cruel signs of
the Passion of her Son and the signs of her maternal sorrow, cut deeply
within her soul, by means of images that are human in their realism. The
Virgin now exhorts the holy women, "cunctae discipulae Domini," to join
her in lamenting her sorrows. There now ensues a scene, extremely poetic
and very powerful in its dramatic structure, in which the Virgin eagerly

and sorrowfully begs the cross to lean down to her so that she may kiss the wounds of her Son, do him reverence, and embrace in her maternal arms his eyes, his face, his hands, and his mouth. This is one of the most famous scenes associated with the lament of the Virgin, an episode which will be taken up and repeated by the exegetical tradition of the Middle Ages; it finds its pre-eminent expression in the laments from the Abruzzi:

> Tu mihi, jam Crux sanctissima, lignumque benedictum *decumbe:* ut dilectissimi fili mei, ac Dei mei plagas exosculer, propriumque filium salutem: ut filii mei corpus amplectar, et os suavissimum, oculosque ac faciem, manus atque pedes, et caedem iniquissimam deosculer. *Decumbe, o crux veneranda, decumbe.*[18]

It is only toward the end of this sublime lament of the Virgin that the lyrical sense of suffering, which is predominant in it, yields to considerations of traditional dogma, which sees on the cross not the God-Man suffering and dying in sorrow and death, but the God of the redemptive apotheosis, the *Christus triumphans*, in union with the Virgin, who raises words of adoration to the bloody signs of the Passion of her Son because by means of them salvation and eternal glory have been won back for everyone:

> Mi fili, fili mi suavissime atque carissime, honoro tuas illas afflictiones: colo et adoro misericordiam, et magnanimitatem tuam. Veneror lanceam, vulnus, arundinem, clavos, spongiam, alapas, irrisiones atque opprobria, fel et acetum, sputa, colaphos, et verbera, mi fili dulcissime. Sed quoniam cuncta illa, creaturae tuae gratia, perpeti placuit; ignominia tua, mi fili, gloria cunctis facta est: tuaque mors toti mundo vita evasit.[19]

One of the most emotional and lyrical evocations of the lament of the Virgin at the foot of the cross is the one that bursts forth from the sumptuous and exquisitely poetic sensibility of James of Sarug (451–521), the most famous poet of Syriac literature after Ephraim the Syriac. Commonly known as "the flute of the Holy Spirit" because of his abundant and eloquent lyricism, James was involved in the religious controversies of the time. In the aftermath of the opposition to the decisions of the Council of Ephesus (431) marking the beginning of Nestorianism, which spread especially in eastern Syria, a similar opposition to the decision of the Council of Chalcedon gave rise to the Monophysite church, which held the doctrine of a single nature in Christ. This theological position was especially prevalent in western Syria and Osroene.[20] Although the arguments of various scholars, such as Assemani,[21] Martin,[22] Peeters,[23] and Vona,[24] have not yet clearly established the orthodoxy of James of Sarug, the question has no importance within the bounds of our investigation, because even if the Monophysitism of James were sufficiently and explicitly attested, this would not have any influence upon his Marian thought.

Like all of Syriac literature, the work of James of Sarug is marked by its Christian and religious character. His literary activity in prose consists of letters, homilies, funeral discourses, and liturgical works. Of greater significance is his poetic output, especially his metrical homilies—which today number some 231 in Syriac and Arabic manuscripts, although originally there were 763 of them—particularly those devoted to the Virgin. As Vona observes, "James of Sarug was a worthy rival of St. Ephraim in both his literary fecundity, his technical artistry and his great love for the Virgin."[25]

It is precisely in one of the two metrical homilies or poetic discourses, entitled *De transitu Dei Genitricis Mariae*—translated into Latin by Baumstark—that we find mentioned the plaint of the Virgin at the foot of the cross. The *De transitu*, in the Eastern tradition, is a homily that celebrates the apotheosis of the Virgin at the end of her earthly journey. In his *De transitu*, after recalling in exquisite accents the image of the Virgin singing a lullaby to the baby Jesus, James of Sarug passes dramatically to the description of her lament at the foot of the cross and of her sufferings in seeing her Son crucified, then pierced by a lance, and finally buried:

> Multas mater tua passiones propter te toleravit / omnesque afflictiones eam circumdederunt in crucifixione tua. / Quot lamentabiles fletus et passionis lacrimas effuderunt oculi eius, / Cum exequias tuas peragerent et intra sepulcrum inferrent (et) ponerent te! / Quot terrores in sepultura tua mater misericordiae vidit, / cum custodes sepulcri eam avellerent, ne tibi appropinquaret! / Passiones toleravit, quando in cruce te vidit suspensum / et cum

lancea latus tuum tibi in Golgotha perforaverunt, / quando Iudaei sepulcrum obsignaverant, in quo positum erat / corpus tuum vivum et vitam dans et crimina remittens.

Atque huic matri, quae propter te toleravit, / finis advenit, ut in novum mundum migraret.[26]

The contemplation and the description, on the part of Ephraim the Syriac and James of Sarug, of the lament and the sufferings of the Virgin at the moment of the final Passion of Christ, constitute a manifestation of their intense love for the Mother of God. This love is evident in their expressions and their delving into Mariological questions such as the divine motherhood of Mary, her virginity, her sanctity, and her antithesis of Eve. These efforts furthermore find a place in that traditional and pronounced interest of the Syriac church in the Passion of Christ. In two interesting studies, Dahane and Khouri-Sarkis have demonstrated, for instance, the solemnity and the abundance of poetic compositions with which the Syriacs celebrated the memorial recurrence of the Passion, during Holy Week, in the liturgy of both the eastern and western Syriac church, as well as the lyrical accents with which they recall the lament of the Virgin at the foot of the cross and near the sepulcher of Christ.[27]

During the liturgical office of Holy Saturday, for instance, in the western Syriac church, in a lyrical composition recited at vespers—from which we shall reproduce some verses in a French translation made by Khouri-Sarkis—the virgin utters a lament of desolation at the foot of the cross and later at the sepulcher:

> Marie s'approcha de Jésus,
> Et appuya sa tête contre la croix.
> Elle commença à murmurer en hebreu
> Des lamentations, des paroles de douleur.
> "Qui me transformera, mon Fils, en aigle,
> pour que je vole aux quatre coins du monde,
> Que j'invite et amène toutes les nations
> Au grand festin de ta mort?
> Qui t'a jalousé, ô mon doux Fils?
> Qu'a vu en toi l'adultère Sion?

Parce que l'as délivrée de l'Egypte,

. . . .

Voilà par quoi elle te recompense, la folle:
La honte, le mépris, la dérision et la croix!

. . . .

Ton tombeau est semblable à la chambre nuptiale
Et, en lui, mon Fils, tu ressembles à l'epoux.
Les morts ressemblent aux invités de la noce
Qui descendent devant les anges.
Créatures, pleurez, pleurez
Votre Seigneur élevé sur la croix.[28]

One of the most fecund composers of *kontakia*, that is, liturgical hymns—
he wrote about a thousand—is Romanos the Melodos (490–560). Although
he was a Syriac like James of Sarug, he wrote in Greek. Revered in the
Greek tradition as the "princeps canticorum," Romanos composed one of
the earliest *Staurotheotokia:* the hymns of the Virgin at the foot of the cross.
Of particular interest is his *Canticum de Virgine juxta crucem,*[29] which was
sung on Good Friday and is characterized by a decidedly didactic purpose:
from the cross Christ strives to instruct the Virgin and the public in general
on the mystery of the Passion, that is, the necessity of his sufferings for the
redemption of the world:

1. Pro nobis crucifixum,
   venite omnes, celebremus.
   Ipsum enim vidit Maria
   affixum ligno, et aiebat:
   "Tametsi crucem sustineas,
   tu es manifeste
   filius ac Deus meus."

2. Suum ipsius agnellum
   Ut agna aspexit
   Maria sequebatur,
   moerore confecta,
   cum caeteris mulieribus,

Haec lamenta edens:
"Quo vadis, fili?
cur precipitem
nunc cursum agis? . . .

3. Haud putabam, fili, me visuram te esse talia obeuntem, neque id tum
credebam, quum scelestos istos viderem efferatos, perfidas manus ad te
suppliciter tendentes. Adhuc enim eorum pueri clamant: Hosannah! Benedictus! . . . Nosse volo, hei mihi! quomodo lux mea extinguatur, quo
pacto cruci affigatur filius et Deus meus.

4. Pergis o viscera mea, ad iniustam necem, ac nemo tibi condolet. . . .

5. Talia dum Maria prae nimio moerore et ob graves aerumnas ederet
lacrymabunda. . . .[30]

At this point Christ intervenes to explain in simple but clear words the
essential character of the mystery of the Redemption. It is a profoundly
human scene when Christ explains to the Virgin in her maternal anguish
the ontological and theological significance of his Passion and death.

conversus ad eam eius natus, ita locutus: "Cur lacrymaris, o mater? Quid
una cum caeteris mulieribus mente excedis? Quomodo Adamum salvabo
nisi passus ac mortuus? . . . Profecto, ut novisti, cruci affigar, et morior.
Cur fles, o mater? . . .

6. Dimitte igitur, mater, dimitte luctum. Te enim lugere minus docet, quae a
gratia cumulata nomen habes; quod ergo noli gemitu contegere; noli te
insciis connumerare, sapientissima Virgo! . . .

7. Acerbam ne reputes hanc diem in qua patior . . .[31]

Christ kindly reproves his Virgin-Mother and explains to her that only
by his Passion and his death will Adam be saved. He begs her to stop
weeping, not to behave like other women, and not to consider the day of
his Passion a bitter one. Obediently, the Virgin submits to the will of her
Son, after being assured by him that she will be the first he will visit after
his Resurrection: "Confide, mater, quod prima tu me videbis sursum e
sepulchris."[32]

Romanos occupies a notable place in the development of Eastern religious literature because of his vast output of *kontakia*—he is generally regarded as "the Melodos," the greatest poet of the Byzantine church.[33] His hymns are inspired by the metrical homilies of Ephraim the Syriac; many of his *kontakia*, in fact, are direct translations of the poetic compositions of Ephraim.[34] But Romanos is especially important in the history of the religious theater of Byzantium because some scholars have established some thematic relations between a Byzantine drama of the Passion of the thirteenth century and the *kontakia* of the paschal cycle composed by him.[35] The text of this so-called *Passione palatina* was published in 1916 by the Greek scholar Spiridion Lambros, who transcribed it from a manuscript of the Vatican Library (*Pal. Graec.* 367).[36] The French Byzantinist Albert Vogt published a second edition in 1931.[37] Since the internal evidence of the text suggests that Cyprus was its original site, its most recent editor calls it *The Cyprus Passion Cycle* and assigns its date of composition to the period between 1260 and 1270.[38]

Of unquestioned historical, philological, and religious value, within the orbit of our research and of the literary tradition of the *Planctus Mariae*, is a little-known text, *The Lament of the Virgin*, which is known to us through an Arabic text written in Syriac characters but which is assuredly of Coptic origin.[39] This lament of the Virgin, one of the most ample in the Eastern tradition, is presented as a homily of Ciriac, the bishop of Bahnasa, who lived at the beginning of the fifteenth century. The lament is important in two respects. First, although the paleographic evidence assigns its composition to around 1450, the text represents the account of the Gospel of Gamaliel, which is connected, in its turn, with the apocryphal *Acta Pilati* or the Gospel of Nicodemus, generally attributed to the fifth or sixth century.[40] Second, this lament of the Virgin, which takes place not only at the foot of the cross but also near the empty tomb (that is, after the Resurrection), shows evidence—as do all the apocryphal Gospels, for that matter—of a desire to flesh out the scanty documentation and the scarce information provided us by the synoptic Gospels.

This lament, in fact, is characterized by an emphatic "historicizing" purpose, which places within the lyrical and pathetic structure of the Virgin's plaint a chronological presentation of the several events within the scheme of which the plaint occurs. The lament of the Virgin, whether on

Miniature. *586. Gospels of Rabula.* Florence, Laurentiana.

Fresco. First half of the eighth century. Rome, Santa Maria Antiqua.

Mosaic. Circa 1150. Rome, Basilica of San Clemente.

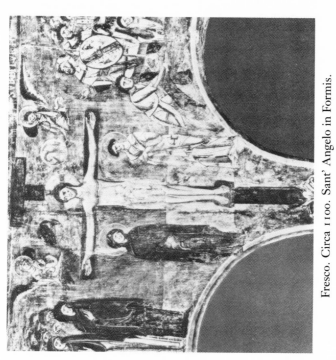

Fresco. Circa 1100. Sant' Angelo in Formis.

Panel painting. Abruzzese School. Circa 1240.
L'Aquila, Museo Civico.

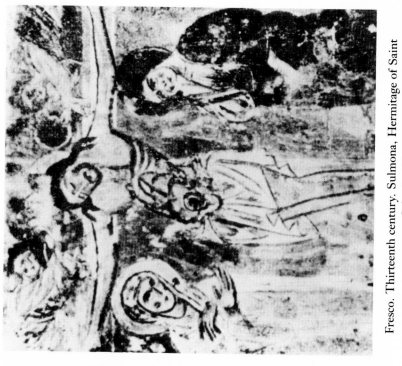

Fresco. Thirteenth century. Sulmona, Hermitage of Saint Celestine V.

Fresco. Thirteenth century. Fossa, Santa Maria ad Cryptas.

Crystal cross. Venetian School, first half of the fourteenth century. Assisi, Basilica of Saint Francis.

Panel painting. Circa 1308–11. Duccio. Siena, ancient main altar of the cathedral.

Fresco. 1350. Barna da Siena. San Gimignano, Collegiata.

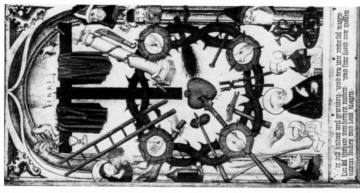

Panel painting. Circa 1500. Daniel Mauch. *Arma Christi* with the five wounds. Ulm, panels from the altar of Buxheim.

Panel painting. Abruzzese School. Circa 1450. Giovanni da Sulmona. L'Aquila, Museo Civico.

Calvary or at the sepulcher of Christ, is quite far from an ideal, rigid, and liturgical presentation, emblematic and self-contained; instead it occurs in a logical and impressively causal sequence, since the lament is fixed in the precise order of the events which produce it. We shall here present the salient moments of the *Lament of the Virgin* in an English translation of the original text.

The homily begins with an indication that its argument will be "the tender lament of the Virgin the day of the crucifixion of our Lord . . . and the day of his holy Resurrection when the Virgin went to the door of the sepulcher of her Son and did not find his body there because he had risen."[41] The account justifies the lament of the Virgin with the observation that if Rachel mourned for her children whom she had never embraced, it is logical that the Virgin would mourn for him whom she had carried as a baby in her arms; and if Jacob had mourned for Joseph, bound by his brothers and then thrown into a well, even if he had not seen it happen, it is even more logical that the Virgin should mourn for her Son when she saw him hanging on the cross between two thieves.[42] Chronologically, the lament of the Virgin begins at the house of John; there a messenger brings her the sad news that her Son is being led on the road of Kranion and Golgotha. She leaves the house of John and walks through the streets of the city in search of a disciple who would accompany her to Golgotha. When she asks that Peter accompany her, she is told that he has gone into hiding after having denied her Son. When she asks for James, they tell her that he fled after the seizure of Christ. When she asks for Andrew, they explain to her that he had not come with her Son into the city. When she asks for Thomas, they tell her that he has fled after throwing away his clothes. When she asks for Philip, they answer that he was frightened at the sight of the torches and took to flight. When she asks for Matthew, they tell her that he is more frightened of the Jews than all the others. Finally, after asking for all the other disciples, she discovers that only John had accompanied her Son to the Kranion and to Golgotha. And it is in his own house that John finds the Virgin weeping when he returns from Golgotha:

> I adjure you, O John, to show me the way to the *Kranion*. I adjure you, O John, to accompany me to the Golgotha. I have never seen yet a robber being

crucified, nor have I stood near a robber when he was being beheaded. I shall foresake my town and my great freedom, and shall go bare-footed to the place in which my beloved Son has been crucified like common robbers, because He is alone and not one of His brethren is standing near Him. . . . O my child, the sorrow of a mother for her beloved son is something, and the sorrow of a friend for his friend is another thing; the pain of the heart of a mother weeping over her beloved son is something, and the weeping of a friend over his friend is another thing. My sorrow, O my child, is today greater than that of the world, and of all the inhabitants of Jerusalem, and my weeping is more bitter than that of all who shall gather near me.[43]

After reaching Golgotha, the Virgin moves forward through the crowd of different nationalities—the Aorites, the Balachites, the Moabites, the Cabarites—who have gathered at Jerusalem for the slaughter of the paschal lamb and then, attracted by the extraordinary event, have gone to Golgotha. The Virgin advances through the milling crowd and finally, lifting her face to the west, she sees her Son hanging upon the cross. Making her way with great difficulty, she finally reaches the cross and places herself at her Son's right:

> When God saw His mother He looked towards John and said to him: "O man, this is your mother," and then He said to His mother: "O mother, this is your son." And John held the Virgin's hand in order to take her to his house, but the Virgin, his mother said: "O John, let me weep over Him, as He has no brother and no sister, and do not deprive me of Him. O my Son, would that I had with you a crown of thorns on my head, and would that I could make it as painful as yours. . . . O John, look at my wretchedness . . . and at the pains of my heart. . . . Let me look at His sufferings. . . . Let me weep over Him, because my sufferings are today greater than His sufferings. . . . This is the wailing indulged in by the Virgin while she was at the right side of her Son . . . because of the greatness of her sorrow . . . she was only bent on weeping.[44]

The homily says that the lament of the Virgin was especially intense at the moment of her Son's death; when at the home of John she recognized in the earthquake and the darkness which covered the whole city the signs which announced it, she wept bitterly. The lament of the Virgin continues, with ever greater tenderness and trembling *pietas*, on Sunday morning, when she went to the tomb after Magdalene and found it empty. There follows a lament full of suffering and sweet composure, of a mother distraught by her inability to pay her buried Son the last homage of a mother's love.

One of the most extended considerations and exegetical interpretations of the compassion of the Virgin at the foot of the cross is found in the *Oratio VIII* of George of Nicomedia (d. after 880), entitled *In SS. Mariam assistentem cruci*. In this homily George offers a metaphorical interpretation of Mary "juxta crucem Jesu," based upon her *fortitudo* and her *compassio*. Glossing the biblical text "Stabant autem juxta crucem Jesu, Mater ejus, et soror Matris ejus Maria Cleophae, et Maria Magdalene,"[45] George emphasizes the strength of soul and the constancy of the Virgin at the moment of the Passion of her Son, especially during his crucifixion at Golgotha.

While everyone else had fled and the holy women observed the agonizing spectacle from a distance, "Mater vero proprius semper assectata, propinquior erat ac immobilis perseverabat. Pro ratione enim incensi in Filium miserantis animi affectus, fortitudinem audentisque animi constantiam ostendebat."[46] The impassiveness and the constancy of the Virgin at the foot of the cross are justified by George, at the beginning of this homily, with the observation that the Virgin was fully conscious of the necessity of the redemptive work of her Son: "Quia ergo Filium videbat ad salutarem properantem passionem."[47] This initial stoicism of the Virgin illumines and offers essential continuity to one of the most peculiar components of George's Mariological thought: his theological conviction—expressed in his homilies on the presentation of the Virgin in the temple—that the Virgin was not only free of all sin and every defect, but that from the tender age of three years she had possessed a perfect *apatheia*, that is, a freedom from all emotions.[48] Even if the articulation of this doctrine creates disturbing confusion on occasion, it does not prevent George from attributing to the Virgin intense manifestations of sorrow and compassion during the dire agony of her Son on Calvary:

Postquam autem deicidae homines venissent ad Calvariae locum, ac sollicite quae ad salutarem mortem inferendam erant urgentes, crucem fixissent, ac eum vestimenta quibus indutus erat, nudassent; clavorumque immanitatem acuentes, ipsi se suppedaneum gradum ad ascendendam crucem, sanguinaria voluntate fecissent, tunc durior in Mariam gladius adactus est; tunc doloris in eam recta ibant spicula. Quo autem modo anima non a corpore recessit? Quomodo non fuit divulsa illa ejus conjunctione? Quomodo ferre potuerint oculi, cum suum lumen viderent conscendere crucem? Quomodo pupillae non diffugerunt, cum intemeratas palmas parricidis sponte manibus exporrectas aspicerent? Quomodo non sunt dissolutae compages, coafixis cruci ejus membris, qui universum continet? Proh! quomodo clavus manui infigebatur, ejus autem cordi impungebatur plaga lethalis? Quomodo dum interim singula membra perforarentur, miserabilius animo sauciabatur? Quomodo stillabant e vulneribus guttae sanguinis, acerbiores autem ab oculis lacrymarum rivi fluebant?[49]

Obviously not disturbed by the incongruity of the juxtaposition of such agonizing sentiments and his concept of the Virgin's *apatheia*, George, faithful to the Eastern tradition, gives even greater emphasis to the sufferings and the compassion of the Virgin. He achieves this end by using material taken from the apocryphal Gospels and by giving a detailed description of the suffering of the Son and the lament of the Mother which, in their startling realism, both figurative and evocative, match the tortured realism suggested by Gothic painting. It suffices to mention, for example, that shortly after the Crucifixion, when some soldiers had returned home and others were busy eating, the Virgin took advantage of the situation to begin kissing the feet of Christ and the dreadful wounds. As she did so, alone under the cross, she gathered in her eyes and on her breast the blood that ran down from his wounds and uttered these words in her plaint:

Utinam vero liceret, tua in me, Fili, cruciamenta recipere! Utinam clavi illi meis possent infigi membris! Utinam tormentorum tuorum dolores in meo ipsa sentirem corpore! . . . At, o fili, dulciores deliciae! . . . Nunc sola venerabilibus tuis cruciamentis affecta, crucior: sola acerbiores dolores tuos in pectore meo recipio. Nemo enim est, qui tristium mihi sit particeps; nemo qui mecum vulnera dividat . . . acutior passionis tuae gladius animum pervadit. . . . Plane vero desideratissimum habuissem, ac mitius prae doloribus qui tenent, ut in me clavi penetrassent: ut tuos cruciatus recepissem in membris meis.[50]

The Virgin utters another lament at the foot of the cross after the death of her Son. And, contrary to the biblical account of the canonical Gospels, George writes that she was present when Christ was taken down from the cross. In tears she received him in her arms; she also took part in his burial and remained near the sepulcher until the day of her Son's resurrection. With George of Nicomedia the description of the sorrow and of the compassion of the Virgin reaches levels of unbounded drama and of heart-rendering pathos, even if they are outside the traditional account of the Gospels.

Simon Metaphrastes (who died toward the end of the tenth century), a *magistros* and logothete for whom we have scanty biographical details, has the honor of having composed one of the most singular and original laments of the Virgin in the Eastern tradition, the *Oratio in lugubrem sanctissimae Deipare pretiosum corpus Domini Nostri Christi amplexantis.*[51] The Virgin's lament of Metaphrastes, in its thematic and chronological structure, develops progressively in a temporal scheme similar to the temporal phases of Augustine's vision of history: *tempus ante legem, sub lege,* and *sub gratia.* In fact, the Virgin begins her plaint, as she clutches the lifeless body of her Son in her arms, with a sorrowful realization of Simeon's prophecy: "Hoc illud est, gladium meam ipsius animam penetraturum, ut Symeon praedixerat."[52] The Virgin remarks on the difference between the glad tidings of Gabriel and the present moment when she beholds the body of her Son in the tomb. "Vae mihi miserae! in lapide demortuus jaces, qui ex lapidibus filios suscitas Abraham."[53] Seeing the evil of her Son's death and the bloody signs it had left on his body, flesh of her flesh, she exclaims, "namque antiquum debitum sufficientissime restitui."[54] She then bursts forth in an overwhelming expression of suppressed maternal grief, as she mentions the various tortures her Son had experienced; they reverberate with a renewed sorrow in the sanctuary of her heart:

O divinum mihi caput spinis perfossum, easque cordi meo infigens! O venerandum sacrumque corpus, quod olim non habebas, ubi declinans quiesceres:

nunc solum ad sepulturam inclinatum est, quietem consecutum, et ut Jacobus aiebat, veluti Leo obdormivisti! O desideratum concupitumque mihi caput calamo percussum, ut calamum imbellis demonis artibus disruptum, longeque a paradiso factum, instaurares! O maxillae alapis foedatae! O os mellis alius favus, licet amarissimum fel degustasti, et acerrimum acetum potionem sump-sisti! O os intra quod dolus inventus non est, etsi dolosum osculum te prodidit ad mortem! O manus, quae hominem creastis, et nunc cruci affixae, et ad inferos protensae, manum illius arripitis, quae olim lignum tetigit, et a lapsu Adamum universum excitatis! O latus lancea perforatum propter eam, quae ex latere creata fuerat, primam matrem! O pedes, qui per aquas, veluti per terram processistis, et fluidam naturam manifeste sanctificastis!

Vae mihi, Fili, ipsa parente antiquior, quas sepulchrales lamentationes, et quas laudationes funebres decantavero?[55]

The emotional outpourings of maternal love expressed in the lament of the Virgin by Metaphrastes anticipate the extensive and tortured images of maternal compassion realized in the twelfth and thirteenth centuries precisely because they flow from the special effort of Metaphrastes, through a deep probing of the heart of the Virgin, to reveal in a concrete way the feelings of *com-passio* which take control of this mother's heart. This effort shines through in the perfect use of verbal forms and of a language which suggests, or rather which makes visible, both semantically and materially, the participation and compassion of the Mother with the Passion and the sufferings of the Son:

Quomodo probrosam sustines mortem, Fili sceleris expers? Perforatae sunt manus tuae, pedesque, sed clavos ipsa in mediam animam meam puncturis dirissimis adactos persentio. Latus tuum confossum est, sed et meum cor eodem ipso tempore confodiebatur. Doloribus una tecum cruci affixa sum, et una tecum tormentis commortua, una tecum sepelior.[56]

The lament concludes with the Virgin adoring the Passion of her Son, kissing his body and receiving the water and the blood pouring from his side, visible and tangible signs of his work of salvation, by means of which even the good thief had been saved.

Passionem tuam adorans, quod reliquum est, corpus deosculor. Accipio aquam, quae e latere tuo effluxit per quam mihi regenerationis lavacrum exprimitur: accipio quoque sanguinem, qui simul effluxit, per quem et baptismus martyrium effingitur, qui et benevolum latronem aspergens sanctum effecit, ablutum ipsum baptismo, qui in te acciderat.[57]

CHAPTER IV

MARIAN EXEGESIS:

MEDIATION AND MATERNITY

OUR investigation of the development, within the Eastern church, of the lament of the Virgin and her compassion at the moment of the Passion of Christ, raises a question of both historical and religious dimensions. This development occurred, after all, as a liturgical and spiritual attitude of considerable novelty, within the confines of a church characterized for centuries by an unbreakable religious unity, quite foreign to any emotion or subjectivity. This church was also distinctive for the classical idealism of its imperial cult; it was governed by rites and ceremonies founded upon the permanence of their liturgical function; it was also based upon a language of artistic and Hellenizing character, a language protected with the dams of a style at once metaphorically impassive, immobile, immaterial, and extraordinarily disciplined.

The emergence and evolution of this new theological attitude broke the traditional stylization of the liturgy of the Eastern church and placed in relief the emotions, the sensibilities, and the maternal feelings of the Virgin. This was all animated and favored by the flowering of the apocryphal Gospels and especially of the apocryphal works involving Mary, composed between the second and the seventh centuries. The patristic tradition of Mary, extending over the first eight centuries of the Christian era, often dwelt, as we have seen, with particular intensity upon the description of the maternal feelings of the Virgin during the Passion of her Son.

But it is only by a chronological analysis of the Marian exegetical tradition that we grasp the change in theological attitudes which led to the humanization of the sufferings of the Virgin at the foot of the cross. During the first years of the Christian era the principal characteristic of the Virgin was her human nature, because the Church wanted to emphasize the reality of the Incarnation. In these early centuries the formal concept of the physical maternity predominated over her spiritual maternity, even though this latter, in an obscure and implicit fashion, had been taught by the early fathers of the Church.[1] During the patristic period, however, precise intellectual efforts were made to define more clearly the role of the Virgin in the mystery of the Redemption. This process began toward the end of the second century with Justinus (c. 100–c. 165), one of the great apologists of Christianity, in his *I* and *II Apologia* and his *Dialogus cum Tryphone*. He presents Mary as the new Eve, a parallel which corresponds on the whole to that between Christ and Adam, for, just as Eve at the moment of her disobedience brought death to the human race, so through her obedience Mary brought salvation. The action of Eve resulted in death and that of Mary in deliverance from death. Justinus thus explains the Eve-Mary antithesis, which he is the first to mention:

> Et cum eum Filium Dei esse . . . legamus, et Filium Dei dicimus illum et esse intelligimus . . . et ex Virgine hominem esse factum, ut qua via initium a serpente inobedientis accepit, eadem et dissolutionem acciperet. Eva enim cum Virgo esset et incorrupta, sermone serpentis concepto, inobedientiam et mortem peperit. Maria autem Virgo, cum fidem et gaudium percepisset, nuntianti Angelo Gabrieli laetum nuntium, nempe Spiritum Domini in eam superventurum, et virtutem Altissimi ei obumbraturam, ideoque id quod nasceretur ex ea sanctum esse Filium Dei, respondit: "Fiat mihi secundum verbum tuum." Ex hac ille genitus est, . . . per quem Deus serpentem, eique assimilatos angelos et homines profligat.[2]

Irenaeus (c. 125–c. 202) developed the Mary-Eve parallel even further. He delved into the moral aspects of the redemption of man and indicated that the influence of Eve in producing the sinful condition of man was equaled by the influence of Mary in freeing him for this condition; that is, from the bondage brought on by the disobedience of Eve man was set free by the obedience of Mary:

> Consequenter autem et Maria Virgo obediens invenitur, dicens: "Ecce ancilla tua, Domine, fiat mihi secundum verbum tuum." Eva vero inobediens: non

obedivit enim, adhuc cum esset virgo. Quemadmodum illa virum quidem habens Adam, virgo tamen adhuc existens . . . inobediens facta, et sibi et universo generi humano causa facta est mortis; sic et Maria habens praedestinatum virum, et tamen virgo, obediens, et sibi, et universo generi humano causa facta est salutis. . . . Sic autem et Evae inobedientiae nodus solutionem accepit per obedientiam Mariae. Quod enim alligavit virgo Eva per incredulitatem, hoc virgo Maria solvit per fidem.[3]

Irenaeus affirms that the bond of our first parents, Adam and Eve, a bond that produced sin and death, was replaced by the indissoluble linkage between Christ and Mary, which brought restoration and salvation.[4] The Mary-Eve parallel did not undergo significant developments after the third century, although it was often reaffirmed. For instance, Tertullian (160–240), that magnificent apologist, emphasizes the contrast between the two women in terms of the faith of Mary in God and the trust of Eve in Satan: "Crediderat Eva serpenti; credidit Maria Gabrieli; quod illa credendo deliquit, haec credendo delevit."[5]

Epiphanius (d. 403), the bishop of Salamis and a defender of the Nicene faith, affirms in this context that Mary and not Eve is the true mother of the living, because while Eve brought death to the human race, Mary instead offered life:

Siquidem Eva tum viventium est appellata mater . . . post admissum videlicet peccatum. Quod quidem admiratione dignum est, post illam offensionem, tam praeclarum cognomen attributum. Ac si exteriora duntaxat et sensibus obvia consideres, ab eadem hac Eva totius est in terris humani generis origo deducta. Revera tamen a Maria Virgine vita ipsa est in mundum introducta, ut viventem pariat, et *viventium Maria sit mater* . . . siquidem Eva generi hominum causam mortis attulit, per quam mors est in orbem terrarum invecta; Maria vitae causam praebuit, per quam vita est nobis ipsa producta.[6]

Ambrose (340–97), the great preacher and exegete, who established a parallel between the two women more generally on the basis of their virginity, called Mary the mother of salvation in contrast with Eve, the mother of the race.[7] John Chrysostom (354–407), an Antiochene doctor of the Church and the greatest of the Greek fathers, offers an interpretation of the

Eve-Mary antithesis within the limits of an eschatological vision that sees the substitution of Mary for Eve; the devil, who had at first conquered because of a woman, was in turn overcome by Christ by means of a woman. Through Eve mankind had gained the wood of death, but, with the substitution of Mary for Eve, the tree of the knowledge of good and evil was exchanged for the wood of the cross and of victory:

> Per quae enim diabolus vicerat, per eadem Christus devicit, et acceptis quibus usus fuerat armis, eum debellavit: et quomodo audi, Virgo erat Eva, necdum enim virum cognoverat; lignum erat arbor; mors mulcta Adami. At ecce iterum Virgo et lignum et mors, illa cladis symbola, ipsius victoriae facta sunt. Nam loco Evae est Maria; loco ligni scientiae boni et mali lignum crucis.[8]

The parallelism between the two virgins is even more vividly presented in his *Expositio in Psalmum XLIV* when he declares: "Virgo nos paradiso expulit, per virginem vitam aeternam invenimus. Per quae condemnati sumus, per ea fuimus coronati,"[9] and in his *Homilia in sanctam Drosiden*, where he asserts: "Per virginem olim Adamum diabolus interemit, per virginem deinde Christus diabolum superavit."[10] Jerome (377–420), the eminent classicist, declares in his customarily terse style, "Mors per Evam, vita per Mariam" (death through Eve, life through Mary).[11] Augustine (354–430) echoes this concept when he writes, contrasting the corruption of Eve with the integrity of Mary, "Per feminam mors, per feminam vita: per Evam interitus, per Mariam salus."[12]

This theme was constantly repeated during the patristic age. Particularly after the Council of Ephesus (A.D. 431), which proclaimed the Virgin the Mother of God (*Theotókos*), the Western church emphasized the grandeur of Mary and her influence, in virtue of her maternal authority, upon her omnipotent Son. It is probable that Origen (185?–254) had coined the term *Theotókos;*[13] it is indisputably certain that this term is found for the first time in the work of Alexander, the bishop of Alexandria, in his *Epistola ad Alexandrum episcopum Constantinopolitanum;*[14] and the term *Theotókos* has been in common use since the fourth century. Nevertheless, it is only in the fifth that the Mother of God receives the consideration and the liturgical recognition that involves her sublime and exalted status and not her maternal and human nature.

Exalted above the angels and saints of heaven, she was acclaimed and called, by virtue of her co-redemptive association with Christ, the second Eve. Identified with *Mater Ecclesia*, she soon was considered the mediatrix of all graces, the one who intercedes as a suppliant at the throne of God. This concept of the mediation of Mary developed more slowly across the centuries by means of an evolution that began with the Eve-Mary parallelism, passed through the Church-Mary comparison, and finally, all very gradually, culminated in the concept of Marian mediation. As Coathalem observes, "Durant les premiers siècles, on ne trouve aucune allusion à l'intercession de la Sainte Vierge."[15] The theme of Marian mediation was touched on ever so slightly in the fourth and fifth centuries[16] in terms that were not too clear; language that was somewhat more pronounced but still not couched in precise doctrinal terms was used at the beginning of the eighth century, especially by Germanus of Constantinople.[17]

Paul the Deacon, in the same century, seems to have been the first in the Western world to refer to the Virgin as the *"mediatrix Dei ad homines,"*[18] while in the Eastern world, as we have already seen, John the Geometer in the tenth century proclaimed her "a second mediatrix next to the first mediator."[19] The doctrine of Marian mediation as elaborated by the Geometer is spiritually interesting because it is inspired by the idea of the maternal activity of Mary toward men and founded upon the concept of Marian co-redemption.[20] But it is only with Ambrogio Autperto (d. 784), the abbot for one year (777–78) of the monastery of San Vincenzo at Volturno, that we encounter a decided progress in the definition of the concept of Marian mediation. Autperto connects Mary's acquisition and distribution of graces with her universal motherhood (which is an extension of her role in the Incarnation) and with her participation in the Redemption, even if he does not explicitly state that Mary intercedes for all graces:

Cum toto mentis affectu beatissimae Virginis nos intercessionibus committamus, omnes eius patrocinia omni nisu imploremus: ut dum nos supplici eam obsequio frequentamus in terris, ipsa nos sedula prece commendare dignetur in coelis. Neque enim dubium, quae meruit pro liberandis proferre pretium, posse plus sanctis omnibus, liberatis impendere suffragium.[21]

In his *Sermo CXXIV*, on the Sunday of the Annunciation, after declaring that the Virgin is the "spes unica peccatorum," Autperto exclaims:

> Sancta Maria, succurre miseris, juva pusillanimes, refove flebiles, ora pro populo, interveni pro clero, intercede pro devoto femineo sexu. Sentiant omnes tuum juvamen, quicumque celebrant tuam commemorationem. Assiste parata votis poscentium.[22]

There is no doubt that in the eighth century Autperto, by the amplitude and originality of his thought on the mediation of Mary, is an exception. In the ninth and the tenth centuries, in fact, exegesis will do nothing but repeat the parallelism Eve-Mary and Church-Mary, set forth by patristic tradition. It is true that the mediational role of Mary can be seen for the first time during the eleventh century, in the hymns, homilies, and sequences of such authors as Fulbert of Chartres (d. 1029), Berno of Reichnau (d. 1048), Odilo of Cluny (d. 1049), Peter Damian (d. 1072), Anselm of Lucca (d. 1086), Alberic of Montecassino (d. 1088), Radbod of Noyen (d. 1098), and many others.[23] But it is principally in the twelfth century, at Citeaux, within the confines of Benedictine monasticism, that we encounter the full flowering and the theological crystallization of the mediation of Mary. Monastic figures such as Serlon of Savigny (d. 1148), Guerric of Igny (d. 1151), Aelred of Rievaulx (d. 1167), Nicholas of Clairvaux (d. 1176), Alan of Lille (d. 1202), and Helinand of Froidmond (d. 1212) compose sermons for the Virgin which comment not only on all the mysteries of the Redemption but in particular on her universal mediation.[24]

To Anselm of Canterbury, however, is due the honor of having defined the principal characteristics of the mediation. He indicated that Mary is the gate of life and the door of salvation for everyone: "mater restitutionis omnium."[25] Druwé declares that Anselm "est le premier à faire passer dans la conscience chrétienne, dans la piété vécue, l'idée . . . que Marie est vraiment notre mère."[26] Anselm not only establishes a parallel between the fatherhood of God and the motherhood of Mary but puts a greater emphasis, in the Incarnation, upon the motherhood of Mary than upon the condescension of the Logos. He even goes to the point of declaring that both damnation and salvation depend as much upon the will of Mary as upon the will of Christ.[27]

Bernard, on the other hand, while he recognizes that Christ is the true mediator, emphasizes the necessity of the mediation of Mary. Because men fear Christ, their Judge, they need "a mediator with that Mediator"; Mary is kind and amiable ("nihil austerum in ea, nihil terribile: tota suavis est") and incapable of judging anyone:

> Et quidem sufficere poterat Christus . . . sed nobis bonum non erat esse homi-
> nem solum. Fidelis plane et praepotens mediator Dei et hominum homo
> Christus Jesus, sed divinam in eo reverentur homines majestatem . . . opus
> est enim *mediatore ad Mediatorem iustum*, nec aliter nobis utilior quam Mar-
> ia. . . . Quid ad Mariam accedere trepidet humana fragilitas? Nihil austerum
> in ea, nihil terribile: tota suavis est . . . age gratias ei qui talem tibi media-
> tricem benignissima miseratione providit.[28]

It is important to note, in this context, that the mediation of Mary assumes a theocentric aspect for Bernard. He specifically affirms that this mediation is in keeping with divine intention. In a metaphor of symbolic brilliance, Bernard observes that Christ is the spring of living water that must provide drink for the *civitatem Dei*, that is the Church and her members, but that this vein of celestial water will not reach the city except through the aqueduct of Mary:

> Vita aeterna, fons indeficiens, qui universam irrigat superficiem paradisi.
> Nec modo irrigat, sed inebriat, fons hortorum, puteus aquarum viventium,
> quae fluunt de Liban: et flumen impetus laetificat civitatem Dei. Quis vero
> fons vitae, nisi Christus Dominus? . . . Descendit per aquaeductum vena illa
> coelestis, non tamen fontis exhibens copiam, sed stillicidia gratiae arentibus
> cordibus nostris infundens, aliis quidem plus, aliis minus, plenus equidem
> aquaeductus, ut accipiant caeteri de plenitudine, sed non plenitudinem
> ipsam.
>   Advertistis iam, ni fallor, quem velim dicere aquaeductum, qui plen-
> itudinem fontis ipsius de corde Patris excipiens, nobis edidit illum, si non
> prout est, saltem prout capere poteramus. Nostis enim cui dictum sit: *Ave,*
> *gratia plena.* An vero inveniri potuisse miramur, unde talis ac tantus fieret
> aquaeductus. . . . Sed quomodo noster hic aquaeductus fontem illum attigit
> tam sublimem? Quomodo putas, nisi vehementia desiderii, nisi fervore de-

votionis, nisi puritate orationis? Sicut scriptum est: *Oratio justi penetrat coelos* (Eccli. xxx, 21). Et quis justus, si non Maria justa?[29]

The humanity of Mary, then, came to be associated generally with her earthly suffering; the most evident image of her humility and her most immediate cooperation with the redemptive act came to be joined with her motherhood. The role of Mary is not expiatory in quite the same sense as that of Christ, but "the inner dispositions of Mary, characterized as they were by a universal love and a perfect obedience to the Father, were perfectly oriented to sacrifice and allowed her to participate in her own way in the immolation, on the part of Christ, of himself."[30] Bur asserts that Mary "comprit parfaitement le plan salvifique de Dieu et . . . elle adhéra au sacrifice du Christ, non par une simple compassion toute naturelle, mais par l'oblation volontairement consentie de sa souffrance."[31] Arnauld of Bonevalle, for example, in the twelfth century, expressed in these terms the idea of this complete and integral adherence, of this participation and cooperation in the realization of the redemptive work of the Son:

> Dividunt coram Patre inter se mater et Filius pietatis officia, et miris allegationibus muniunt redemptionis humanae negotium, et conducunt inter se reconciliationis nostrae inviolabile testamentum.[32]

In considering the sacrifice of Christ as a liturgical action, Arnauld even arrives at suggesting the idea of the priesthood of Mary. Mary is an associate in the work of Redemption because she is also an associate in the mystery of the Incarnation: the *Fiat* of the *Mater gaudiosa* preannounces and prefigures in itself the mission of the *Mater dolorosa*. But in the maternity of Mary the exegetes of the time preferred to accentuate her vulnerability to human suffering, to tears, to sorrow.

As a consequence, just as the initial impulse toward the production of a drama of the Passion was furnished by the intense Christocentric mysticism of the eleventh and the twelfth centuries, so too the embryonic nucleus of the *Planctus Mariae* sprang forth from the meditations on the sufferings of the Virgin. Beginning in the eleventh century, these meditations reached their height in the twelfth century, and, by virtue of their pathetic comments upon the sacrifice of the cross, they betray the natural ties that exist between the *Passio* and the *Compassio*. Although patristic writings had generally commented on Mary's instrumentality in the Passion by indicating that she had cooperated in a proximate, direct, and immediate manner in the fulfillment of Redemption, the commentaries of the eleventh and twelfth centuries emphasized her suffering and her human agony; they saw in the Virgin the figure of the *Mater dolorosa*, who experienced in her heart the most sorrowful reality of the sufferings of her Son.

CHAPTER V

THE MARIAN CULT

AND DEVOTION

THE theory of the *Zeitgeist* will appear even more plausible because it is precisely the twelfth century that shines forth as the period of the richest development in the formulation of a type of Marian liturgy; this finds its most sublime expression in the hyperdulia dedicated to the Virgin.[1] This temporal convergence should come as no surprise in light of the patristic writings, the works of the eighth and the tenth centuries, and those of the eleventh and twelfth, which had affirmed that the Virgin suffered in full association with Christ the sorrows of his Passion. It was logical that the same spiritual sensibility that had dwelt, in the eleventh and twelfth centuries, with such intensity upon the meditation of the Passion of her Son should confer upon the Virgin her own peculiar cult. In their various exegetical works men of that age would grant her the most exalted status as the Mother of Christ and would celebrate her suffering motherhood at the moment of the Passion of her Son.

The logic and the validity of this temporal convergence are pointed out, for instance, by Vandenbroucke, when he asserts that "la dévotion au Christ ne pouvait qu'entrainer une recrudescence de la dévotion à Marie. Pour être plus populaire, celle-ci ne manqua pas d'exercer une réelle influence sur les conceptions des théologiens et des grands auteurs spirituels. La place de premier plan que tint Marie dans la Rédemption leur parut un titre sans pareil à un culte spécial."[2] Druwé agrees and indicates, from his perspective, that "l'ardente dévotion du Christ dans son humanité—a

l'Enfant de la crèche et au Supplice du Calvaire,—que l'on voit apparaître
à la fin du XIᵉ siècle, devait s'attacher, du même élan, à la mère de Jésus."[3]

More than in any other period, in fact, the Virgin became, in the eleventh century and even more so in the twelfth, the object of ardent veneration. Numerous were the forms of devotion that rose in her honor.[4] Of
particular interest for the purposes of our investigation is the formulation
in this period of devotions intended to celebrate the profound sufferings of
the Virgin during the Passion of Christ, sufferings and sorrows which not
only make manifest and visible the reality of the sacrifice of Christ upon
the cross but also project the tortured tragic vision and the intensely dramatic emotions of the compassion of the Virgin.

Toward the middle of the eleventh century there appeared, for instance,
the liturgical development of the cult of the five joys of the Virgin; in the
twelfth century the number of joys reached seven. Toward the middle of
the same century there arose, perhaps under the inspiration of the cult of
the five joys, the devotion to the five sorrows that the Virgin suffered on
seeing the five wounds of her Son.[5] Symptomatic of this devotional intensity to the sorrows of the Virgin are the cult of the seven sorrows of the
Virgin, which existed at the beginning of the fourteenth century; the
Order of Servites, approved by Benedict XI in 1304 and consecrated from
its very foundation to the veneration of the sorrows sustained by the Virgin under the cross;[6] and the Confrérie de Notre-Dame des Sept-Douleurs, founded in Flanders in 1490 at the instance of John of Coudenberg,
dean of the Church of Saint-Gilles in the city of Abbenbroek. Generously
supported by Philip the Handsome (1478–1506), the Confrérie received
pontifical approval in 1495 and thereafter Leo X (1513–1521) showed himself quite munificent to it.[7] But already at the beginning of the fourteenth
century the devotion to the Seven Sorrows of the Virgin is amply documented.[8]

The cult of the five sorrows and the wounds of the Virgin—the manifestation of her *compassio*—was a direct response to the needs of the conso-
latory emotionalism elaborated by the spirituality of the eleventh and
twelfth centuries; it found expression not only in prose compositions but
also in lyrics. The specifically emotional and dramatically expressive aspects, as yet not properly studied, of the *preces compassionis* are of unques-

tionable importance for an appreciation of the development of the theme of the *Compassio* and the *Planctus Mariae* in the Middle Ages. The earliest of the *preces* date from the time of Pope John XXII (1316–34),[9] to whom is attributed the composition of an *Officium horarum de dolore Beatae Mariae Virginis*.[10] Extremely interesting, for instance, because of their tragically tender and dolorous language, are the two *orationes*—the one *de doloribus Virginis*, the other *de planctu Virginis*—which appear in an *Officium* of the fourteenth century, preserved in the Bibliothèque Mazarine in Paris. This *Officium* offers "septem orationes . . . ad honorem VII cardinalium doloris transverberantium gladiorum, que virgo benedicta Maria seu eius felix anima passa fuit in captione et passione filii sui die Veneris Sancta."[11]

In the *Oratio de doloribus Virginis*, the author recalls the vision of the Virgin at the foot of the cross and lists the sorrows that were cut into her mother's heart at the sight of the tragic Passion of her Son:

> Propter illius doloris gladium qui pertransivit animam tuam virgo clementissima, quando cernebas filium tuum delicatissimum, dulcem Ihesum, nudum in cruce levatum, clavis perforatum, cruore perfusum ac per omnia plagis et vulneribus laceratum: adiuva, suppliciter deprecor, me peccatorem miserum, ut animam meam compassionis gladius perfodiat, divinique amoris lancea vulneratur: ut omnis peccati causa noxie effluat a pectore meo.[12]

In the *Oratio de planctu Virginis*, the author expresses the lament of the Virgin in plangent accents and with telling effect:

> Propter illius acerbi eiulatus planctum, quem de profundo pectoris erumpentem abscondere non valebas, virgo castissima, quando, . . . in amplexus ruebas exanimi corporis filii tui dulcis Ihesu de cruce depositi, cuius genas ante nitentes et ora rutilantia mortis conspiciebas perfundi palloribus ipsumque cernebas totum tumidum livoribus ac concisum vulnere super vulnus: auxiliare, suppliciter deprecor, me miserum peccatorem.[13]

Distinctive for its complete apprehension of the *compassio* is an *Officium* of the seven sorrows or *tristitiae* of the Virgin, also preserved in a text of the Bibliothèque Mazarine but once in the possession of the Celestines of Paris. This *Officium* is fundamentally a reworking by Philippe de Maizières (d. 1405), chancellor of Cyprus and counselor of France, of passages taken from the famous *Speculum humanae salvationis*. In its sixth *tristitia* it offers one of the most moving and emotional descriptions of the lament of the Virgin at the moment of Christ's being taken down from the cross:

VI^a Tristicia

> *Ave Maria, mater Christi pia, celestis imperatrix. Tu es, virgo dya, tristium in hac via clemens consolatrix.*
>
> *Sextam tristiciam, mater dulcissima, tunc habuisti, quando dulcissimum filium tuum de cruce suscepisti,*
>
> *Quando ipsum brachiis tuis, mitissima virgo Maria, mortuum et lividum imposuit Ioseph ab Arimathia.*
>
> *Quem olim crebro dulciter et letanter vivum portaveras, heu nunc mortuum cum magna tristicia portabas.*
>
> *Novus luctus et novus gemitus in corde tuo oriebatur, et tristicia tua semper magis ac magis accumulabatur.*
>
> *O quantus erat, pia mater, tuus luctus et ploratus, O qualis erat, dulcis virgo, tuus planctus et ululatus.*
>
> *O quam modicam quietem et consolacionem, domina, habuisti, antequam dilectum filium tuum resurrexisse conspexisti.*
>
> *Tantam habuisti, pia mater, tristiciam et dolorem quod libenter pro filio tuo dilecto vel cum eo subiisses passionem.*
>
> *Die noctuque luxisti, planxisti, doluisti et flevisti, quamdiu illa melliflua presencia filii tui caruisti.*
>
> *O quam durum et quam lapideum cor habere videretur, qui tue tristicie tam immense, virgo pia, non compateretur.*
>
> *Per hanc tristiciam, mater clementissima, rogo te.*[14]

In the context of the prose compositions of the fourteenth century we encounter the *Speculum humanae salvationis*, a treatise in rhymed prose that sets forth, according to the figurative, allegorical fashion of the Middle Ages, the story of the fall of man and of his redemption. The *Speculum*, which was composed in 1324 among the Dominicans of Strasburg, most probably by Ludolph of Saxony,[15] in its earlier chapters provides a biblical and exegetical commentary on the Passion of Christ; then in the twenty-seventh chapter it gives a deep and penetrating presentation of the lament of the Virgin. The *Speculum* explains the predominantly human character of the plaint and affirms that its intensity, sadness, and devotion were so moving that the bystanders were stirred "ad compatiendum et complorandum." The author of the *Speculum* presents the lament of the Virgin in its co-redemptive context, the perfect association of the Mother with the Passion of her Son; the background is the prophecy of old Simeon, who had foretold the participation of the Mother in the sorrow of her Son:

> In praecendentibus audivimus Salvatoris nostri passionem,
> Consequenter audiamus dulcissimae matris eius dolorem.
> Quando Salvator noster *passionem* toleravit,
> Affuit Maria et secum omnia per *compassionem* portavit.
> Tunc impletum est quod dixerat ei Simeon justus:
> "Tuam ipsius animam pertransibit gladius!"[16]

The lament of the Virgin is initially discussed in the twenty-sixth chapter, in its typological symbolism and in contrast to the lament of Jacob and in particular to the lament of Adam and Eve over Abel. The author declares that, although they had wept for Abel for "centum annos," the sorrow of the Virgin was greater: "Tamen dolor Mariae comprobatur major existitisse."[17] In its thematic and lyrical essence the lament begins in the twenty-seventh chapter, at the moment when the body of Christ, wrapped in a shroud, is laid by Joseph of Arimathea and Nicodemus upon the sepulchral stone:

> Maria affuit cum miserabili planctu et lamentatione
> Et cum luctu et multarum lacrimarum effusione.
> Nulla lingua sufficit ejus dolorem enarrare,
> Nec aliqua mens sufficit ejus tristitiam cogitare.
> In tantum tota nocte et die planctu fatigata erat,
> Quod vix exsequias Filii sui ad sepulchrum sequi poterat.
> Tot osculis et amplexibus corpus Filii constringebat,
> Quod omnis populus sibi compatiens, quaerulando dicebat:
> "O quam crudelitatem impiissimi exercuere
> In hac tam pulchra delectabili muliere!"

In tantum planxit, luxit, genuit et ploravit,
Quod omnes ad compatiendum et complorandum provocavit.
Quis enim tam turbatissimae matri non compateretur?
Quis ad tantarum lacrimarum effusionem non emolliretur?
Nunc manus Filii, nunc pedes ejus deosculabatur,
Nunc collum ejus, nunc latera stringendo amplexabatur,
Nunc pectus proprium pugnis percutiebat et tundebat,
Nunc manus cum effusione lacrimarum constringebat,
Nunc intuebatur vulnera Filii sui, nunc oculos,
Nunc osculis oris super pectus ejus corruit, nunc super os.[18]

The notion of the *compassio* of the Virgin, that is, of her association and involvement with the Passion of Christ, is exhaustively detailed in chapter 30, where the profound agony of the Mother in sharing the sorrows and tribulations of her Son confers upon her the special title and privilege of being a companion in the Passion and a conqueror with him of Satan:

Omnia, quae Christus in passione sua tolerabat,
Haec Maria per maternam compassionem secum portabat.
Clavi, qui pertransiverunt pedes Filii sui et manus,
Per compassionem penetraverunt sanctissimae Mariae pectus.
Lancea, quae latus Filii sui mortui perforavit,
Per compassionem cor Matris viventis penetravit;
Aculei spinarum, qui caput Christi pupugerunt,
Per compassionem cor genitricis eius vulneraverunt;
Gladius acutissimarum linguarum, quas Christus audivit,
Per compassionem intimam Mariae animam pertransivit;
Et sicut Christus superavit diabolum per suam passionem,
Ita etiam superavit eum Maria per maternam compassionem.[19]

Very important in their mystical perfection and felicitous expression are the *preces compassionis* of Anselm. Born of his intense Marian devotion, they employ powerful images to describe the extraordinary feeling of the very human tenderness of the Virgin during the Passion of her Son. Although the impressive contribution of Anselm to the development of the *Planctus*

Mariae will be examined later in the course of our investigation, I would like to offer here some evidence of his devotion in a passage from his *Oratio XX*, which mirrors with lyrical immediacy the compassion of the Virgin:

> Domina mea misericordissima, quos fontes dicam erupisse de tuis pudicissimis oculis, cum attenderes unicum filium tuum innocentem coram te ligari, flagellari, mactari? Quos fletus credam perfudisse piissimum tuum vultum, cum susciperes eundem filium tuum Deum et Dominum tuum in cruce sine culpa extendi, et carnem de carne tua ab ipsis crudeliter dissecari? Quibus singultibus aestimabo purissimum pectus vexatum esse, cum tu audires: "Mulier, ecce filius tuus"; et discipulus: "Ecce mater tua." Cum acciperes in filium discipulum pro magistro, servum pro Domino?[20]

Commenting on the luminous and profound humanity of the compassionate sentiments expressed in this *Oratio*, Du Manoir affirms that "avec ce thème de la compassion, Anselme nous introduit dans une nouvelle voie de la piété, qui n'a guère été explorée avant lui."[21]

The cult of the sorrows of the Virgin finds an even more intense elaboration and illustration in the lyric. The five sorrows suffered by the Virgin traditionally embody those which were most profoundly imprinted upon her maternal heart by these biblical events: the prophecy of old Simeon, the loss and discovery of Jesus after three days in the temple, the betrayal and arrest of Jesus, the contemplation of Christ on the cross, and his being laid in her lap after being taken down from the cross. A hymn of the fifteenth century from the *Codex Iosephini* of Hildesheim, although it surely reflects an older tradition, offers us a profoundly lyrical version of the five sorrows:

> *De V Doloribus Beatae Mariae Virginis*
>
> 1. Recordare, O Maria,
>   Quo dolore tua pia
>   Perfusa sunt intima,
>   Dum narrante Simeone
>   Transigenda cum mucrone
>   Tua fertur anima.

2. Recordare, virgo clemens,
   Tuum natum quantum gemens
   Quem quaerebas triduo
   Flens, dum illum perdidisti,
   Qui est salus, invenisti
   Cum cordis desiderio.

3. Recordare, quod turbatum
   Est cor tuum, dum artatum
   Cognoscebas filium,
   Quo detento liberabar,
   Qui in culpis captivabar
   Praesenti in exsilio.

4. Recordare, quantum flebas,
   Dum in cruce hunc cernebas
   Moriens deficere,
   Quia ventris tui fructus
   Sic sanare nostros luctus
   Volens ac deicere.

5. Recordare, o praeclara,
   Quam immensa, quam amara
   Tua fuit anxietas,
   Dum in cruce est levatus
   Et in tuas ulnas datus,
   Qui est vera pietas.

6. Recordare quinque horum
   Tormentorum ac dolorum
   Perenni memoria,
   Ut omnes, qui te invocamus,
   Per te sisti valeamus
   In caelesti gloria.[22]

An example of the poetic compositions on the seven sorrows of the Virgin is offered us by a text of the thirteenth century. At its conclusion the poet unites his feeling of commiseration with the compassion of the Virgin.

De VII Doloribus Beatae Mariae Virginis

1. Christi matris animam
   vicibus et horis
   Septenis pertransiit
   gladius doloris.

2. Te, Maria, gladius
   doloris anxiavit,
   Quem in templo Simeon
   primum prophetavit.

3. Secundus, cum parvuli
   Bethlehem necantur
   Et per matres flebiles
   voce deplorantur.

4. Tertius, cum triduo
   Iesum amisisti
   In doctorum medio
   eumque invenisti.

5. Quartus, cum in spiritu
   scires captivari
   Iesum [atque] vinculis,
   sputis, flagris dari.

6. Quintus, cum in medio
   latronum pendentem
   Crucifixum cerneres
   atque morientem.

7. Sextus, cum depositum
   de cruce tulisti,
   Fletum et suspiria
   gravia dedisti.

8. Septimus, cum tumulo
   corpus abscondisti,
   Flens et quasi mortua
   inde recessisti.

9. Fac me, virgo, plangere
   tecum ac turbari.
   In extremis ut queam
   per te consolari.

10. Hos dolores recolo
    dolens cum Maria;
    Christe, me caelicolam
    fac cum matre pia.[23]

Examples of lyrics on the five wounds of Christ, that is, the wound in
his side and those on his hands and his feet, are offered us by a codex of
the fourteenth century from Karlsruhe in Germany and by a codex of the
fifteenth century preserved in Mantua. The hymn to the five wounds in
the German codex is particularly interesting because the aesthetic and
dramatic tension, established by the reality of the five wounds, is communicated to us with a vibrant actuality, spiritually manifest in a fundamental
appreciation of the sufferings of Christ in which the Virgin participates by
her motherhood and her implied presence on Calvary:

De Vulneribus Christi

1. Ave, fructus O Mariae
   Et caelestis vas sophiae,
   Circumcisus qui in die,
   Fac nos salvos, Iesu pie.

2. Ave, cuncta qui creasti,
   Dum in monte qui sudasti,
   Quando patrem exorasti,
   Nos exaudi, quos plasmasti.

3. Ave, caput Christi gratum,
   Duris spinis coronatum,

Nos conserva, ne peccatum
Poenae ducat ad reatum.

4. Ave, dextra manus Christi,
Perforata plaga tristi,
Nos ad dextram iube sisti,
Quos per dextram redimisti.

5. Ave, palma Iesu laeva,
Sic confixa plaga saeva,
Nos ab aevo malo leva,
Quod produxit mater Eva.

6. Ave, latus lanceatum,
Unde fluxit flumen gratum,
Praebe nobis conducatum
Ad aeternae vitae statum.

7. Ave, vulnus dextri pedis,
Aedem mentis pie laedis,
Dum ad eam saepe redis,
Esto nobis spes mercedis.

8. Ave, plaga laevae plantae,
Qua virtutum crescunt plantae,
Nos ab hoste supplantante
Contuere post et ante.

9. Ave, tota denudata
Caro Christi flagellata,
Nos conserva, ne peccata
Vita privent nos beata.

10. Ave, Iesu, cruce pressus,
Fatigatus, lassus, fessus,
Tu pro nobis post excessus
Laxa malos cordis gressus.

11. Ave, Iesu, tu frumentum,
In Maria quod inventum,

> Crucis venit ad tormentum,
> Cordis nostri pascementum.
>
> 12. Ergo nostri miserere,
>   Hic nos pasce et tuere,
>   Tu nos bona fac videre,
>   Ubi dies, quies vere.[24]

Hymns which celebrate the seven sorrows of the Virgin are particularly plentiful in the fourteenth and fifteenth centuries[25] and are indicative of the popularity this cult had achieved in that period. But it is especially through the vast flowering, from the twelfth to the fourteenth century, of the *Planctus Mariae* and of lyrical compositions on the theme of the *De compassione Beatae Mariae Virginis*[26] that we attain a full and detailed picture of the fine array of clearly literary compositions dedicated to exploring, describing, and communicating the agonized and tormented maternal emotion of the Virgin at the foot of the cross.

CHAPTER VI

PLANCTUS MARIAE *AND*

COMPASSIO VIRGINIS

N their finished state the composi-
tions of the *Planctus Mariae*, which are frequently the fruit of an inspired
aesthetic sense and an uncommon intellectual ability, often let transpire an
apparent inconsistency in wishing to provide a biblical event with an aesthetic undertone, to transfigure poetically one of the most moving moments of the liturgy of the Passion, the *Stabat Mater juxta crucem*. Despite
the solemnity of its content and of its spiritual power, the *Planctus Mariae*
invariably emphasizes the contrast of the logic of the maternal heart as it
contemplates the awful intensity of the bloody drama of the Son upon the
cross with the affirmation of the dogmatic elements of the Redemption, of
which the *Planctus Mariae* represents nevertheless an ennobling spiritual
crystallization.

The liturgical tradition of the earlier *Planctus Mariae* stretches from the
eleventh to the fourteenth century; we have already had occasion to refer
to them in this study. They are the *Planctus ante nescia* of Geoffrey of
Breteuil and the *Maestae parentis Christi* of Adam of St. Victor,[1] both of the
twelfth century; the "Flete fideles animae" of the thirteenth century; the
two laments of the fourteenth century preserved in the Biblioteca Civica
of Bergamo, the *Planctus Sacratissime Virginis Mariae Matris Yhesu Christi*
and the *Planctus Virginis Marie Matris Dei*;[2] and the *Planctus* of Cividale and
the *Planctus* of the *Ordinarium ecclesiae Patavinae*, which also belong to the
fourteenth century. In this tradition one can also include another *Planctus*
of the twelfth century, little known to students of medieval drama; it is
preserved in a Latin manuscript, also of the twelfth century, in the Biblio-

teca Civica of Turin (Laudes. 749.91). Our presentation is based on the version of 1439, written in Florence but surviving in the Hofbibliothek of Karlsruhe in Germany as a manuscript written on paper.[3] The profound thematic unity of this *Planctus* is composed of the human and spiritual tension of the dialogue or, better, the contest between the Virgin and the cross, born of the anguished desire of the Mother to take her Son away from the cross:

> Crux redde meum filium,
> totum meum solatium
> jam non expecto alium,
> ut scripturae nuntiant

and of the cross's firm if deferential refusal to restore the Son to his Mother before the completion of the redemptive sacrifice:

> Virgo tibi respondeo,
> pro mundo Ihesum teneo,
> hunc tibi non restituo,
> ut mundum morte redimat.

At the conclusion of the *Planctus* a human and spiritual balance is reached between the love of the Mother and the spiritual resolution of the cross, so that the redemptive work of Christ for the salvation of the world may take place:

> Pacem simul habeamus,
> amplius non contendamus,
> totum Deo committamus,
> cui sit laus et gloria.

The complete version of the lament underscores for us the harmony and proportion existing between its spirituality and the vast range of human feelings of the Virgin in her sufferings:

> *Planctus et lamentatio beatae Mariae*
>
> I
>
> Ante crucem virgo stabat
> Christi poenas cogitabat,

totam se dilaniabat,
   vultum lavat lacrimis,

II

dixit "Fili: quid fecisti?
quod delictum commisisti,
quare crucem ascendisti?
   me dolentem respice!

III

O vel heu, Christe, deus,
heu heu amor meus,
te damnavit phariseus
   viventem sine crimine.

IV

Jam pendes in patibulo,
juvare te non valeo,
mori tecum desidero,
   Ihesu pie dulcissime!

V

Orbata sponso filio,
apostolos non video,
sola quo vadam nescio,
   non possum ultra vivere.

VI

Vos, Judei, per errorem
occidistis redemptorem,
mundum sanat per amorem
   sua sancta passio.

VII

O gens caeca Judaeorum,
ad te venit rex coelorum
totam summam debitorum
   solvens magno pretio.

VIII
Jhesum meum condempnastis,
spinis, clavis perforastis,
me pro illo contristastis
 fellis dantes pocula."

IX
Respondet Christus Mariae
Dixit Christus: "Mater mea,
non te turbet poena mea,
praecedam vos in Galilea,
 resurgam die tertia.

X
Johannes sit tuus filius,
custos tibi et famulus,
eritque tibi bajulus
 in hac mundi miseria.

XI
Pater misit me ad mortem,
jam vici draconem fortem,
super me miserunt sortem
 Judaei, gens incredula.

XII
Mors est pavor damnatorum,
visus, gaudium sanctorum,
communis porta viatorum
 ad poenam vel ad gaudium.

XIII
Dixit Maria ad crucem
"O crux dira, quid fecisti?
multum certe praesumpsisti,
Jhesum deum suscepisti,
 qui creavit omnia.

XIV

Crux, redde meum filium,
totum meum solatium,
jam non expecto alium,
    ut scripturae nuntiant.

XV

Crux, aperte respice,
vide terram tremere,
solem et lunam claudere,
    haec Ihesum deum nuntiant."

XVI

Respondet crux Mariae
"Virgo, tibi respondeo,
pro mundo Ihesum teneo,
hunc tibi non restituo,
    ut mundum morte redimat.

XVII

Haec est certa lex naturae,
jugum grave geniturae,
omnes vivunt isto jure,
    ut mors omnes rapiat.

XVIII

Mors est quies viatorum,
finis omnium laborum
per mortem Christi redemptorem,
    oportet quod sic transeat.

XIX

Christus mortem ordinavit,
mundum morti subjugavit,
propter hoc ipse gustavit,
    quod aliis ordinaverat.

XX

Nichil convenientius
quam Christus Adae filius
patri succurrat penitus,
    ut secum ad coelum redeat:

XXI

Virgo, tu Evae filia
morte damnata libera
solve serpentis vincula,
    mundus te laudet et serviat.

XXII

Mundus totus te laudabit,
paradisus exultabit,
Christus Adam liberabit,
    resurget die tertia."

XXIII

Dixit Maria ad crucem
"Crux, verba tua audio,
sub umbra tua doleo,
Ihesum pendere video
    inter latrones viliter.

XXIV

In me se deus humiliavit,
et infernum exspoliavit,
per me coelum reseravit
    Christus clamans fortiter.

XXV

Coeli scala sum ordinata,
per mortem Christi consecrata
et Adae praedestinata,
    vexillum victoriae."

XXVI

Respondet crux Mariae
"De hoc debes tu gaudere;
non debet mundus sic jacere,
sed per crucem subvenire
    voluit rex gloriae.

XXVII

Mundus debet me amare,
me devote salutare,
se totum mihi inclinare
    pro Christi reverentia.

XXVIII

Pacem simul habeamus,
amplius non contendamus,
totum Deo committamus,
    cui sit laus et gloria.

XXIX

Mortem jam non timeamus,
Deo devote serviamus,
crucem Dei diligamus
    in hac vita misera."[4]

Also pertaining to the twelfth century is the *Maestae parentis Christi*,[5] a *Planctus* of wide-ranging lyricism, of clear power of expression and of explosive emotionalism. Attributed to Adam of St. Victor, despite the variety of its metrical schemes, the *terminus ad quem* of this lament of the twelfth century finds confirmation not only in the liturgical language from which it draws its inspiration but also in the fact that, as Adalbert Daniel notes, this *Planctus* is a sequence, "partim Notkeriana est, partim Victorina."[6] The lyrical structure of *Maestae parentis Christi* is profoundly effective and dramatic because it derives its impetus from the aesthetic contrast of two distinct perceptions of the same sorrow. There is, on the one hand, the representation of tender maternal feelings as the Virgin, contemplating her Son upon the cross, gives direct utterance to her plaint; on the other hand, there is the image of the grieving and afflicted Virgin, shortly after her Son has been taken down from the cross, as she "in gremio tenet exuvias" and caresses with her tender hands each of his wounds and kisses his pallid face, marked with pain and suffering. This lament is very reserved and intimate, but, all the same, it finds physical expression in a torrent of uncontrollable tears that bathes the body of the Son:

> Manus extorquens exclamavit
> Fletuque corpus irrigavit
> Stillas ut rivos lacrimans.[7]

This lament is compared with those of Rachel, Naomi, Anna the mother of Samuel, and Anna the mother of Tobias; but their plaints were not similar in intensity, as the author observes, to that of the Virgin:

> Sed ad lacrimas amaras
> virginis Mariae,
> Matris Christi crucifixi
> verique Messiae,
> non erat planctus
> similis.[8]

Completely dominated by the plaint of the Virgin is the *Virgo plorans filium*, a *Planctus* of the fourteenth century.[9] It totally internalizes and then projects the agony and the sorrow of Mary; it thus represents the sublimation of the *compassio* of the *Virgo moerens* by means of an emotional crescendo of most delicate sensitivity. It is the plaint of a mother who uses agitated and vibrant words as she feels herself imbued with alternate emotions set loose by the memory of the baby Jesus in her arms:

> Ecce, mater misera,
> Quae te parvum tenera
> Nutrivit ad ubera,
> Fili mi, O Deus!

Then there is the vision of her Son suffering on the cross:

> Moreris et morior,
> Pateris et patior,
> Moerore afficior,
>   Tecum volo mori;
>   . . . .
> Cum in te considero,
> Certe pati video
> Crucis in patibulo
>   Sine culpa poenas;
> Quanta fers supplicia,
> Verbera, ludibria,
> Habens in opprobria
>   Tuas sputa genas.

Her mother's sorrow grows even stronger when she considers the denial of Peter, who had shattered and abandoned the "firma petra" emblematic of his name and of his declared resolution; he had denied the Lord for whom he had sworn to die:

> Heu, Petre, cur frangeris,
> Firmam petram deseris?
> Pro quo mori asseris,
> Iuramentis nega.

Planctus Beatae Mariae Virginis

1. Virgo plorans filium
     Ductum ad supplicium:
     Dic, O rex humilium,
       Fili, quid fecisti?
     Quia gens incredula,
     Mordax velut vipera
     Te traxit ad vincula
       Et crucem subisti?

2. Te in cruce video
   Fixum clavo ferreo,
   Dulce, fili, defleo,
      Dulcis amor meus.
   Ecce, mater misera,
   Quae te parvum tenera
   Nutrivit ad ubera,
      Fili mi, O Deus!

3. Moreris et morior
   Pateris et patior,
   Maerore afficior,
      Tecum volo mori;
   Dans Iohannem filium
   Sed parvum remedium
      Materno dolori.

4. Cerne matrem miseram
   Virginem puerperam,
   Quam in annis teneram
      Tibi dedicasti,
   Ut pupillam oculi
   Te servavi saeculi,
   Qui peccata populi
      In cruce portasti.

5. Fili venerabilis,
   Multum delectabilis,
   Non est dolor similis
      Sicut dolor meus;
   Matrem tuam respice,
   Fili mi dulcissime,
   Noli me deserere,
      Dulcis amor meus.

6. Fili mi, tu loquere
   Et mori me patere,

Cur me solam linquere,
  Fili, vis Iudaeis?
Heu, mors amarissima
Te rapit, O misera,
Iam recedat gratia,
  Moreris pro reis.

7. Vadis, vera hostia,
   Mortis ad supplicia,
   Solus fers stipendia
     Ad salvandas gentes.
   Ubi Thomas Didymus
   Vel Petrus apostolus,
   Qui dixerunt "Ibimus
     Tecum morientes?"

8. Sed tu plagas pateris
   Manuum ac lateris,
   Et tu solus duceris
     Ad crucifigendum.
   Natus sine crimine
   De me matre virgine,
   Agnus sine murmure
     Is ad redimendum.

9. Cum in te considero,
   Certe pati video
   Crucis in patibulo
     Sine culpa paenas;
   Quanta fers supplicia,
   Verbera, ludibria,
   Habens in opprobria
     Tuas sputas genas.

10. Tamquam latro caperis
    Et ligatus duceris
    A Iudaeis miseris
      Mortem crucis pati.

. . . .

11. Heu Petre, cur frangeris,
    Firmam petram deseris?
    Pro quo mori asseris,
        Iuramentis negas.
    Ante multum loqueris,
    Postea mulieris,
    Naeh, a verbo sterneris
        Atque vitam negas.

12. Solus pastor caeditur,
    Totus grex dispergitur,
    Pastor bonus patitur,
        Et crux fugat mortem.
    Mors morte destruitur,
    Dum sic vita moritur,
    Manus crucifigitur
        Et destruxit sortem.

13. Quare tanta pateris,
    Cum nihil peccaveris,
    Quare nunc sic moreris,
        Dulcis amor meus?

Of piercing and painful lyricism but of utter and absolute realization, even in their terse structure, are two brief *Planctus* of the fourteenth century from a German manuscript.[10] In the first of them, entitled *Prolem in cruce pendentem*, the lament of the Virgin is presented within the context of her existence and is focused on two principal events: the prophecy of the aged Simeon, which foretold the lament; and the Crucifixion of her Son, of which the lament constitutes a sorrowful and overwhelming crystallization. The distraught and agitated lament of the Virgin fits harmoniously within the lyric action, which summarizes temporally the two essential and unified boundaries, the Incarnation and the Redemption upon the cross, within which the lament of the Mother finds its theological and eschatological embodiment:

PLANCTUS MARIAE *AND* COMPASSIO VIRGINIS

Planctus Beate Virginis Mariae

Prolem in cruce pendentem
   moesta mater aspiciens,
lacrimatur incessanter
   pectus suum percutiens.

II

Plures movit ad moerorem
   suo ploratu querulo,
natum videns cruentatum,
   tensum crucis patibulo.

III

Animam moestae parentis
   tunc pertransivit acrius
juxta verbum Symeonis
   compassionis gladius.

IV

Sic deplorat mortem prolis
   quam blasphemavit populus
solus erat consolator
   ejus custos discipulus.

In the second of the two laments, which begins *Cum de cruce deponitur,* the relationship between the poetry and the liturgy is created by the internal component, a more visual presentation of the sorrow and the compassion of the Virgin as she contemplates, after Christ has been taken down from the cross, the bloody and cruel evidence of the torment suffered by her Son. The smothered lament of the Virgin is conveyed wordlessly to us as she tries to delay the sorrowful experience of being separated from the body of her Son, as she begs the bystanders to let her remain a little longer, "paululum," to bewail her sorrow and to touch and kiss her Son:

Sustinete, quod paululum
   dolorem meum plangam,
et quod meum dulcissimum
   deosculer et tangam.

The lyrical drive of this sorrow delineates the dimensions of a soul that has shared so fully in the sufferings of her Son that she wants to plumb the very depths of the tragic violence to the point of sharing his death and burial:

> Mihi meum carissimum
> subtrahere nolite,
> Si sepeliri debeat
> me secum sepelite.

Planctus Beatae Virginis Mariae

I
Cum de cruce deponitur,
ad tumulum portatur,
inter dolores anxios
portantes sic precatur;

II
"Sustinete, quod paululum
dolorem meum plangam,
et quod meum dulcissimum
deosculer et tangam.

III
Mihi meum carissimum
subtrahere nolite,
Si sepeliri debeat
me secum sepelite."

IV
Accessit sic exanimis,
et super corpus jecit,
Et sacrum vultum lacrimis
ubertim madefecit.

We can understand the poetic and formal character of the *Planctus Mariae* in its development and evolution by examining a body of lyrical compositions, the thematic and expressive content of which is focused, as in the *Planctus Mariae*, upon the interpretation and lyrical expression of the sorrow and the lament of the Virgin during the Passion of her Son. From a specifically thematic point of view the literary and historical value of the compositions entitled *De compassione Beatae Mariae*—which flourished particularly between the thirteenth and fifteenth centuries—corresponds approximately to the *Planctus Mariae*. Nonetheless, substantial differences exist between these two lyrical embodiments of the same theme. These differences, in general, reflect each author's adherence to a different means of poetical probing of the Virgin's lament.

The literary structure of the *Planctus Mariae* is generally dominated by an imaginative vision of the *Virgo moerens;* there is no limitation here to the description, in coherent but static forms of rhetoric, of the lament and the sorrow of the Virgin. In the *Planctus Mariae* what predominates is the effort to capture the inward movements of the soul of the Virgin and to express them sorrowfully and tragically by the mournful lyricism of her own words. The method of lyrical representation in the *Planctus Mariae* rests upon the Virgin's direct communication of her inner tribulation. The Virgin does not remain inaccessible, as she does in the lyrics of the *De compassione;* instead, she reveals her inner self to the reader directly, as she formulates and presents *coram populo* the here and now of her plaint and her agony. The suggestive power of the *Planctus Mariae* and of its extraordinary emotionalism derives from the vivid description of the plaint of the Virgin. By breaching the figurative barrier of the lyrical composition, the Virgin expresses in her own voice the immediacy of her agony, so that from an artistic representation we reach an instantaneous perception of her lament.

The compositions of the *De compassione* are marked, on the other hand, by an internalization of the Virgin's plaint and sorrow, which is purely descriptive. Thus an understanding of her plaint and sorrow requires the desire of a sensitive soul to grasp them. A characteristic purpose of the rhetorical and poetic journey of the lyrics of the *De compassione* is to establish intimate correspondences of commiseration between the compassion of the Virgin and the sensitivity of the Christian for whom the *De compassione* is intended. In general, the theme of the *De compassione* may be defined as the *Compassio animae devotae super contritione et dolore Beatae Mariae Virginis*, the actual title of a lyric of this genre written in the fifteenth century.[11]

A typical example of this process and expressive attitude is found in a *De compassione Beatae Mariae Virginis* of the fourteenth century.[12] Here the sorrow of the Virgin is recalled in an informative and didactic fashion. The devout author, in exquisite lyrics of great verbal power that suggest and illumine the tormented sorrow and plaint of the Virgin during the Passion, begs of her that he may be allowed to mourn with her. The violent representation of the death of Christ, experienced by his Mother with inner anguish, contains even within its attitude of dramatic compassion a certain detachment, a certain distance from the incomparable and unique reality of a direct contemplation of this scene by means of the words of the Virgin. The lament of the Virgin and her maternal feelings are controlled by the omnipresent devout author, who enters personally into the realistic violence of the events recalled and thereby diminishes the profound power that a presentation in the first person would have emphasized:

> Post haec Christus exclamavit
> Et in cruce exspiravit,
> Sol se totum obscuravit,
>   Quasi lugens Dominum;
> O quis possit cogitare,
> Quaenam lingua explicare,
> Quam tu flebas tunc amare
>   Videns unigenitum!

But even if this composition is not tinted with the direct expression, on the part of the Virgin, of her lament and her sorrow, it is completely suffused with an overpowering lyricism and mournful meditation that contribute to a dramatic quality of the most exquisite variety. The lyric offers memorable pictures of the agitated compassion of the Mother projected upon the background of the unavoidable and already prophesied death of her Son, *ut salvetur saeculum:*

> *De compassione Beatae Mariae Virginis*
>
> 1. O Maria, mater Christi,
>   Quem dolorem habuisti,

Cum in cruce conspexisti
Contemplando filium!
Fac me totum condolere
Et de Christo semper flere
Qui est passus pro me vere
Peccati patibulum.

2. Tota eras dolorosa
Et plorabas lacrimosa,
Velut nubes pluviosa,
    Dans cordis suspirium,
Quia Christus, tuus natus,
Spinis erat coronatus
Et irrisus et velatus
    In conspectu hominum.

3. Vultus eius gloriosus
Et decore speciosus
Erat turpis et lutosus
    Sputis infidelium,
Corpus eius candidatum
Totum erat denigratum,
Quia fuit flagellatum
    Manibus crudelium.

4. Quem tu, virgo, dum vidisti,
Prae dolore defecisti,
Sed nec loqui potuisti
    Per cordis martyrium;
Corde vero tu dolebas
Et amare nimis flebas
Propter natum, quem videbas
    Verberatum nimium.

5. Tantus dolor abundavit,
Qui te totam conquassavit,
Sed et mentem laniavit
    Scindens tuum animum,

Tu videbas patientem
Christum crucem deferentem
. . . .
Ad perdendum unicum.

6. Post hoc Christus denudatur
. . . .
Ut salvetur saeculum;
Per manus ipse pendebat,
Qui iam mundum redimebat,
Tibi mater condolebat
Per cordis incendium.

7. Nimis dure tu plorabas
Et te totam laniabas,
Quia Christus, quem amabas,
Ferebat supplicium;
Non est mirum, O decora,
Si plorabas sine mora,
Iam videbas illa hora
Sanguinem sanctissimum.

8. Post haec Christus exclamavit
Et in cruce exspiravit,
Sol se totum obscuravit,
Quasi lugens Dominum;
O quis possit cogitare,
Quaenam lingua explicare,
Quam tu flebas tunc amare
Videns unigenitum!

9. Stabas, virgo, cum dolore
Iuxta crucem cum maerore,
Quasi virga sine flore
Et amittens lilium,
Nec a cruce recedebas
Et in corde perferebas

. . . .
Passionis poculum.

10. Intus eras cruciata
Et in mente vulnerata,
Tota quoque denigrata
Perdens vultum roseum,
Duras plagas Iesu Christi
Sola corde pertulisti,
Vere martyr tu fuisti
Per doloris gladium.

The feeling of commiseration and of participation in the lament and in the compassion of the Virgin is a constant image of the *De compassione*, even in those lyrics remarkable for their restraint. This motif, for instance, occurs in a *De compassione Beatae Mariae Virginis* of the fourteenth century,[13] preserved in a Czechoslovak manuscript. There, participation in the plaint, in the sadness and the sorrows of the Virgin, is sharply expressed:

Te precamur supplices,
quatenus illorum
Fletum, tristitiae,
omnium dolorum,

17. Quibus ut compatiens
pia mater Christo
Toto plena saeculo
fueras in isto
Digneris perfundere
nos una saltem stilla,
Ut nostrae memoriae
sit infixa illa.

18. Jesu poena vulneret
tuique doloris
Gladius nos qualibet
die septem horis.[14]

One of the singular and interesting deviations from this attitude of perceiving and narrating the plaint and the compassion of the Virgin, through
an external texture and an indirect illumination of them, is found in a *De
compassione Beatae Mariae Virginis* of the fourteenth century, from a German
manuscript.[15] This lyrical composition, which is one of the most spacious
on the theme of the *De compassione*, also begins with an invitation to the
devout soul to consider the sorrow of the Virgin at the foot of the cross, to
experience her inner wounds, and to mourn with her:

> 1. Iam nunc matri virgini,
>   anima, intende,
> Quantum ipsa doleat
>   sub cruce, perpende,
> Ut te secum vulneret,
>   preces mox impende,
> Et quod illi condoles,
>   lacrimis ostende.[16]

But very quickly the consciousness of the sorrow suffered by the Virgin
during the Passion of her Son sharpens the desire and the aspiration of the
devout soul for a more introspective vision of that sorrow. The soul then
turns directly to the Virgin and begs that Mary concede to her the grace of
hearing and understanding from the Virgin's own lips the pain and sorrow
she endured during those bloody moments:

> 21. Meas preces, domina,
>   digneris audire
> Et nunc et in posterum
>   semper subvenire,
> Tuas atque Domini
>   plagas fac me scire
> Et in corde iugiter
>   devote sentire . . .
>
> 22. O mea fiducia
>   mater salvatoris,

Me transfige gladio
tui mox doloris,
Dita me ex munere
perfecti amoris
Ac dic meae animae
vim tui maeroris.[17]

The devout soul is so insistent upon obtaining these intimate revelations of the maternal travail that the Virgin, after initially reproving the soul and calling her "importuna anima" for having turned to her in such a bold, "*audacius*" spirit, nevertheless consents; in thirty-nine stanzas of piercing lyricism and powerful psychological penetration the Virgin offers a poetic transfiguration of her sorrow and her lament during those agonizing and ruthless hours of the Crucifixion of her Son. It is an evocation of the heartrending event in which the contemplation of the torments and tribulations of her Son is harmoniously realized and universalized in her maternal heart, which savors in its innermost recesses the cruel suffering of her Son. She then communicates, at extraordinary levels of intuition and illumined sensitivity, all of its sacredness and humanity:

26. Modo si audire vis
      poenas meae mentis,
   Crucifixo filio
      meo condolentis,
   Vanitates abice
      cordis discurrentis
   Et lamenta animi
      da compatientis.

   . . . .

38. Stabam sub patibulo
      mater verbi Dei,
   Videns pati Dominum
      universae rei,
   Condolebam intime
      eius speciei,

Quam deformem fecerant
torquendo Iudaei.

39. In languore maximo
et dolore gravi
Ad natum saepissime
oculos levavi,
Vere vae, ut poteram,
vae, fili, clamavi
Ego te ad poenas has,
fili, generavi.

. . . .

41. In dolore maximo
filium videbam
Et iuvare penitus
eum non valebam,
Gemitus, suspiria,
singultus edebam,
Lacrimas multiplices
amare fundebam.

. . . .

44. Sanctum caput filii
lassum dependebat,
Nam, ubi quiesceret,
locus non manebat,
Praeter spinas minime
pulvinar habebat,
Cuius dolor multiplex
multum me torquebat.

45. Manus sacratissimas,
quas saepe tractavi,
Laceratas graviter
tunc consideravi,

> Quas augebant nequiter
> perforatas clavi,
> Quos in his transfixerant
> tunc Iudaei pravi.
>
> . . . .
>
> 52. Tecum fac obire me
> per istum agonem,
> Quae te ipsum alui
> ad hanc passionem;
> Ergo, heu, lactavi te
> ad occisionem,
> Fac me, precor, commori
> per compassionem.
>
> . . . .
>
> 64. Anima, si rumines
> pie hunc dolorem,
> Possidebis forsitan
> lacrimarum rorem,
> Et si tu devota sis
> cupiens honorem,
> Meditare saepius
> hunc meum maerorem.[18]

Consistent with the traditional type of the *De compassione* is a *De compassione Beatae Mariae Virginis* of the thirteenth century,[19] rapid and concise in style. With fine and spirited insights it presents an evocation of the compassion of the Virgin in a fully celebratory fashion. To intensify the sorrow of the Virgin, the author blends into the poetic structure of this lyric, with increasing coherence, four verses taken from the second stanza of the most famous of all the *Planctus Mariae*, the *Stabat Mater* of Jacopone da Todi:

> *De compassione Beatae Mariae Virginis*
>
> 1. Compassa filio
> mater Maria

veneratur hodie
quamvis semper sit digna laudibus.

. . . .

5. Simeonis
   praesagio
   hodie
   orbata, mater, solacio,
   cum dulcissimam
   gladius
   tuam pertransivit animam.

6. Quam, mater,
   anxia stetisti
   quando passionem
   innocentis
   filii
   conspexisti incliti,
   cruci affixi!

7. Cor matris
   lancea filio
   mortuo transfixit,
   passionem
   filius
   dum gustavit corpore,
   mater anima.

. . . .

9. *Quam tristis et afflicta fuit*
   illa benedicta!
   Maerebat et dolebat
   mater unigeniti.
   Perpendat hoc quaevis
   genetrix.[20]

The thematic structure of this *De compassione* is based, in its entirety, on
an eschatological vision in which there is imagined and lyrically expressed

the profound mystery of the Redemption. The central role of the Virgin in the economy of the Incarnation is prefigured not only by her unsullied purity—

> 2. Virgo sine macula
>   nec in radice
>   infecta crimine
>   actuali neque foedata

—but also by her free and glad assent to the Annunciation, which predestined her to divine motherhood:

> 3. Fungebaris
>   obsequia
>   placido,
>   cum peperisti, angelico;
>   quem genuisti,
>   filius
>   tibi adplausit vultu hilari.

Her profound and indissoluble association with her Son's Passion is prefigured not only in the prophecy of Simeon—

> cum dulcissimam
> gladius
> tuam pertransivit animam[21]

—but signified, in a sacred and official manner, by her intense, profound and concrete participation in the sorrows of her Son,

> passionem
> filius
> dum gustavit corpore,
> mater anima.[22]

In the light of the attitudes of Marian devotion expressed in the writings of the fathers in the East, in authors of the early Middle Ages in the West, and especially in the expressions of Latin Marian spirituality of the eleventh and twelfth centuries (which we have examined and illustrated with the aid of the vast outpouring of the *Planctus Mariae* from the twelfth to the fourteenth century, and of the immense dissemination of the *De compassione Beatae Mariae Virginis* from the thirteenth to the fifteenth century) we find some of the affirmations of distinguished scholars completely anachronistic. Lipphardt, for instance, says, "Nicht nur in der liturgie und in den evangelien, in der gesamten patristichen und frühmittelalterlichen literatur, sei sie nun lateinisch oder nationalsprachlich—finden wir keine erwähnung der klage Marias unter dem Kreuze."[23] Mâle, too, asserts, "De même que l'on dit *Christi Passio* on commence à dire dès le XIVe siècle, Mariae Compassio."[24]

As we have shown in this excursus on the theme of the *Compassio* across the centuries, these statements do not correspond at all to reality. To be critically precise, the pitiful expressions on the sufferings of the Virgin are more frequent during the thirteenth and the fourteenth centuries, but the theme of the *Compassio*, in its modern meaning, begins in the eleventh,[25] flourishes in the twelfth,[26] and finds its most intense lyrical effusion in the thirteenth century with the current of Franciscan piety: Bonaventure, Peckham, and Jacopone da Todi.

Jacopone (1230–1306) in particular, with his *Stabat Mater dolorosa*, created the most sublime and profound lyrical expression of the lament of the afflicted Mother at the foot of the cross. It has been variously attributed to Jacopone, John XXII, Saint Bernard, Innocent III, Bonaventure, Gregory XI and even to Gregory the Great. Now it is generally considered the work of the mystic from Todi, on the authority of students of Franciscan history and medieval hymnology, such as Wadding, Wharton, Gerbert, Ebert, Mohnike, Ozanam, Tiraboschi, Sorck, Daniel, Mone, Venturi, Kayser, Clement, Ermini (who wrote a stupendous study of this plaint from both the historical and the hymnological perspective[27]), and Pacheu, who declared that "nul autre competiteur que Jacopone da Todi n'est admissible, parmi ceux qu'on met en avant."[28]

Composed between 1303 and 1306, the *Stabat Mater* of Jacopone reproduces the Victorine arrangement of strophes and meters, the *versus tripartitus caudatus.* Adam of St. Victor (d. 1192) used this system in his lyrics *De Trinitate,*[29] *Heri mundus exultavit,* and *Gratulemur ad festivum.*[30] Prescinding from the complexity of the various critical judgments intended to ascertain and evaluate the authenticity of the poetic experience of

Jacopone—D'Ancona, for instance, referring to his "uncivilized and disorderly" nature, considers him a "popular poet" but not a "mystical poet,"[31] while Sapegno, on the other hand, defending his refinement and originality, declares that his poetry "pertains without doubt to the history of cultured literature"[32]—we feel that the value of the *Stabat Mater* consists fundamentally in its agitated and tender vision of the plaint and the sorrow of the Mother, of which it has harvested the fullness and the universality. Sapegno's judgment, therefore, seems to stray from the thematic reality of the lyric and from the Christocentric and Marian spirit of Jacopone's spirituality, when he observes that the agitation and the grandeur of the *Stabat Mater* derive not from the "silent and motionless agony of the Virgin" but from the "extremely rapt and reflective prayer" which constitutes the second part of the lyric.[33]

In fact, on both the theological and the emotional plane, the predominant intellectual perception of the *Stabat Mater*, fusing as it does the senses with the intellect, derives precisely from the explosive embodiment and the aesthetic as well as psychological contemplation of the plaint and the sorrow of the Virgin. The utter penetration and self-involvement with the sorrow of the Virgin at the foot of the cross is a typical characteristic of Jacopone.[34] He offers us one of its most sublime dramatic realizations in his *Lauda, Donna del paradiso,* "the most successful and exalted expression of Jacopone's poetry,"[35] which, by preferring to set the vision of the sorrowful humanity of the Mother before the contemplation of the sacredness of the divine torment, draws its inspiration from "a humanism characteristically Franciscan, a humanity profoundly imbued with a Christian sense of life."[36]

With good reason, then, Ermini observes that "the poetic merit of the *Stabat Mater* is fully apparent in the imaginative significance of this immense sorrow."[37] Furthermore, it seems evident that even in the second part of the lyric, the prayer emphasizes the sorrow of the Mother by inviting her to allow the supplicant to share in her grief:

> Fac me vere tecum flere,
> Crucifixo condolere,
> Donec ego vixero.

THE PLANCTUS MARIAE

Although the lament and the sorrow of the Virgin are principally illumined and revealed in their fullness in the first nine stanzas, the remain-
ing eleven derive their inspiration from the stirring prayer of the suppliant, who wishes to share in, to immerse himself in, the sorrow of the
Virgin by a concrete and intimate participation and experience of it:

> Sancta mater, istud agas,
> crucifigi fige plagas
>   cordi meo valide;
>
> . . . .
>
> Virgo virginum praeclara,
> mihi iam non sis amara,
>   fac me tecum plangere,
> Fac ut portem Christi mortem,
> passionis eius consortem,
>   et poenam recolere.

Planctus Beatae Mariae

1. Stabat mater dolorosa
   juxta crucem lacrimosa,
       dum pendebat filius;

2. Cuius animam gementem,
   contristantem et dolentem
       pertransivit gladius.

3. O quam tristis et afflicta
   fuit illa benedicta
       mater unigeniti.

4. Quae moerebat et dolebat
   et tremebat, dum videbat
       nati poenas incliti.

5. Quis est homo, qui non fleret,
   matrem Christi si videret
       in tanto supplicio?

6. Quis non posset contristari,
   piam matrem contemplari
   dolentem cum filio?

7. Pro peccatis suae gentis
   Iesum vidit in tormentis
   et flagellis subditum;

8. Vidit suum dulcem natum
   morientem, desolatum,
   cum emisit spiritum.

9. Eia, mater, fons amoris,
   me sentire vim doloris
   fac, ut tecum lugeam;

10. Fac, ut ardeat cor meum
    in amando Christum Deum,
    ut sibi complaceam.

11. Sancta mater, illud agas,
    crucifixi fige plagas
    cordi meo valide;

12. Tui nati vulnerati,
    iam dignati pro me pati
    poenas mecum divide.

13. Fac me vere tecum flere,
    crucifixo condolere,
    donec ego vixero.

14. Juxta crucem tecum stare,
    te libenter sociare
    in planctu desiderio.

15. Virgo virginum praeclara,
    mihi iam non sis amara,
    fac me tecum plangere,

16. Fac, ut portem Christi mortem,
    passionis eius sortem
    et plagas recolere.

17. Fac me plagis vulnerari,
    Cruce hac inebriari
    ob amorem filii;

18. Inflammatus ac accensus
    per te, virgo, sim defensus
    in die iudicii.

19. Fac me cruce custodiri,
    morte Christi praemuniri,
    confoveri gratia;

20. Quando corpus morietur,
    fac ut animae donetur
    paradisi gloria.[38]

Of particular interest, in our context, is an inspired translation of the *Stabat Mater* into Italian, taken from the *Melodie sacre* of Biava, which reproduces faithfully and with extreme poetical balance both the tortured tragic vision of the maternal sorrow and the lyrical rhythm which vivify the original:

1. Appiè della croce si stava dolente la madre
   piangendo pel figlio dolente.

2. Del cuore affannato gemeva l'afflitta,
   siccome da colpi di spada trafitta.

3. Oh quanto era mesta, languente nel lutto,
   la già benedetta per l'unico frutto.

4. D'angoscia atteggiata, con ansio lamento
   del figlio divino guardava il tormento.

5. Chi fuvvi e non pianse, lo spasimo visto,
   che allora sofferse la madre di Cristo?

6. Chi mai sosterrebbe mirare la pia
   col figlio straziata per tanta agonia?

7. Ahi scempio, ella scorse per l'empio Israello
   Gesù tra martiri, soggetto al flagello!

8. Ahi scorse quel caro sul legno confitto,
   la vita lasciando, giacer derelitto!

9. O fonte d'amore, deh fammi sentire
   con te lagrimando, quel sommo patire!

10. Deh fa, che nel cuore mi avvampi l'amore
    devoto ai voleri di Cristo signore!

11. O santa, concedi, ch'io pur le ferite
    di quel crocifisso mi senta scolpite!

12. Per quelle sue piaghe, qual tu l'hai provato,
    il duolo dividi con me del tuo nato!

13. Quest'anima teco, dal duolo contrita,
    deplori la croce per tutta la vita!

14. Jo bramo, alternando la funebre voce,
    star teco compagno dinanzi la croce.

15. O donna suprema, qui tristo son io
    per gemere insieme, fa' pago il disio!

16. Fa' qui sul costato, che adora la mente,
    ch'io m'abbia di Cristo la morte presente.

17. Quel sangue, che stilla, supplizio mi sia,
    ebbrezza d'affetto pel figlio, o Maria!

18. In te mi confido, mi salva nel punto,
    o nostra signora, del mondo consunto!

19. Stendardo la croce mi guidi qual forte,
    sia grazia vegliante di Cristo la morte.

20. E quando il mio spirto dal corpo si sciolga,
    per te fra gli eletti nel cielo mi accolga.[39]

CHAPTER VII

THE COMPASSIO IN

MEDIEVAL SPIRITUALITY

ALTHOUGH, as we have ascertained historically, the theme of the compassion of the Mother at the foot of the cross had been sporadically expressed across the centuries by the early patristic tradition, especially that of the East, this theme did not receive wide dissemination—given the general characteristics of the solemn and hieratic spirituality of antiquity—as a vivid liturgical or Marian motif, nor was it articulated with any emotional intensity, mystically or lyrically, until the early days of the eleventh century. Peter Damian (988–1072), in his exegetical commentary on the prophecy of Simeon, seems to have been the first to use the term *compassio* in exactly the sense and significance that would be prevalent and predominant in the subsequent centuries.

> Beata vero Maria, cum filium ad templum deferret et hunc Simeon in ulnis acciperet, audivit: "Et tuam ipsius animam pertransivit gladius." Ac si aperte diceret: dum Filius tuus senserit passionem in corpore, te etiam transfiget *gladius compassionis* in mente.[1]

But it is essentially with Anselm of Canterbury in the eleventh century and with Bernard in the twelfth that there is realized and defined that luminous, fruitful, and triumphant period of meditations upon the sufferings and the compassion of the Virgin at the foot of the cross. The work of Anselm "exerça une influence profonde sur le renouveau de la piété chrétienne à la fin du XIᵉ siècle,"[2] and especially upon the theme of the compassion of Mary. Its first fruits are unquestionably found, as we have already noted, in his famous *Oratio XX*, where the generous space given by Anselm to compassion places him "à l'origine d'un courant de piété destiné à devenir presque predominant vers la fin du moyen âge."[3]

Anselm, by virtue of his famous *Dialogus Mariae et Anselmi de Passione Domini*[4] and especially through his *Oratio XX*,[5] and Bernard, by means of his *Liber de Passione Christi et doloribus et planctibus Matris eius*,[6] introduced to Christianity a new current of piety which emphasized the sorrow and the compassion of the Mother. This piety made more intelligible and more human the relationship between the Mother and her Son and later became of inestimable importance in the creation of the dramas of the Passion in the vernacular; it also took an unchallenged pre-eminence in contemporary monastic works.

The *Liber de Passione Christi et doloribus et planctibus Matris eius*, generally believed to be the work of Bernard, has been convincingly attributed by various scholars to the Italian Cistercian Ogero (1136–1214), the abbot of Locedio in the province of Vercelli.[7] Born at Trino in the Piedmont, Ogero (variously known as Oglerius, Ogerius, and Occlerius) was attracted by the Cistercian ideal and soon entered as a novice the nearby abbey of Locedio, of which he became abbot in 1205.[8] Barré declares that the *Liber de Passione Christi et doloribus et planctibus Matris eius* "n'est rien d'autre, en réalité, qu'un extrait, détaché de . . . De Laudibus Sanctae Dei Genitricis du cistercien Ogier."[9] Barré shows how the treatise known as the *Liber de Passione Christi et doloribus et planctibus Matris eius*, separated from its original text because of the *Planctus*, which interested contemporary spirituality, fits logically and coherently within the structure of the *De laudibus Sanctae Dei Genitricis* of Ogero.

This latter work presents chronologically the following events: the conception and the birth of the Virgin; her life in the Temple; her marriage to Joseph; the Annunciation, the Visitation, the anguish of Joseph; the birth and the Passion of Christ; his Resurrection and Ascension; and finally the death and assumption of the Virgin. Barré concludes with the assertion that an analysis of the text makes clear how the *Planctus Mariae*, that is, the *Liber de Passione*, "s'insère parfaitment dans cet ensemble et n'apparaisse pas comme une pièce rapportée après coup."[10]

The first man to discover the existence of the *De laudibus Sanctae Dei*

Genitricis was the cardinal Jean Bona (d. 1674) of the Cistercian order. In 1873, J. B. Adriani published in their entirety both the *De laudibus* and the *Sermones* of Ogero.[11] Barré ends his essay with the remark that in the light of the fact that "le *Dialogus Beatae Mariae et Anselmi*, par exemple, dépend manifestement d'Ogier, ainsi que le *Stimulus amoris* et le *Meditationes vitae Christi*, attribués à saint Bonaventure . . . le thème de la Compassion aurait donc fleuri d'abord dans l'Italie du Nord, pour se repandre ensuite dan les pays voisins."[12]

Beyond these considerations of a philological and historical character, we must observe that the thematic structure of the *Liber de Passione Christi et doloribus et planctibus Matris eius* is characterized by a perception of the compassion of the Virgin that is devoid of all theological, doctrinal, and intellectual content. The primary and authentic value of the *Liber* consists of the revelation of the immediacy of the Virgin's affliction and plaint, and it provides in poetic images the fathomless amplitude and intimacy of that affliction. We shall provide a concrete instance of this by citing a passage in which the Virgin evokes the image of her Son on the road to Calvary, under the weight of the cross:

> Erant et mecum meae sorores et feminae multae, mecum plangentes eum quasi unigenitum, inter quas erat Maria Magdalena, quae super omnes alias, excepta illa quae loquitur tecum, dolebat, et dum Christus Deus clamante praecone, imperante Pilato, sibi bajulans crucem ad supplicium traheretur, et factus est concursus populorum post ipsum euntes, alii super ipsum plangentes, alii eum illudentes ridebant. Sequebatur et ipsum, prout poterat, ejus moestissima mater cum mulieribus, quae secutae fuerant a Galilaea ministrantes ei, a quibus trahebatur, et tenebatur velut emortua, quousque perventum est ad locum ubi crucifixerunt eum. Ante oculos ejus fuit in cruce levatus, et ligno durissimis clavis affixus. . . . Aspiciebat ancilla Dominum suum, intuebatur mater filium suum in cruce pendentem, morte impiissima morientem, et tanto dolore vexabatur in mente, quanto non posset explicari sermone. Nec mirum, manabat ejus sanguis ex quatuor partibus rigantibus nudis, ligno manibus, pedibusque clavis confixus, de vultu illius pulchritudo effluxerat omnis. . . . Volebam loqui, sed dolor verba rumpebat, quoniam verbum jam mente conceptum, dum ad formationem praetenderet oris, ad se imperfectum revocabat

dolor, non inimica cordis vox tristis sonabat, non lingua vocis magistra per-
diderat usum. Loquendo videbam morientem, quem diligebat anima mea, et
tota liquefiebam prae doloris augustia. Aspiciebat et ipse benignissimo vultu
me matrem plorantem, et me verbis paucis consolari voluit. Sed ipsis consolari
non poteram, sed flebam dicendo, et dicebam plorando: Fili mi, fili mi, quis
mihi dabit, ut ego moriar pro te? Moritur filius, cur non secum misera moritur
mater ejus? Amor unice, fili mi dulcissime, noli me derelinquere post te, trahe
me ad te ipsum, ut ipsa moriar tecum.[13]

Particularly intense and emotively rich are the feelings of the suffering
of the Virgin, probed to the depths, as she contemplates her Son on the
cross. These feelings reveal a soul torn apart by sorrow, sorrow that
springs physically and uncontrollably from the anguish of the Mother.
The language is indelibly charged with the weariness of humanity and the
inexpressible tenderness of the Mother as the Virgin kisses the ground
bathed by the blood of her Son:

> Juxta crucem stabat Maria considerans vultu benigno Christum pendentem
> in crucis ligno, stipite saevo, pedibusque flexis, junctis manibus levabat in
> altum, amplectens crucem, ruens, et oscula ejus, Christi qua parte sanguis
> nuda rigabat, ut Christum valeret amplecti, quae non poterat sursum volebat
> tendere manus. Sperat amor impatiens credit, volebat amplecti Christum in
> alto pendentem; sed manus inde frustra tensae in se complexae redibant. Se
> levans a terra sursum se erigebat ad Christum, et quia tangere nequibat illum,
> male collidebatur ad terram; ibi prostrata jacebat doloris immensitate de-
> pressa, sed eam erigere compellebat vis magni amoris incensam. Impetu
> amoris surgebat intensis manibus attractare cupiens Christum. Erat enim
> vero magno cruciata dolore, terram iterum petere cogebatur. O quam male
> tunc illi erat, gravius erat illi vita vivere tali, quam mortis gladio saeve necari,
> tamque mortis pallor ejus perfuderat mentem, vultum tamen perfuderat, et
> genis, et ore rubra erat Christi cruore. Cadentes guttas sanguinis ore tan-
> gebat, terram deosculans, quam cruoris unda rigabat.[14]

Beginning with the end of the eleventh century, the theme of the compassion was taken up in its fundamental lines by the contemporaries of
Anselm and Bernard. Jean of Fécamp (990–1078), for instance, one of the

most intense Christocentric mystics and a contemporary of Anselm, in his prayer "Ardens desiderium ad Christum," comments in this way upon the compassion of Mary: "Cur, o anima mea, non es compassa sanctissimae Matri ejus, dilectae Dominae meae, cum ineffabilibus singultibus Unigeniti sui dilectissimi membra coram se cruci confixa vehementissime defleret?"[15] Anselm of Lucca (1036–86), who had habitually contemplated *interiore oculo* the mysteries of the life of Jesus and Mary, asserts that the Virgin "non potuit sine incomparabili dolore videre in crucis patibulo gloriosissimum filium clavis affixum."[16] Arnauld of Bonnevalle (d. 1156), in the twelfth century, emphasizes the co-immolation of Christ and of Mary in the mystery of Redemption. Particularly in his *De laudibus B. Mariae Virginis*, Arnauld offers the contemplation of the Passion of Christ and of the compassion of Mary and "considerant avant tout la Passion, sacrifice du Christ, comme une action liturgique, il est conduit à suggerer l'idée du sacerdoce de Marie."[17] The Virgin shares in the Redemption not only because she immolates her own Son but also because she immolates herself along with her own Son, and in this common immolation the Mother and Son offer a unique holocaust to God. And it is especially through the compassion, suffering in her heart all the corporeal Passion of her Son, that the Virgin shares and cooperates in the Redemption.

> Dividunt coram Patre inter se mater et filius pietatis officia et miris allegationibus muniunt redemptionis humanae negotium, et conducunt inter se reconciliationis nostrae inviolabile testamentum. Mater Christo se spiritu immolat, et pro mundi salute obsecrat, Filius impetrat, Pater condonat. . . . Expiraturus Jesus matrem tanto affectu honoravit, victor suppliciorum, et quasi sui immemor, ad matrem de cruce convertitur, et colloquitur, intimans quanti apud eum meriti esset et gratiae, quam solam in illo puncto respiceret, cum jam capite vulnerato, fossis manibus et pedibus, in ultimis esset. Movebat enim eum matris affectio, et omnino tunc erat una Christi et Mariae voluntas, unumque holocaustum ambo pariter offerebant Deo: haec in sanguine cordis, hic in sanguine carnis. . . . Una est Mariae et Christi caro, unus spiritus, una charitas. . . . Unitas divisionem non recepit, non secatur in partes, et si ex duobus factum sit unum, illud tamen ultra scindi non potest, et Filii gloriam cum matre non tam communem judico quam eamdem. . . .

Fugientibus apostolis, in faciem Filii se opposuerat mater et gladio doloris animae ejus infixo, vulnerabatur spiritu, et concrucifigebatur affectu: et quod in carne Christi agebant clavi et lancea, hoc in ejus mente compassio naturalis et affectionis maternae angustia.[18]

Eadmer (1060–1141), the most famous of Anselm's English disciples, dwells upon the suffering of the Virgin in his *De compassione Beatae Mariae pro Filio crucifixo*. After noting with "quibus doloribus, quibus gemitibus, quibus suspiriis" the Virgin was afflicted when her Son was betrayed, seized, and condemned to death, he presents the image of the Mother *juxta crucem* in these terms: "Vere pertransivit animam tuam gladius doloris, qui tibi amarior extitit omnibus doloribus cujusvis passionis corporeae; quidquid enim crudelitatis inflictum est corporibus martyrium leve fuit, aut potius nihil, comparatione ipsius tuae passionis, quae nimirum sua immensitate transfixit cuncta penetralia tui benignissimi cordis."[19]

Richard of St. Victor (1105–1173), accentuating the most immediate cooperation of Mary in the salvation of man, refers to the sorrow she bore at the foot of the cross as a more intense martyrdom than that suffered by the martyrs to the Faith:

Super haec martyrio decorata fuit. Ipsius enim animam pertransivit gladius, non materialis, sed doloris. Quo martyrio gravius passa fuit quam ferro. Quanto enim incomparabiliter amavit, tanto vehementius doluit. Unde sicut non fuit amor sicut amor ejus, ita nec fuit dolor similis dolori ejus. In martyribus magnitudo amoris dolorem lenivit passionis, sed beata Virgo quanto plus amavit, tanto plus doluit.[20]

But it is above all in the mysticism of Bernard that the theme of the compassion acquires a particular and exceptional distinction thanks to his refined and exquisite sensitivity. He emphasizes the element that is decisively human and personal in the sublime emotion felt by the Virgin at the moment of her Son's sufferings. The mystical insight into the compassion of the Virgin flows in the thought of Bernard from the emotions and the maternal feelings that accompany it. The luminous interpretation that Bernard offers of the compassion of the Virgin is filtered through and decanted from words that probe deeply the inconceivable mystery of this mother's anguish; they reveal and communicate all the emotions and all the pathos that trouble her.

In his *Dominica infra octavam Assumptionis Beatae Virginis Mariae sermo*, commenting on the compassion of the Virgin, in the context of her role of mediation and Redemption, Bernard defines her sorrow as an inward *martyrium* that makes her "plus quam martyrem." He indicates that without any doubt this inward martyrdom, due to the physical Passion of her Son, was overcome by virtue of the intensity of her compassion. Bernard observes further that the lance that did not reach the soul of Christ, who was already dead, pierced the soul of the Virgin:

> Martyrium sane Virginis . . . tam in Simeonis prophetia, quam in ipsa Dominicae passionis historia commendatur. . . . Vere tuam, o beata mater, animam gladius pertransivit. . . . Et quidem posteaquam emisit spiritum tuus ille Jesus (omnium quidem, sed specialiter tuus), ipsius plane non attigit animam crudelis lancea, quae ipsius (nec mortuo parcens, cui nocere non posset) aperuit latus, sed tuam utique animam pertransivit. Ipsius nimirum anima jam tibi non erat; sed tua plane inde nequibat avelli. Tuam ergo pertransivit animam vis doloris, ut plus quam martyrem non immerito praedicemus, in qua nimirum corporeae sensum passionis excesserit compassionis effectus.[21]

The meditations on the lament and the compassion of the Virgin, developed by the Marian spirituality of the eleventh and the twelfth centuries, find a vast resonance in the writings of monastic authors of the subsequent centuries. With an inexhaustible fertility they develop one of the most imposing and universal aspects of medieval spirituality: the theme of the compassion of the Virgin. Of remarkable impact, beginning with the thirteenth century, is the extraordinary contribution, both emotional and intellectual, brought to this theme by the luminous mysticism of the Franciscans, whose *pensée mariale*, as de Dieu asserts, "avait été orientée par saint François vers la considération des qualités et des mérites, des joies et des tristesses de Marie."[22]

This Marian thought of the Franciscans is one which in its psychological realism and its dramatically poetic language is reflected in the loving consideration of the sorrow of Mary expressed by, among others, Giacomo da Milano, Ubertino da Casale, and Bernardino da Siena. Giacomo da Milano (d. c. 1275), known also under the name of Giacomo Capelli, is known for the warmth of the Marian piety which characterizes many pages of his *Stimulus amoris*, for a long time attributed to Bonaventure.[23] Giacomo, who in his *Stimulus* draws inspiration from the spirituality of Bonaventure, whose prayers and meditations he adopts, in the fifteenth chapter of his book, entitled *Meditatio in parasceve*, offers a contemplation of the bitterness and compassion of the Virgin at the foot of the cross, which presents immediately and simultaneously the suffering of the Son, *Dominum meum vulneratum*, and the participation of his Mother, *convulneratam*, in that suffering:

> *Stabat iuxta crucem Iesu mater eius.* O domina mea, ubi stas? Nunquid iuxta crucem? Immo certe in cruce cum Filio, ibi enim crucifixa es secum. Hoc restat, quod ipse in corpore, tu autem in corde; nec non et vulnera per eius corpus dispersa sunt in corde tuo unita. Ibi, domina, lanceatum est cor tuum, ibi clavatum, ibi spinis coronatum, ibi illusum, exprobatum et contumeliis plenum et aceto et felle potatum. O domina, cur ivisti immolari pro nobis? Nunquid non sufficiebat nobis Filii passio, nisi crucifigetur et mater? O cor amoris, cur conversum es in globum doloris? . . . *amaritudine repleta es*, totum cor tuum versum erat, domina, circa Filii tui passionem. O mira es, tota es in vulneribus Christi, totus Christus crucifixus est in intimis visceribus cordis tui. . . . Verecundum et opprobriosum est mihi videre Dominum meum vulneratum et, te, o domina mea, convulneratam.[24]

One of the most exalted and profound expressions, in the Middle Ages, of Christocentric and Marian spirituality is the *Arbor vitae crucifixae Jesu* of Ubertino da Casale (1259–1329). Begun on March 9, 1305, and completed on September 28 of that same year, the *Arbor vitae*, the title of which was probably suggested by the *Lignum vitae* of Bonaventure, is made up of five books and one hundred and eleven chapters. Shot through with spiritual and temporal preoccupations and pervaded with a profound, albeit frenetic, mystical spirit, the *Arbor vitae* offers a doctrinal interpretation of the mysteries of the life, Passion and death of Christ and a notable presentation of the sorrowful Virgin. The joys and the sorrows of the Virgin are set forth by means of an explosive lyricism, metaphorical as well as visual, which transcends the intellectual strength and the complexity of the traditional language of mysticism.

The compassion is initially discussed by Ubertino in chapter 14 of book 4, where he speaks of the pre-eminence granted by Christ to the Virgin and the good thief. Ubertino declares that at the moment of his Passion on Calvary, Christ granted to the Virgin the "primatum compassionis: ut esset mare magnum omnis deplorationis et lamentationis mortis sue" and to the good thief the privilege of being crucified with him, "primatum associationis . . . cum ipsum . . . iuxta latus suum crucifixum elegit."[25] While the good thief was the only one to be associated with his Crucifixion, the Mother was the only one to be associated with the sorrowful lament of "morientis filii pro sceleribus nostris."[26] Ubertino presents a more complete picture of the significance, spiritual and human, of the compassion of the Virgin in chapter 15 of the same book, entitled "Jesus matri compatiens." By inverting the order of perception, Ubertino reveals the intensity of the compassion of Mary through the compassion that Christ shows for the sufferings inflicted upon his Mother by his Passion:

> Quamvis bone Iesu posset exprimere quando compassionis feriebaris telo: quando materna viscera contuebaris omni amaritudine tue passionis repleta. Nec non et ipsam faciem pallidam et quasi sine morte mortuam: et tui sanguinis aspersione manibus et vestibus et faciem cruentatam gemitibus anxiam: voce raucam: lachrymis perflusam: et totam in tuis doloribus inabysatam . . . et Iesu novam et magnam amaritudinis crucem ex tue matris tali consortio pro nobis peccatoribus assumpsisti: unde cum nulla creatura minor ipsa dolores cordis eius mensurare sufficiat: tu solus tue dilectissime matri pro te et pro nobis miseris et indignis filiis fuisti debita mensura compassus. Et hoc bone Iesu fuit ad tui doloris augmentum: quod non solum in te sed in altero hoc est in materno corde fuisti sic letaliter crucifixus.[27]

The sorrow and the compassion of the Virgin acquire a universal value of mediation and reconciliation, because the sacrifice of her Son in sustaining the greatest possible sorrow for the redemption of the world finds an acknowledgment in the sufferings of his Mother, who takes upon herself the sorrow of all:

Et sicut ipse maiores dolores assumpsit propter redemptionem humani generis . . . sic et beata virgo Maria sibi magis condoluit quia dolores omnium in
se portabat: immo sicut ipse fuit omnium redemptor: ita ipsa fuit omnium
genitrix: mediatrix: reconciliatrix.[28]

Ubertino asserts that the Virgin was utterly intent "ad compassionem
morientis filii" and that the privilege of experiencing within herself the
sufferings of her Son was granted her because she was worthy of being a
participant in his Passion: "Ipse etiam Iesus qui sciebat quod dignum erat
matrem suam participare passionem: eam plenissime suis doloribus
coniungebat."[29]

In this profound and uninterrupted rhythm of Christocentric and Marian
piety of Franciscan spirituality there is found the experience, both ascetic
and contemplative, of the famous German mystic, the Dominican Henry
Suso (c. 1295–1366). Under the impulse of the cultural matrix of speculative mysticism provided by his masters, Bernard, Thomas, and Eckhart,
Suso broke forth in some of the most ardent and fiery meditations on the
Passion of Christ and the compassion of the Virgin that have ever been
written. Especially known in the history of medieval piety as the originator
of the devotion known as the Hundred Meditations on the Passion of
Christ, Suso is remarkable also for the great place he gives to the compassion of the Virgin.[30] The tender pages of Suso on the sorrows and the
sufferings of the Virgin appear in his *Horologium sapientiae*, composed probably between 1334 and 1338.[31] It is generally regarded as a reworking in
Latin of his *Das Büchlein der ewigen Weisheit*.[32] In the *Materia sextadecima* of
the *Liber primus* of the *Horologium*, entitled *Commendatio singularis Beatae
Virginis, et dolore eius inaestimabili, quem habuit in Passione Filii*, Suso displays
a great power of evocation and uses a language free of all the restrictions
imposed by the traditional formalities of contemplations; his language,
instead, is characterized by its semantic concreteness and its employment of
torturous poetic images. Suso converses with the sacred text to find and to
transmit the most profound echoes of the inward stress and the irresistible
anguish overflowing in the heart of the Virgin:

Stabat namque iuxta crucem Iesu mater eius. O verborum totius compassionis.
Quamvis enim, o viscera mea, ex intimis movere vos debeant dolores et afflic-

tiones tam pii salvatoris in cruce pendentis, iure tamen singulari nobis . . . convenit tantae matri iuxta crucem stanti et immensum dolorem patientis Filii in corde suo plenissime sustinenti specialius quodam modo ac peculiarius compati ex medullis cordium nostrorum. . . .

O Maria, quid cordis erat tibi, cum iuxta crucem stabas et *Iesum benedictum fructum ventris tui,* sic suspensum cernebas? . . . Multum dolebas, quia multum diligebas.[33]

But it is particularly by a direct citation of the inward feelings of the Virgin at the foot of the cross that Suso allows us to harvest the agitations that are harrowing her soul, as *viva voce* she recounts all the intensity of her maternal bonds in images that are almost visible and explode with their humanity:

Hunc igitur Filium unigenitum, cordis mei thesaurum pretiosum, cum oculis elevatis vidissem sic contemptibiliter in cruce cum latronibus suspensum, et doloribus mortis angustiatum; ah quam intolerabilis mihi hic aspectus erat, o quam lamentabilis et poenosa haec mihi visio fuit. Anima mea prae dolore cruciabatur, viscera materna sauciabantur, et commoriebantur omnia ossa mea. Virtus omnis evanuit, sensus a me recessit, et calamitas me oppressit immensa. Oculos lacrimosos sursum levavi, dilectum meum suspensum vidi, nec sibi in aliquo solatium ferre potui. . . . O quantum anima mea in me angustiabatur, quam magno cruciabatur dolore. Corde privata eram, quia ipse mihi cor abstulerat et simul secum crucifixum tenebat. Vocem prae clamore et eiulatu multo amiseram, quod vix loqui poteram. Defeci prae dolore, corrui prae moerore.[34]

Until this moment the sorrow and the suffering of the Virgin have been made manifest by a vision of the inner recesses of her soul and the succession of her agitations and palpitations, but now they are put in terms and images more concretely explicit, at the moment when her Son, a little before his death, commends his Mother to the beloved disciple. At the voice of her dying Son, the "*gladius* maeroris *pertransivit* animam fidelissimae matris," awakening in her heart a recall, in a language quite Gothic in its morbidity, of the blood which ran from the wounds of her Son, "sanguinem

fumantem . . . ex vulneribus Filii," which the Virgin kissed with all eager-
ness, until her face was completely smeared:

> Cumque vocem Filii loquentis cor maternum percepit, dolore vehementissimo
> aestuare coepit, et *gladius* maeroris *pertransivit* animam fidelissimae matris.
> Levavi manus sursum prae cordis desiderio, tangere cupiens dilectum meum,
> ut vel sic dolori et amori melius consulere potuissem. Cumque aliud solatium
> non haberem sanguinem fumantem et ex vulneribus Filii ad terram usque
> stillantem nimia cum aviditate deosculabar in tantum, ut facies matris de
> cruore Filii occisi sanguinolenta redderetur.[35]

No less rich in agitated yet concrete expressions of compassion are the
scenes of Christ being taken down from the cross and of his burial, in
which the Virgin kisses the lifeless arms of her Son and then takes him
into her lap, as she tries to keep him from those responsible for his burial.
The iconography of the scene is grafted onto an expressive process that
establishes a symbolic but exquisitely realistic connection between word
and vision, between letter and perception: the evocation of the cruel torments inflicted upon the body of her Son flows toward the projection of
her compassion, which mirrors and sums up quite lyrically the immense
pathos sealing the scene:

> Post expirationem Filii, cum de cruce deponeretur, o quam affectuosissime
> brachia eius dependentia suscipiebam, et mortuum Filium gremio materno
> colligebam, affectu materno ipsum amplexabar, rigabam lacrimis faciem mor-
> tui et recentia vulnera frequentibus osculis leniebam. Res miseranda. . . .
> Loquebar ei, et non respondit mihi. . . . Astabant namque, qui mihi mor-
> tuum meum, thesaurum meum, auferre et sepelire volebant; tunc flebam et
> gemebam, et voces lamentabiles dabam. Cor prae dolore concutiebatur, cum
> dilectum Filium brachiis maternis constrictum avellere conabantur. Faciem
> meam lacrimosam ipsius vultui applicabam; faciem suam saepius inter manus
> accipiens, crebrius inspiciebam, et gemebam, quoniam *amaritudine repleta*
> *eram*. Nec erat, qui haec intueretur, et matri patienti non compateretur.[36]

Of particular significance on account of the keenness of its doctrinal and
pedagogical content and of its rhetorical and eloquent orientation is the

Christocentric and Marian thought of Bernardine of Siena (1380–1444), who was one of the principal champions of the "Observance" within the Franciscan order. Trained in the school of spirituality of Bonaventure, Ubertino da Casale, John Scotus, and François de Meyronnes, Bernardine followed their intense, Christocentric speculative mysticism. He deepened the significance of the Passion and illustrated, in particular, the doctrine of and the "devotion to the Name of Jesus, which he considered as the banner of his ministry and which he understood not as a simple cultural and devotional expression, but . . . as a sign and token of recognition that someone is leading a sincere, coherent Christian life."[37] The devotion of Bernardine to the Name of Jesus and to his Passion is a coherent reflection of the original mysticism of the Franciscans, who considered meditation on the Passion of Christ and on Christ's sorrowing and suffering upon the cross as the center of their spiritual exercise and of inward progress. This profound Christocentric ideal is exhaustively and lyrically repeated, for instance in a *Planctus de Passione Domini* of the fifteenth century:

> Absit nobis gloriari
> Aut quacumque re laetari
>   Nisi cruce Domini,
> Sine qua nemo salvari
> Quit in magno mundi mari,
>   Istam contemplemini.
> . . . .
>
> Hoc est proprium Minoris,
> Recordare vim doloris,
>   Quam rex Christus pertulit,
> Et sectari vias moris,
> Quas repletum vas amoris
>   Franciscus his intulit.
>
> Opus erat hoc Francisci
> Cruci Christi reminisci
>   Et plagas recolere,
> Nunquam planctus oblivisci,

Sed in cruce revivisci
Corde, ore, opere.[38]

The thought of Bernardine on the compassion of the Virgin, still within the orbit of his own particular contribution, is expressed in perfect conformity with the warm devotion of Anselm, Bernard, Eadmer, and the pseudo-Bonaventure, to whose works he refers in his discussion of the compassion of the Virgin. The more properly theological and doctrinal aspect of the compassion of Mary is discussed by Bernardine in his *Sermo II: De glorioso nomine Mariae, et quod interpretatur "amarum mare."*[39] Bernardine says that during the time of the Passion the sorrow inflicted upon the Virgin by the "separatio et subtractio filii sui" was extremely intense because it lasted continually for four days, from Wednesday to Holy Saturday:

> Nam maxime incepit dolor eius feria quarta, quia tunc mors Christi fuit tractata et confirmata; continuatus autem fuit feria quinta, eo quod in nocte fuit captus, colaphizatus atque delusus; augmentatus autem fuit usque ad feriam sextam, quia tunc filius eius crucifixus est; dilatatus vero usque ad diem sabbati, quia tunc filius suus in sepulchro clausus est.[40]

Bernardine says that there are three qualities that distinguish the "compassio" of the "compatiens" for him "cui compatimur": "primum, vehementia; secundum, ipsius vehementiae in compatiente notitia: tertium, ipsius ad compatientem amor et amicitia."[41] Referring almost literally to the words of Eadmer in his *De compassione Beatae Mariae pro Filio crucifixo*,[42] Bernardine declares that the sorrow of the Virgin was in proportion to her love:

> Propterea summe passa est, quia summe dilexit eum. Non tantum quippe afflicta fuisset, si illius cruciatus non vidisset; sed cum "Prolatam suae mortis sententiam audiret; cum crucem, cum qua suspendi debebat, humeris ad locum passionis subvehere gemebunda conspiceret," immo cum iam lividum, verberatum, vulneratum, cruentatum, in cruce pendentem videret, "est ne, precor, quis, qui percipere possit qualitatem doloris pectoris eius"?[43]

Bernardine evokes the depth of maternal sorrow and bitterness through an emotional crescendo which summarizes all the agony she had suffered during the Passion of her Son; from the very beginning she had contemplated the awful reality when she saw

> Dominum mundi, ut latronem comprehensum . . . arctioribus vinculis constrictum . . . ad columnam vinctum . . . ictibus lividum . . . flagellis diruptum et laniatum . . . a scelestissimis spretum . . . a sceleris illusum . . . arundine percussum et sic rivulis sanguineis cruentatum, spinis coronatum et . . . morti iudicatum. . . . Vidit insuper quod candet nudatum pectus, rubet cruentatum latus, quod tensa arent viscera . . . quod regia pallent ora . . . quod crura pendent marmorea, quod rigat tenebratos pedes beati sanguinis unda. Vere igitur in amaritudine erat anima Mariae spectans haec et contemplans.[44]

But the most tormented vision of the maternal compassion appears in his long *Sermo LV: De sanctissima Passione*,[45] especially at the moment when Christ is taken down from the cross and is buried. There the Virgin, with an emotional participation and a compassionate lament, allows her feelings of all-consuming humanity to appear. Bernardine heightens the dramatic sense of the scene of Christ's deposition from the cross at the crucial moment when, citing the *De Passione Christi* of Bernard, he pictures the Virgin with her arms stretched forth to receive the lifeless body of her Son:

> Stabat et mater Iesu in altum brachia levans, et manus Christi et caput dependentia recipiebat super pectus suum. Quem cum attingere parumper valuit, iam non sinebat eum, sed in eius amplexus et oscula ruens, de suo dilecto, licet exstincto, satiari non poterat.
>
> Dumque de cruce in terram corpus depositum fuit, prae incontinentia doloris et immensitate amoris irruit maesta mater super faciem eius et faciem suam faciei Christi coniunxit, et oscula devota imprimens, quasi mortua stetit. . . . Stabat ad caput exstincti Virgo Maria, vehementer plangebat, et faciem eius rigans, per diversa suspiria torquebatur.[46]

Bernardine expresses the compassion of the Virgin with greater intensity at the moment of the burial, when the Virgin, in the grasp of uncontrollable surges of sorrow, embraces and kisses the stone and then, with

her face already covered with blood and ceaseless tears, is tenderly removed from the tomb by the holy women and accompanied toward the
house of John:

> Ponitur tandem Dominus in sepulcro ac revolvitur lapis super illud. Lapidem
> sepulchri amplectitur et deosculatur ac madefacit irriguo lacrimarum
> maestissima mater . . . quando a sepulcro filii dolorose avulsa, pallens facie,
> aspersa sanguine, cum anhelosis suspiriis et gemitibus interruptis et fletibus
> lacrimosis versus reducitur, adiuta manibus illarum fidelium mulierum. Ver-
> tebat se saepius maesta mater, dum tardo gressu rediret Ierusalem et, locum
> in quo extinctum filium reliquerat prospiciens, gemitus renovabat.[47]

This capacity to penetrate, both psychologically and spiritually, into the
compassion of the Virgin, so brilliantly performed and expressed by the
Franciscan Marian piety of Giacomo da Milano, Ubertino da Casale, and
Bernardine of Siena, would once again appear in Italy a few years later.
With an unmistakable compactness of expression and with exalted and
luminous images, Bernardino de' Bustis (c. 1450–c. 1513), in his Marian
theology—especially his *Mariale*, compiled in 1492—would provide an
inexhaustible treasure of doctrinal exegesis on the mediation of the Virgin.[48] This capacity to penetrate, both psychologically and spiritually,
would also be present in the field of the lyric. A century and a half after
the composition of the *Stabat Mater* by Jacopone, an agitated and anguished *Planctus Mariae*[49] would be written by Paracleto Malvezzi (c.
1408–1487), a man of letters at home with both the Bible and the classics,
who provides evidence of the vast resonance and the wide dissemination
enjoyed, in so late a period of the Western world, by the theme of the
compassion of Mary at the foot of the cross.[50]

CHAPTER VIII

THE PLANCTUS MARIAE

AND THE THEATRICAL

TRADITION

THE inexhaustible fecundity and the universality of the theme of the *Compassio* from the eleventh to the fifteenth century and its presence, in lyrical form, in medieval theatrical presentations, require us to consider, in the temporal and literary perspective of this study, the crucial moment when the relationship between the *Planctus Mariae* and the drama becomes evident and essential. It is that moment when the *Planctus* takes its place as a lyrical and emotional element in the tradition of the religious theater.

The development of the theme of the *Compassio* in the eleventh and twelfth centuries was helped and favored by an artistic factor: a definitive change of attitude in pictorial representations of Christ. As we have had the opportunity to mention, beginning with the eleventh century the representation of the dead Christ on the cross—emphasizing with sharp and heart-wrenching realism the image of the "vir dolorum et sciens humanitatem"[1]—created another eloquent and vital impulse toward artistic and meditative representations of the Virgin grieving at the foot of the cross. Some of the most intensely lyrical meditations on the sorrow and the *Compassio* of the Virgin were taken up and made part of *Planctus*. (Among these is the famous *Planctus ante nescia* of the twelfth century.)[2] This was made possible by the fact that in this period terms such as *compassio*, *planctus*, *lamentatio*, and *transfixio* had the same significance.

Later these *Planctus* were incorporated, with little or no variation, in religious dramas as independent lyrical compositions. It seems logical to assert, therefore, in the light of these considerations, that the usual and widespread presence of the *Planctus*, as a theme in the religious poetry and the meditations of the time, shows that this custom constitutes only one of the manifestations of the vast cult dedicated to the Virgin in the twelfth century.[3]

We can, then, with a consciousness of theory and with sound confidence, suppose that when a *clericus* or a monk of the twelfth century outlined a drama of the Passion of Christ, he would have included in its structure a lament of the Virgin to reinforce and to cast into strong relief the intensity and the reality of the scene of the Crucifixion. And this throbbing note of warm humanity, able to fuse in a single image both the divine and the human, could be achieved only by the projection of the anguish of Christ's Mother. Diller has a fine comment, in this connection, on the new dimensions and dramatic possibilities inspired by the compassion of the Virgin:

> Es waren vor allem die Kreuzesklagen der Mutter Maria, die es vermochten, dem liturgischen Drama durch das Moment der Anteilnahme eine neue Erlebnis-dimension zu öffnen. Als die lyrischen Planctus des 12. Jhs., in denen Maria selbst auftrat und ihnen eigenen Schmerz kundtat, in die Liturgie und das liturgische Drama aufgenommen worden, war ein bedeutender Schritt zur Humanisierung dieser Feiern vollzogen. Maria, die als Gnadenmittlerin verehrt wurde, konnte auch in emotionalen Bereich die Brücke zwischen menschlichem und göttlichem schlagen. Ihr mütterlicher Schmerz ist in dieser frömmigkeitsgeschichtlichen Periode leichter nachvollziehbar als das Leiden des göttlichen Heilands.[4]

This possibility is reinforced by the consideration of the relatively minor importance of the *Planctus* in various dramas and by the fact that the earliest drama of the Passion still existent, the Passion of Montecassino of the twelfth century, and the two dramas of the Passion of Benediktbeuern, in Germany, of the thirteenth century, both of them also in Latin, present both the Passion of Christ and a type of *Planctus*.

Later, however, with a greater flowering and a fuller development both of the drama and the lyric, the *Planctus* would acquire a pre-eminence and a centrality in the dramatic structure. Its internal prevalence would be due to its emotional power:

> The expression of an inconsolable sorrow proceeds to free itself from the spectacular encumbrances of the traditional accompaniment of the Passion: the crowd of Jews, the soldiers, the thieves, in a word the spectacle of the throng that could in the phantasmagoria of the Passion neglect and sometimes completely forget the humanity of the religious sentiments. . . . Everything is focused on the protagonist, the Madonna; everyone else is put at a distance, their voices stilled. All light and color is extinguished, in the darkness of the death of Christ.[5]

In fact, although the commemoration of the Passion of Christ always remained the most solemn, emotional, and sublime moment of dramatic representation, slowly the popular imagination became ever more fascinated by the most human suffering of Golgotha, that of the Mother for her Son. Realizing that the vision of the grieving figure of the *Virgo moerens* could excite emotions of piercing agitation and produce a more intense participation of the people in the representation of the Passion of Christ, the dramatic authors of later centuries emphasized the pathos of that scene. They elaborated the available Latin sequences on the maternal sorrow of Mary and created new ones. This is the way in which extensive and dramatic *Planctus*, like the plaint of Cividale, of the fourteenth century, were produced.[6]

Especially in England, in this period, the motif of the grieving Mother became the subject of vigorous sermons and touching lyrics.[7] It was also one of the principal and liveliest dramatic moments in the numerous religious poems written in the vernacular toward the end of the thirteenth century and the beginning of the fourteenth. From the *Cursor mundi* to the *Northern Passion*, from the *Southern Passion* to the poem *A Stanzaic Life of Christ*, we find documentation for the exceptional popularity of the supreme expression of love and of compassion of the Mother for her Son.

Just as important in France is the large role assigned to the Virgin in the poems *La Passion de jongleurs* and the *Ystoire de la Passion* and in the vernacular Passions, from the *Passion du Palatinus* to the *Passion d'Arras*, from the *Passion Semur* to the *Passion d'Autun*. In Germany, beginning with the poems *Erlösung* and *Alt Passional* and continuing with the dramatic tradition in the vernacular, the role of the Virgin was even more incisively and extensively developed than in the vernacular dramas of the Passion from France and England. In such German dramas as *Das Tyrol Passionsspiel, Das St. Galler Passionsspiel, Das Frankfurter Passionsspiel*, and *Das Alsfelder Passionsspiel*, the Virgin occupies a central place in the entire scene on Calvary.

In Italy, in the *Sacre Rappresentazioni* and especially in the *Laude*, the Virgin rises to a significant pre-eminence, thanks to her fundamental dramatic function in the culminating moments of the divine tragedy. In Spain, a country whose tradition of medieval drama is not as rich as that of England, France, Germany, and Italy, whether one considers *Las lamentaciones fechas par la Semana Santa* of Gómez Manrique, the *Planto o duelo que fizo la Virgen de la Pasión de su Fijo Jesu Christu* of Berceo, the *Pasión trobada* or some of the more advanced *Autos Sacramentales*, the compassion and the plaint of the Virgin are always illumined in the dramatic action with an extraordinary richness of pathos and rhetoric, exalting their universality and humanity.

In a sensible study of the medieval Spanish theater, for instance, Iglesias asserts that "en el *Duelo* de Berceo . . . la Virgen tiene un sitio señalado" and that "también la Virgen es figura sobresaliente en las representaciones castellanas de la Pasión. . . . La Virgen protagoniza tanto y más que Cristo estas 'Pasiones.'"[8] *El duelo que fizo la Virgen Maria el día de la Pasión de su Fijo Jesu Christo* and, for that matter, the *Milagros de Nuestra Señora* of Berceo (c. 1198–1246), are literary expressions that mirror the cult and piety devoted to Mary which developed in the West during the twelfth century. In Spain they reach their apex during the years of the artistic maturity of Berceo. The route was the profound influence exercised by the Cistercians, whose order had been introduced to Spain in 1137.

A critical examination of the basic structure and the liturgical as well as spiritual patrimony of the *Milagros* provides us in fact with "une idée assez exacte de ce qu'a été la piété mariale dans l'Espagne du XIIIᵉ siècle."[9] The *Duelo*, for its part, forms an element of the vast devotional context generated by the Marian spirituality of Bernard, whose influence is evident in everything written by Berceo. The *Duelo*, in particular, shows the direct influence of the *Liber de passione Christi et doloribus et planctibus Matris eius*[10] of Bernard, whose stylistic devices and formal pattern it adopts. Like the *Liber de Passione*, the *Duelo* is cast in the form of a dialogue between Bernard and the Virgin. Like the *Liber de Passione*, the *Duelo* is built on the "notion de compassion et sur le principe de l'assimilation de la Mère au Fils."[11] All of this is expressed in 197 quatrains and 13 distichs of unequal lyrical level and diverse aesthetic impulse. For their stylistic refinement and the unmistakable transparency of their lyrical accents, the most remarkable quatrains are those numbered 137–46. There the revelation and the projection of maternal sorrow are emphasized by the image of the inner isolation of the Virgin, which directly communicates her anguished emotional state at the foot of the cross. The poetic sensibility of the moment is further transmitted by the simultaneous correspondence of words and rhymes; the thematic motifs are linked with the harmony of the rhyme and create a simultaneous relationship of images between the verbal element and the sonorous element of the various quatrains:

> De cerca de la cruz yo nunqua me partía,
> lo qe rebolbién ellos, yo todo lo bedia,
> yo catava a todos e todos a Maria,
> teniénme por sin seso del planto qe facía.

> Abraçava la cruz hasta do alcançava,
> besavali los piedes, en eso me gradava;
> non podía la boca ca alta me estava,
> nin facía las manos qe yo más cobdiciava.

> Bien ploren los mis ojos, non cesen de manar,
> el coraçón me rabia, non me puede folgar,
> acïago es oy, bien nos debe membrar,
> los siervos de mi Fijo dévenlo bien guardar.

> A los del nuestro vando miémbrelis esti dia,
> día tan embargoso, tan sin derechuría,
> día en qui yo pierdo mi sol, Virgo Maria,
> día qe el sol muere non es complido día.

Día en qui yo pierdo toda mi claridat,
lumne de los mis ojos et toda pïadat,
ploran los elementos todos de voluntat,
yo mesquina si ploro non fago liviandat.

Yo mesquina si ploro o si me amortesco,
o si con tan grant cueita la vida aborresco,
non sé por qé me viene ca yo no lo meresco,
mas a Dios pos quien vino, a El gelo gradesco.

Fijo qe más alumnas qe el sol ni la luna,
qe governavas todo yaciendo en la cuna,
tú, Sennor, qe non qieres perder alma ninguna,
miémbrete como fago de lágremas laguna.

Miémbrente las mis lágremas tanta como yo vierto,
los gemidos qe fago ca non son en cubierto;
tú penas e yo laçdro, non fable bien en cierto,
qe tuélleme la fabla el dolor grant sin tiento.

El dolor me embarga, non me dessa fablar,
qui bien me entendiese non me devié reptar,
qa quánt grant est el duelo e quánt grant el pesar,
la qe tal fijo pierde lo puede bien asmar.[12]

   This spontaneous and agitating dwelling, in the late Middle Ages, upon
the sufferings of Mary is especially due to the enormous influence enjoyed
by the *Meditationes vitae Christi* of pseudo-Bonaventure, composed at the
beginning of the fourteenth century and now attributed by scholars to the
Franciscan Giovanni de Caulibus of San Gimignano.[13] The entirety of the
Meditationes—which were written by a *clericus* for a spiritual daughter of
his, quite probably Giovanna Cattani, the prioress of the Poor Clares of San
Gimignano—although based upon the Gospels and the Acts of the Apostles, avoids the parables and the miracles contained in them. The *Meditationes* amplify the scanty profiles contained in the canonical account and
invent new scenes of the Passion, while clothing and investing them in the
glow of a mounting emotionalism, liveliness, and concreteness of detail.
They elaborate the anguish of Mary, increase the hyperdulia of the *mater*

dolorosa, and omit the dogma to offer the contemplative the spectacle of a personal and intense human experience. While the Gospels were directed to the intellect, the *Meditationes* make an appeal to the heart.[14] In his presentation and evocation of Jesus and Mary, the author seems unable to describe the divine, to hold to the cold points of doctrine; instead, he prefers to emphasize the immediacy and not the historicity of a scene. He succumbs to the profound drives of a language which is dramatically lyrical and emotional, one that captures and then presents the fullness of human reality and feeling. This is especially apparent in the evocation and the concrete representation of the sorrow of the Virgin not only at the foot of the cross but at the moment when Christ was taken down from the cross. Nicodemus and Joseph of Arimathea had taken the nails from the hands of Christ. The author recounts that the Virgin, weeping, took the dangling right hand of her Son and covered it with kisses: "Tunc pendentem manum dexteram Domina suscepit reverenter, et ponit ad vultum suum, intuetur, et osculatur cum lacrymis validis et suspiriis doloris."[15]

The sense of sorrow and of compassion are particularly acute at the moment of burial, when the Virgin begs Joseph of Arimathea not to take her Son away from her so quickly for burial or at least to bury her along with him:

> Nolite, amici mei, tam cito filium meum accipere, vel me cum ipso sepelite. Flebat autem lacrymis irremediabilibus, aspiciebat vulnera manuum et lateris, modo unum, modo aliud; aspiciebat vultum ejus, et caput, et videbat spinarum puncturas, depilationem barbae, faciem sputis et sanguine deturpatam, et caput tonsum; et de fletu et aspectu non poterat satiari.[16]

The contemplation of the Virgin's maternal compassion, her anguish, torment, and bitterness, and the repercussions within her soul of the bloody death of her Son were ineradicably etched on the soul of Bonaventure. "Psychologue et poète, saint Bonaventure avait été attiré par le mystère des souffrances et des joies de Marie et par celui de sa vie intérieure. Joies et appréhensions de l'enfance de Jesus, joies et douleurs de la Passion. Devant celles-ci surtout, il laisse parler son âme."[17]

Bonaventure allowed his soul to speak, with all the force of his impassioned, emotional intellect, in his *Officium de compassione B. Mariae Virginis*,

where he offers us a concrete poetic representation of her bloodied maternal heart. He projects, with a loving spontaneity, the holy and intangible
reality of the Virgin's anguish during the most gruesome moments of the
Passion of her Son and, especially, at the moment when he is taken down
from the cross. There, Bonaventure turns directly to the Virgin, identifies
himself with her and feels himself shot through with her sorrow; he then
considers the

> planctum acerbi ejulatus, quem profundo pectoris fonte manantem abscon-
> dere non valebas, Virgo castissima, quando . . . in amplexus ruebas exan-
> imis corporis Filii tui de cruce depositi, cujus genas ante nitentes, et ora
> rutilantia, mortis conspiciebas perfundi palloribus, ipsumque totum con-
> cussum cernebas, lividum livoribus, ac concisum vulnere super vulnus.[18]

And it is precisely these lyrical accents, this pathos, the concrete detail
and the palpitating images, at once human and humanizing, of the *Meditationes* which dominate the dramas of the Passion, the art, and the literature
of the late Middle Ages.

The investigation we have conducted across the unexplored reaches of
the theme of the compassion of the Virgin, one of the fundamental motifs in
medieval liturgy, art, and literature, has clearly shown how deeply rooted in
the Greco-Latin tradition are the vision and the idea of the *Virgo moerens*. As
we have reviewed the testimony of authors from the patristic age to the
fourteenth century, we have been able to verify the continuity of the theme
of the *Compassio*. In its specifically contemplative, lyrical, and dramatic
significance, it constitutes an inalienable inheritance of the medieval literary tradition. Born in the bosom of the Eastern spiritual tradition and
developed, through vital redefinitions, in the orbit of the intense emotionalism and Marian sensibility of the Latin spirituality of the eleventh and
twelfth centuries, the theme of the *Compassio* is illumined, from the beginning of the twelfth century, by the wondrous fruitfulness of the literary
tradition of the *Planctus Mariae*. Through the verbal splendor of its lyrical
form, the *Planctus* invests the theme of the compassion of the Virgin with a
fullness of artistic beauty and the sublimity of dramatic efficacy. And it is
this emotional power of the *Planctus Mariae*, able to project, with lyrical
energy and personal accents, the immediate fullness of the sorrows of her

maternal compassion, that the medieval authors of dramas of the Passion will tap to intensify poetically and dramatically the bloody sacrifice of Golgotha.

The separation and the isolation of the *Planctus*—a lyrical form—from the Passion—a narrative, dramatic form—and the fact that numerous *Planctus* have come down to us, have contributed to the birth of the idea that the dramas of the Passion are derived from the *Planctus*. We know, however, that no existent *Planctus* antedates the refined and extensive Passion of Montecassino; we know, too, that this drama includes only a rudimentary *Planctus* of three verses. So we may justly and logically conclude that the *Planctus* cannot be considered the germ or the starting-point of this drama of the Passion, nor probably of other dramas of the twelfth and thirteenth centuries. The *Planctus* should be considered only a lyrical composition which could be used to intensify the emotionalism and the drama of the scene of the Crucifixion, or it could simply co-exist with the drama of the Passion as a distinct and autonomous type of lyric.

The objective justification for this separation of the *Planctus* from the organic structure of the drama of the Passion may be found, in part, in an observation made by Mone in 1854, that the lyrics of the sorrow and the lament of the Virgin were called in the Eastern tradition *Staurotheotokia*, because they were recited at the foot of the cross; in virtue of this particular characteristic, shared with Greek lyrics, the *Planctus Mariae* in Latin and in German were often introduced as lyrical monologues in dramas of the Passion.[19] There are, furthermore, numerous instances offered by the Latin liturgy, from the twelfth century on, in which the *Planctus* was performed during the ceremony of the *Adoratio crucis*, in which a simple cross was emblematic of the scene on Calvary.

To confirm this coexistence of the lyrics of the *Planctus* with the dramas of the Passion, but in an autonomous and separate mode, it is sufficient to remark that the *Planctus* of Montecassino does not proceed chronologically and synchronically with the development of the episodes of the central theme of the Passion of which it is a part. Rather, it takes place at the end of the Passion, after the *consummatum est*, and precisely, as in the *Staurotheotokia*, at the foot of the cross:

Mater . . . stans cum Ioanne et aliis mulieribus ante crucem . . . versus . . . quasi ostendens ei ventrem in quo christum portavit. Unde dolens beata virgo quia loquendo latroni et matri sue flenti numquam loquitur cum ingenti clamore ipsa beata virgo vocat filium crucifixum et coram loricatis . . . mag . . .

> . . . te portai nillu meu ventre
> Quando te bei [mo]ro presente
> Nillu teu regnu agi me a mmente.[20]

According to Mancini, the intervention of the Mother in the Passion of Montecassino is furthermore logically and tightly connected with the episode of the good thief, which determines it and to a certain degree makes it plausible, by means of the relationship established between the *pietas in latronem* and the *charitas in matrem*.[21] The interpolation and the grafting of the lament in the vernacular onto the Latin drama demonstrate the desire of the author to secure an increasing psychological participation of the Virgin in the divine sacrifice, to "confer an official investiture to a genre particularly dear to popular devotion"[22] and to interject within the dramatic tension of the Latin text "a violent shout of peasant passion"[23] and of popular emotion.

In the Passion fragment of Sulmona, the *Officium quarti militis* of the fourteenth century, which, as has been shown, formed a part of the complete original text of the Passion of Montecassino-Sulmona,[24] the *Planctus* of the Virgin is also recited *ante crucem*. In fact, the Virgin, who does not seem to have been at all involved in the dynamics of the theatrical action, intervenes in the dramatic time after the death of her Son and only at the moment of the scenic presentation of her *Planctus:*

> Quando venit Maria ad crucem, quartus milex dicat:
> Solus:
>> Que est mulier que plorat
>> et plorando semper orat
>> ut reddatur filius?[25]

O uiat q̃ dicit primo. Vidar tristaȳ milex nobileiṅ
oiuȝ uȝ armoȝ ꝩocreṁ fiut ſarmite hic iuctoꝛ p̃maiṡ.
ṙille ꝗ dicēs · pꝛopt̃ eſiſto · q̃ oiao uacat ꝛo pꝯt̃ aȝ ů ꝩcoieſt ſoaꝗ
oiat. parata uobiſ mictio. · q̃ onliṫ. dicit iſimĺ
Ergo caṁ ꝛo illa regalia · ꞇ cū pilaꝟ habeaṁ cõſilia que ualɖ
noꝑ ſuꝺ moꝯ utilia. Cuȝ fuerint coꝛaȝ pilato dicit
O pilate maɡ̃ uir eꝗgie · auoi mie ůba ꝛeſꝑatoꝛie que moꝯ
tibi uciṁ dicē⁊
Cuȝ ꝛo huic ille ſeꝯuctoꝛ uiuēt nobis ꞇ miꝪs ꝛuſiuȝ fiut dicā
poſt moꝛteȝ iſtaȝ ꝛebeo ꝛeſ⸝gē.
ſleſiqua arte uale⁊t ſ⸝ipe ꝯnoꝭ trī q̃ miciat auc̃ iꝏminne et
dicat illuꝭ amoꝛte ꝛeſ⸝gē
Tũc eēt ẽoꝛ uȝ̃ṅe nouiṡimṁ ſat peioꝛ pꝛṁo ꞇ autoꝛ perṁi ſi
r⸝ipeꝭ uciuo uoꝑ oi⸝iṁ. pilat̃ ꝗ · O cheꝯoꝛ ſociuim.
Auṅ ſiɡl̃ ꝗ · ꞇ quiſꝯ oꝭ dicit ·
Eṅſe uibꝛaꝯ ꝛo ſepuleȝ ueꝪa · ſi īpiſetes aliꝗs ꝛepiaȝ capiꝯo
coꝛ meo onſe ferias · pꝪa ꝛioꝛ · ꞇte no ꝗ̃ · onilıⱥ eſt ꝛo ſepuleⱥ dicēo
Ergo caṁ ꞇ quoꝯ oiȝ ſacaṁ uigilaūo cuſtooiaȝ · ne ſepuleȝ ꝛo
micaꝏ · ꝙ̃ ſóce uciat ei oiſaplṫ r⸝ipṁ coꝛ capiat̃ ſigli ne
ſıc īmuⱥ apena patibuli · Cuȝ uenetẽ pilaeꝟ ꝛo ſepuleȝ dicēs
oniuⱥ dat̃ · aȝĺ daivēt ſepuleȝ dicātes
ſle ſoꝛꝯ uciant ei oiſaplı ꞇ ſurtioo ꝛꝛaſſⱥiiⱥ alibi iuaⱥaṁ coꝛ
auȝ lincuꝭ ꞇ ueberemꝰ eoꝛ glaoıꝯſ
Cuȝ fuerint ꝯ⸝atali ꝛo ſepuleȝ · qlibȝ eoꝛ dicat. heu miſi · heu
miſꝭꝭ · heu miſꝭ ꝯoletoꝭ heu miꝭꝭ plaꝛgētᷓ caṁ ꝛo pꝛnapeȝ.
pꝛ⸝imuⱥ ꞇ ꝑꝭ auleꝭ · dicſc. Dira celĺ · trī ꞇ quiⱥ⸝ ꝩ⸝
pꝛoſꝑciⱥ⸝ īquā ꝯomⱥ⸝ apilaꝯo ualⱥ boiⱥ ſeq̃ṁ iuiīȝ.
oeꝏeo eſt ꞇ iactura pluiṁa ītharc fuiⱥā ſigliⱥ obpꝛobꝛia ·
O⸝ꝛ ꝑꝪ dicat · r⸝ual ē ꝗ eⱥⱥⱥiⱥuⱥ · quiⱥ⸝ ꝩ⸝
Cu ṅoꝰ cruciat pilaeꝟ · eᷓ⸝ṅ mⱥⱥ patet latꝯ ꝛo ꝗ qȝ flagina
oiuuⱥⱥo aɡat ꝗeꝯo dicat̃ meꝯoꝭ nᷓꝯ nuꝗȝ plicat · ut
diⱥaṁ alia · pꝛꝁ ꝁꝭo dicat̃ · Jꝭ latea · trī ꞇ quiⱥ⸝ ꝩ⸝
Ooc teſtaṁ hoc fateṁ neqȝ uey oiffiⱥⱥṁ o uioei crevtⱥ ·
Jꝑꝭ tecꝰ uaſe pulɡ̃ ꝛebꝛeꝭ ꝛe ſepuleȝ alliⱥa aṅⱥ ·

Fragment of the *Officium quarti militis*. Sulmona, Archivio Capitolare of
San Panfilo. Fasc. 17, n. 9.

This technique of representation is also used in the other two dramas of the Passion in Latin, preserved in the manuscript *Carmina burana* of Benediktbeuern, the *Ludus breviter de Passione* and the *Ludus de Passione*. In the *Ludus breviter de Passione* the action of the recitation of the *Planctus* is inserted in the course of the drama in a manner similar to that observed in the Passion of Montecassino. The stage directions which introduce the scene are quite precise in detailing and describing the exact moment when the Virgin should make her entry. After Christ has been crucified and his side pierced by the lance, and after the God-Man has uttered his heart-rending "Deus meus, Deus meus, quid dereliquisti me?"—only at this point is the entry of the Virgin contemplated, *ante crucem:* "Tunc Maria mater Domini veniat et due alie Marie et Iohannes. Et Maria planctum faciat quantum melius potest."[26]

In the *Ludus de Passione* the episodic disposition of the dramatic action again indicates that the Virgin appears at the moment of the *Planctus* after Christ has been hung on the cross: "Tunc veniat Mater Domini lamentando cum Iohanne evangelista, et ipsa accedens crucem respicit crucifixum."[27]

On the basis of these examples it seems logical that the justification for the presence of the *Planctus* in a drama of the Passion must be found in its evident decorative function, intended to intensify, through the representational efficacy of the lament and the compassion of the Mother, the immensity of the drama of the Son upon the cross. Rather soon, however, the increasing complexity of the dramas of the Passion and the desire, on the part of the playwrights, to amplify the scene of maternal sorrow by a progressive enrichment of the lyrical and dramatic tension created by the *Planctus*, confer on the various *Planctus* their precise scenic individuality and increase their autonomy. That is, the *Planctus*, to use Ugolini's words, is detached "from the trunk, where it had first blossomed as the more intense participation of the people at the culminating and conclusive moment, when the human affliction of the Mother flanks the divine tragedy, to undertake the role of dramatic and lyric action within a more restricted frame."[28]

This detachment is visible not only in the Latin *Planctus* of the fourteenth century, such as those of Cividale and those found respectively in the Biblioteca Civica in Bergamo and the *Ordinarium ecclesiae Patavinae* of the Biblioteca Capitolare in Padua, but in the enormous production of *Planctus* in the vernacular. For the purposes of the present study and in the context of the handling of this theme, it is a fact of illuminating and determining historical and literary value that definite relations exist among the primitive and most archaic *Lament of the Virgin* of the Montecassino Passion of the twelfth century, the *Lamentatio Beate Marie de filio* of the Abruzzi from the second half of the thirteenth century, and the *Pianto delle Marie* from the Marches, datable between the end of the thirteenth century and the beginning of the fourteenth.[29] Stylistically, these three laments are associated by the same structure of strophe and meter, monorhymed quatrains of ten-syllable lines.

Of greater importance, however, are their stylistic, thematic and lexical components, which lead one to establish derivations and linguistic as well as literary references. Although the *Pianto* from Montecassino, like the whole Montecassino *Passio*, is an expression of the culture and orbit of the Benedictine order, the *Lamentatio* from the Abruzzi and even more so the *Pianto delle Marie* from the Marches reflect the ideas and the values of Franciscan spirituality which, detaching itself from the spirituality of the preceding centuries, in particular from that associated with Anselm and Bernard, marks the passage, in the commemoration of the *Passio*, from *devotio* to *imitatio*.[30]

Among the themes and stylistic elements which appear in the three *Pianti* and bring us back to the verses in the *Pianto* of Montecassino, we note the latter's first verse, ". . . te portai nillu meu ventre," which is echoed in the *Pianto delle Marie* (v. 210), "Io nove misi en ventre te portai," and also in the Lombard Passion of the thirteenth century, "ke te portai intel me' corpo"; this topos is surely an echo of Bonaventure, "ventris tui viscera / Iesum portaverunt."[31] On the basis of the correspondences of the rhyme *dolente / mente* in *lauda* 17 (vv. 92–95) of the Urbino poem,

> A ccui lassi questa dolente
> ke tte porto, fillo, nel ventre?
> Pregote, fillo, ke tte sia a mmente
> de darme consolatione

and in the *Lamentatio* from the Abruzzi (vv. 49 and 52),

A ccui me laxi, meme dolente . . .
Dili tu, filiu, che m'aia a mmente,

Mancini seems authorized, by virtue of the rhyme with *dolente*, to offer the completion of the Montecassino tristich with the addition of a first verse, in this way:

A ccui me lassi, oi me dolente
ch'eo te portai nillu meu ventre.
Quando te beio [mo]ro presente
Nillu teu regnu agi me a mmente.[32]

The correspondences that exist between the *Lamentatio* from the Abruzzi and the *Pianto* of Montecassino are exceeded by the notable affinities between the *Lamentatio* and the *Pianto delle Marie*, which extend to whole strophes:

Lamentatio	*Plaint of the Marys*
A ccui me laxi, me me dolente?	A ccui me lasse, Christu potente?
Sola remango fra questa gente.	Sola remango fra queste gente!
Ecco Johanne ke tt'e pparente.	Eccu Johani k'e tui parente.
Dili tu, filiu, ke mm'aia 'n mente.	Dilli, hoi filgu, ke m'aia mente.
(vv. 49–52)	(vv. 108–11)

Lamentatio	*Pianto delle Marie*
Dolce meu filiu lu pietusu,	Dolce meu filiu et pigitusu,
fusti a la gente scì caritusu;	ere a la gente si caretusu!
ore te veio scì angustiusu!	Ora te veio sì angostiusu
tapina me me, core doliosu!	ke lu me core multu e doliusu!
(vv. 45–48)	(vv. 267–70)[33]

In the tradition of the *Planctus* in the vernacular the *Lamentatio* from the Abruzzi occupies a fundamental position since "because of the age of the manuscript that contains it, it holds the first place in a group of compositions, which are so tightly bound together by meter and content that they constitute a minuscule literary genre: that of the *Pianto per la passione di Cristo*."[34] Beginning with its source and matrix, the *Pianto* of the Virgin of the Montecassino Passion composed in lines of ten syllables, this verse line will become "the indicator of a literary genre,"[35] the Lament of the Virgin, which will gradually spread beyond the Benedictine orbit, from the Abruzzi to the Marches and Umbria, to Tuscany and northern Italy.

This spread of the *Lamentatio* beyond the confines of the Benedictine tradition of Montecassino was determined by the close ties between the Spiritual Franciscans of the Marches and Umbria and the monks of the Abruzzi of Pietro dal Morrone who observed the rule of Saint Benedict.[36] The influence which the psychological themes, the lyrical dramatic character, and the elements of anguish established by the archaic *Pianto* of Montecassino and amplified, through the dramatic force of maternal *pathos*, by the *Lamentatio* of the Abruzzi, will have upon the *laude* of the Disciplinati and the *laude* of Jacopone has already been emphasized.[37] Within the limits of our investigation we shall restrict ourselves to remarking that the *Pianto* of Montecassino, the *Lamentatio* of the Abruzzi and the *Pianto delle Marie* of the Marches form the first step of a tradition of *Pianti*—with an epicenter, according to Ugolini and Baldelli, in the Abruzzi, in which the role of the Virgin in the sorrowful divine mystery is presented with a poetic uniqueness and an exemplary power of dramatic presentation. These are characters that will be accentuated with special technical and theatrical craftsmanship from the beginning of the thirteenth century.

To offer specific instances of the poetic uniqueness and of the lyrical and emotional distinctiveness of the role of the Virgin in subsequent *Planctus*, it is sufficient for the present purpose to refer to the fourteenth-century *Planctus* of Cividale. According to indications furnished by the text, this *Planctus* took place on Good Friday: "Hic incipit Planctus Mariae et aliorum in die Parasceven."[38] The Virgin Mary, *ante crucem*, accompanied by Mary Magdalene, Mary the mother of James, Mary Salome, and John, sings a good nine of the twenty-one stanzas of this famous *Planctus*, which, by virtue of the abundance of stage directions that accompany it, constitutes one of the most original and extraordinary monuments of the medieval theater.[39]

Furthermore, we have information on a *Planctus* of the fourteenth century which was recited *ante crucem* in the cathedral of Mallorca on Good Friday, shortly after the ninth responsory of the Office of Matins:

Item fari dicantur bona hora propter *planctum*. . . .Finito nono responsorio, dicantur *planctus* a tribus bonis cantoribus. Et sint induti vestimentis et dalmaticis nigris vel violatis, et velati faciebus. Et quilibet dicat unum versum *planctum* in eundo. Et in fine cuiuslibet versus omnes insimul flectendo genua dicant, *Ay ten greus son nostras dolors*. Et cum fuerint in truna, dicat ibi quilibet duos versus *planctus*. Finito planctus dicantur laudes.[40]

Donovan observes that quite probably the "tribus bonis cantoribus" mentioned above represented the Virgin Mary, another Mary, and Saint John, and that the refrain "Ay, ten greus son nostras dolors" is a translation of the Latin refrain "Heu, quantus est noster dolor!" which was sung in the Easter drama of Vich in the twelfth century.[41] We must mention, however, that this refrain was sung three times in the *Visitatio sepulchri* of Narbonne[42] and seven times in the *Ludus Paschalis* of Tours, both of the thirteenth century.[43] What remains unanswered is the question whether this *Planctus* was recited entirely in the vernacular, even though the liturgical context in which it was inserted seems to deny that possibility.

A description taken from the *consueta de tempore* of the same cathedral of Mallorca tells us, however, the way in which the *Planctus* of this ceremony of the Office of Matins was sung toward the middle of the fifteenth century (c. 1440):

Et postmodum accensis cereis procedentur ad faros ut in consueta continetur. Et post nonum responsorium fiat Planctus Passionis Domini nostri Ihesu Christi. Prius veniat unus presbiter indutus cum dalmatica in persona Sancti Petri, et faciat planctum ante crucifixum paratum in media ecclesie. Et postea veniat alius sacerdos ex alia parte, et faciat in persona Sancti Johannis. Et immediate alius sacerdos in persona Sancte Marie Matris Salvatoris, et eciam alii presbiteri in persona Sancte Marie Magdalene et Marie Iacobi, etc. Et facta Representacione Planctuum omnes clerici sint in choro et dicant laudes.[44]

In a manuscript of Regensburg of the thirteenth century we find prescribed the ceremony for the recitation of a *Planctus* that was performed during the rite of the *Adoratio crucis* and recited by two "*scholares*" who, dressed in the appropriate array of lamentation, personified the Virgin and Saint John:

Deinde, si placet, veniant duo scholares, indutis vestibus lamentabilibus, sub typis Beatae Virginis et Sancti Johannis, et plangant ante crucifixum alternatim planctum:

> *Planctus ante nescia,*
> et alium:
> *Hew, hew! virgineus* [flos].[45]

From the first years of the fourteenth century there is a representation, both lyrical and dramatic, of the *Planctus* performed at Gubbio, the night of Good Friday, in a church of the city: "in qua ecclesia lacrimosas laudes et cantus dolorosos et amara Lamenta Virginis Matris vidue proprio orbate Filio cum reverentia populo representent, magis ad lacrimas attendentes quam ad verba,"[46] or that which took place, it too *coram populo* but from a covered pulpit, in a church of Toulouse, France, in the thirteenth century, after the *Officium matutinorum* of the *feria V in Coena Domini*, where the *Planctus Mariae* was recited by two children:

> Officium Matutinorum incipitur hora meliori propter diei (feria V in Coena Domini) et propter gentium multitudinem et etiam propter Planctum Beatissimae Virginis Mariae, quae dicitur a duobus puerulis post Matutinum, et debent esse monachi, si possunt reperiri, ad hoc apti, sin autem dicetur a secularibus ad hoc fundati, monachisque deficientibus. Et omnes candelae extinguntur post Matutinum, scilicet post *Kyrie eleyson* quod dicitur super altare cum versibus, excepta una candela quae remanet accensa usque Planctus finiatur; ad denotandum quod ista die tota fides remanserit in sola Virgine Maria, quia omnes discipuli erraverunt seu dubitaverunt secundum magis et minus, excepta Virgine Maria. Ita Planctus dicitur in cathedra predicatorii, et debet esset cooperta et circumcinta de cortinis albis predicta cathedra ad finem, quod dicentes sive cantantes praedictum Planctum non possint videri a gentibus, nec ipsi videant gentes, ut securius possint cantare sine timore, quia forte videndo gentes turbarentur.[47]

The recitation or the chanting of this *Planctus* is presented, in its cultural context, as an example of that participation in the liturgy, by means of the dramatization of the lament of the Virgin, which will be one of the determining aspects of the *devotio* of the Confraternities of the Disciplinati.[48] The participation of the people in the sorrow of the Virgin is lyrically illustrated, for instance, in a *Dialogus Mariae cum populo* of the fifteenth century, in which the structure of the action by dialogue suggests a scenic presentation *ante crucem* of this *Dialogus:*

Populus

1. O perpulchra domina,
   cur sic perturbaris?
   Nive quae candidior,
   fletu denigraris,
   Luna, sole clarior,
   lugens eclipsaris,
   Singulorum gaudium
   tristis lacrimaris,
   Vita, salus hominum,
   mortua iudicaris?

Maria

2. Dic, quare non debeam
   aspere lamentari,
   Natum meum intuens
   acriter vulnerari?
   Totus sanguis funditur
   manu militari
   Nulli membro parcitur,
   sic commaculari
   Corpus eius video,
   dolens haec effari.

Populus

3. O regina saeculi
   barathri dominatrix,
   Scala caeli splendida,
   hominum imperatrix,
   Virgo mater Domini,
   splendida mediatrix,

Non est sui criminis
    plagula vulneratrix,
Mortem morte liberat,
    haec sunt, dominatrix.

Maria

4. Et si prosit homini
        dura flagellatio,
    Meae tamen animae
        haec est gladiatio,
    Nam non sensus discutit,
        obumbratur ratio,
    Cum matris sit ad filium
        perfecta compassio,
    Quae praedixit fieri
        prophetica narratio.

Populus

5. O fontalis venia,
        parce delinquenti,
    Sanctorum victoria
        gloria praecellenti,
    Malo quinque verbula
        quam mille legenti,
    Secundum tua gaudia
        hoc do paenitenti,
    Quamvis sit aprocrypha
        claret hoc studenti.[49]

Of extraordinary importance in our context—since it is a precious *uni-cum*—is a characteristic *Planctus* of the last decades of the fourteenth century, recently discovered in the musical archive of Florence, the *Opera* of Santa Maria del Fiore. It was performed with the distribution of lyrical material among performers listed as *cantores* and *mulieres*, among whom there was the Virgin Mary.[50] This *Planctus* was sung on the occasion of the *Processio veneris sancti* for the ceremony of the *Depositio*. The reconstruction of the order of the rubrics indicates clearly that there were seven interventions attributed to Mary in the *Planctus:* unfortunately, however, they were not copied in ms. 21. The epicenter of the rite was the *feretrum*, upon which quite probably there was "an image of Christ, unnailed and dead."[51] One of the fundamental questions we have to answer—in view of the discovery of new documents—is the possible relationship between *Planctus* of this type and those belonging to an earlier tradition. To this question must be added the problem of historical research, not only concerning the process of transmission and diffusion of such *Planctus* but also the complex set of themes to which they pertain, as evidence of a lyrical and dramatic expression "between the austerity and the stability of a liturgy transmitted for centuries and the need, felt with ever greater urgency, of visualizing the mystery and making it comprehensible."[52]

In Processione Veneris Sancti

I. [*Maria*] (?)

II. *Cantores prope feretrum*
   Jerusalem, luge,
      et exue te vestimentis iocunditatis:
      indue te cinere et cilicio,
      et deduc quasi torrentem lacrimas
      per diem ac noctem;
      non taceat pupilla oculi tui
      quia in te occisus est Salvator Israel.

III. *Cantores anteriores*
   Vinea mea electa, ego te plantavi;
   Quomodo conversa et in amaritudine,
   ut me crucifiggeres et Barrabam dimicteres?

IV. *Cantores prope feretrum*
   Cum portaretur ad sepulcrum,
   illa sequebatur eum
   amarissime plorando,
      et lamentabatur post eos dicendo:

V. [*Maria*]
[Sinite me osculari
sanctissimum corpus dulcissimi filii.]

VI. *Cantores anteriores*
Cui comparabo te, vel cui assimilabo te,
filia Jerusalem?
Cui exequabo te, et consolabor te,
virgo, filia Syon?
Magna enim velud mare contrictio tua,
et non est qui consoletur te.

VII. *Mulieres*
Vide, Domine, aflictionem nostram,
quoniam erectus est inimicus noster;
nos vero plorantes
et oculi nostri deducentes aquam,
quia longe factus est consolator noster.

VIII. *Cantores prope feretrum*
Omnes amici eius spreuerunt eam,
et facti sunt ei inimici.
Omnes porte ciuitatis Jerusalem destructe,
sacerdotes eius gementes;
virgines eius squalide,
et ipsa oppressa amaritudine.

IX. [*Maria*] (?)

X. *Cantores prope feretrum*
Dixerunt uiri impii:
et deglutiamus iniustum,
et deglutiamus eum uiuum sicut infernus,
auferamus memoriam illius de terra,
et de spoliis eius sortem mictamus inter nos:
ipsi enim amici tesaurizauerunt sibi mala.

XI. *Mulieres*

Quis dabit capi[ti] nostro aquam
et oculis nostris fontem lacrimarum,
et plorabimus die ac nocte?
Quia turpiter mactauerunt filium Dej.

XII. *Cantores anteriores*

Judas merchator pessimus
osculo petiit Dominum:
Ille, ut agnus innocens,
non negauit Jude obsculum;
denariorum numero
Christum Judeis tradidit.
Melius erat illi, si natus non fuisset.

XIII. *[Maria]* (?)

XIV. *Cantores prope feretrum*

Cum autem uenissent ad locum,
ubi crucifigendus erat filius eius,
statuerunt eum
in medio omnis populi,
et vestibus expoliatis
nudum dimiserunt corpus sanctissimum.

XV. *Cantores anteriores*

Sicut ouis ad occissionem ductus est,
et dum male trateretur non aperuit os suum:
traditus est ad mortem
et inter scelleratos deputatus est,
ut ipse saluum faceret populum suum.

XVI. *[Maria]* (?)

XVII. *Mulieres*

Vide, Domine, et considera afflictionem
    nostram:
desolate sumus ac derelicte;
spes nostra a nobis ablata est.

XVIII. *Cantores prope feretrum*
Amici eius elongati sunt,
et noti eius quasi alieni recesserunt ab eo.
Insipientes et maligni oderunt sapientiam,
et rey facti sunt in cogitationibus suis.

XIX. *Cantores anteriores*
Plauserunt super te manibus suis
omnes transeuntes per uiam:
sibilauerunt et fremerunt dentibus
et moverunt caput suum
super te, filia Jerusalem.

XX. *[Maria]* (?)

XXI. *Cantores prope feretrum*
Accingite uos, sacerdotes,
et plangite, ministri altaris,
aspergite uos cinere,
quia recessit pastor noster
et sol obscuratus est.

XXII. *Cantores anteriores*
Ecce hic peccata nostra portauit,
et pro nobis dolens uulneratus est
propter iniquitates nostras:
cuius livore sanati sumus.

XXIII. *[Maria]* (?)

XXIV. *Cantores prope feretrum*
Cum vero venissent ad locum,
ubi seppelliendus erat filius eius,
statuerunt eum
in medio mulierum,
et syndone inuoluentes
sepultum dimiserunt corpus sanctissimum.

XXV. *Mulieres*

O nimis triste spectaculum,

o crudele supplicium impensum filio Dei!

O felix rex,

tam turpi morte coronatur!

O pontifices iniquitatis,

tantumne in uestrum exardescitis Deum?

XXVI. *Cantores anteriores*

Sepulto Domino, signatum est monumentum,

uoluentes lapidem

ad ostium monumenti.

ULTIMA. *Quatuor cantores simul. In recessu a sepulcro*

[A] Consolamini, consolamini, universi populi.

[B] Quoniam Dominus noster Jesus Christus

hodies moriendo mortem occidit,

uitam donavit et uiam ad eternam gloriam

preparavit.

[A] Nos vero peccauimus, inique egimus.

[B] Ipse peccata nostra portauit,

et sanguine suo pretioso nos redemit.

[AB] Leuemus ergo corda nostra cum lacrimis

ad Dominum in celis,

et ipse miserebitur nostri,

qui est benedictus in secula seculorum.

Amen.[53]

The problem of the relations between *Planctus* of this type and their transmission acquires special value and significance in the context of our discussion for various reasons: the perception that the twenty passages of the *Planctus* of ms. 21 created by their compiler constitute, in great part, a labor of stringing together biblical texts, which figured prominently in the liturgy of the time of the Passion; that one of the melodic formulas used for the stanzas of the *Planctus* is a *tonus lamentationum* called the "Benedictine" tone, which recurred time and again in the manuscripts and the publications of the Benedictine congregation of Santa Giustina, which had strong associations with Montecassino;[54] and finally, the realization that the ceremony of the *Depositio*, introduced in Italy during the twelfth century or at the beginning of the thirteenth, soon underwent modifications in contact with various popular devotions of Italy, such as the *laude*, the *sacre rappresentazioni*, and the *Planctus* of several sorts.[55]

The specifically and exceptionally lyrical and emotional character of these several *Planctus*, and in particular of the *Planctus Mariae*, in the dramas of the Passion is confirmed, in every instance, by the arrangement of the stage directions and the text, which prescribe and reveal the nature of the execution: "Cum ingenti clamore ipsa beata virgo vocat filium" (Passion of Montecassino); "Et Maria planctum faciat quantum melius potest" (*Ludus breviter de Passione*); "Tunc veniat Mater Domini lamentando. . . . Mater Domini omni ploratu exhibens multos planctus et clamat" (*Ludus de Passione*); "Que est mulier que plorat / et plorando semper orat" (*Officium quarti militis* of Sulmona). There is also the consideration that the *Planctus* inserted in the dramatic structure of the dramas of the Passion of Montecassino, the *Ludus breviter de Passione*, and the *Ludus de Passione* are supplied with musical notes (neumes). The music that accompanies these *Planctus* does not constitute a simple aesthetic embellishment, but in its adaptability and melodic variety it is a sad, lyrical melody that comments on, accents, and expands with its melody the heartrending and desolate anguish of Mary.

Recently, for instance, in a scenic presentation of the *Ludus de Passione*, it could be observed how the chanting of the *Planctus* was an important instrument for the projection of Mary's inner travail. "The singing itself quite unambiguously established the dominant emotional chord . . . in the Virgin's *planctus* as in the entire play, the range of melodies and the vocal interpretations actually help carry the burden of the action."[56]

The lament of the Virgin breaks away from the compositional scheme of the dramatic representation to form, within the theatrical action, an iconlike contemplation of the tragic pathos of the Mother. This is especially evident in the Passion of Montecassino, where the insertion, at the end of the drama, of a *Planctus* in the vernacular allows the Virgin to detach herself "from the dramatic action and in the context of motion, in a brief moment of general cessation, become a speaking icon."[57] And in her function as an intermediary not closely subordinate to the symbolic canons of the traditional liturgy she can communicate to the faithful her personal experience and offer herself to them "as a real and concrete model."[58]

This iconlike character seems present in an incomplete and little-known French *Planctus* of the twelfth century, preserved in the Laurentiana, with this description, "versus quidam lingua Provinciali in mortem filii ut videntur conscripti." Quite probably it was part of a drama of the Passion. The Virgin laments the loss of her Son in the context of references to the happy event of the Incarnation and of the prophecy of Simeon. Together with the recapitulative structure of the entire fragment, these references suggest the considerable dimensions of the complete text:

> Je plains et plors come feme dolente,
> Quar ie ay perdu ce que plus m'atalente.
> A grant tristour fuie ma iouuente,
> Sans nul confort triste sera ma uie iusques a la mort.
>
> Beau dous cher fis, simple uis, bele bouche!
> La vostre mort, beau fis, au cuer me touche.
> Des ores mais uiuray come une souche.
> Sans nul confort triste sera ma uie jusques a la mort.
>
> Beau dous cher fis, uos deinaistes decendre
> Dou ciel en moy et char umaine prendre.
> Par uostre mort bien me doit li cuers fendre.
> Sans nul confort triste sera ma vie jusques a la mort.
>
> Beau dous cher fils et beau sire et beau pere!
> Quant uos de moi feistes uostre mere.
> Par uostre mort doi ge auoir bouche amere.
> Sans nul confort triste sera ma vie jusques a la mort.
>
> Beau dous cher fis! a lo uostre naissance
> Remes uirge san mal et san greuance,
> Que enpren trop nature sans uengance.
> Sans nul confort triste sera ma uie iusque a lo mort.
> Beau dous cher fis! que grant ioei i'auoie.[59]

The possibility that this *Planctus* had been a part of a drama of the Passion is reinforced by the obviously lyrical and emotive writing that characterizes it: the quality of the language seems dictated by the exigencies of adaptation for scenic recitation. There is the direct discourse of the *Planctus:* "beau dous cher fis," "simple uis," "bele bouche." Then, too, there are the apostrophes and interjections of the Virgin to her Son: "La uostre mort," "beau fils," "au cuer me touche." These are, in general, characteristic of a lyrical, emotive recitation and allow us to suppose that this *Planctus*, like the incomplete *Planctus* of the Passion of Montecassino, was recited at the end of a drama of the Passion. The lyrical, emotive elaboration of maternal anguish is furthermore emphasized by the repetition of the refrain, "Sans nul confort triste sera ma uie jusque a la mort," which serves as an emotive frame for each of the stanzas of the *Planctus*.

Parallels should be noted, for instance, between this refrain and similar interjections in the *Plaint* of the Virgin in the *Passion des jongleurs*—

> Mort volentiers te recevrai,
> A qui me reconforterai
>
> (vv. 1838–39)[60]

—in that of the *Passion du Palatinus*—

> Jehan, que devenrra la lasse, l'essartee
> Que la mort ne veut penrre? Moy vivre plus n'agree.
> Diex, qui confortera certe desconfortee?
>
> (vv. 1222–24)[61]

and in the doleful expressions of the plaint of the Virgin of the *Mystère de la Passion Nostre Seigneur*—

> Triste, dolente! Que feray?
> Bien me devroit le cuer partir.
> He! Mort, car me fay departir.
>
> (vv. 2858–60)[62]

A most striking parallel is furnished by some lines of a *Planctus* of the Virgin, delivered *ante crucem* (this *Planctus* occurs in a recently discovered fragment of a fourteenth-century French Passion play:

Mort, mort, pour quoy tel duel confermez?
Pour quoy m'ouste tu mon enfant
Pour toy d'angoysse tressuant?
Mort, mort, tu li dois obehir:
Je te prie bien a moy venir.

(vv. 110–14)[63]

The existence of a French *Planctus* in the vernacular of the twelfth century sets again, but in a different key and on the basis of different considerations, the problem of the affinities, relationships, and dependencies which Ugolini had suggested, even if with extreme caution, between the versification of the *Pianto* of Montecassino and of the *Lamentatio* from the Abruzzi—a ten-syllable line with a single rhyme scheme—and French or Provençal models of like syllabic schemes, especially the quatrain of assonant octosyllables. Ugolini had suggested that "the more remote antecedents, in the realm of the vernacular, of the Italian decasyllable of two sets of five syllables" were "discernible in one of the most illustrious monuments of the early French literary language: the *Passion du Christ* of Clermont-Ferrand"[64] of the tenth century. Its meter, quatrains of assonant octosyllables, has affinities with the Italian decasyllables of two sets of five syllables.[65]

The hypothesis advanced by Ugolini seems extremely interesting if one considers the chronological difference that exists between the Passion of Clermont-Ferrand of the tenth century and the *Pianto* of Montecassino of the twelfth, a difference which could suggest the possibility of echoes of the earlier French versification in the forms of the early Italian literary culture. Such couplings, however, seem a little too bold, given the structural difference of the meter of the Passion of Clermont-Ferrand, formed of quatrains of assonant octosyllables arranged in a system that dates from the Ambrosian strophe, tetrastich of iambic dimeter,[66] and the versification of the *Pianto* of Montecassino and the *Lamentatio* of the Abruzzi, written in decasyllables of double quinaries.

The couplings suggested by Ugolini, between the culture of primitive Italian literature and Cisalpine models, could be valid and of great critical interest if they were aimed at exploring possible relationships not between

the Passion of Clermont-Ferrand and the *Pianto* of Montecassino, but between our French *Planctus* of the twelfth century on the one hand and the
Pianto of Montecassino, the *Lamentatio* of the Abruzzi, and the *Pianto delle
Marie* from the Marches on the other. This relationship is suggested by the
fact that they are all arranged in the same form of strophe: monorhymed
or monoassonant quatrains of decasyllables.

Whether one supposes that our hypothesis is valid, that is, that the
French *Planctus* of the twelfth century was recited at the end of a drama of
the Passion, and whether such a hypothesis presents difficulties of evaluation, the existence of two laments of the Virgin of the twelfth century, the
Pianto of Montecassino and the French *Planctus*, would surely invite us to
consider a re-elaboration of those couplings between the forms and experi-
ences of literary French and the forms of early Italian literature which
were suggested by Ugolini.

Implicit in our discourse, for instance, is the necessity of offering an
exhaustive and precise response, in the realm of medieval drama, to two
fundamental historical and literary problems. The first is that of identify-
ing—on the basis provided by the *Planctus* in the Montecassino Passion—
the initial stage when an early French *Planctus* was inserted in an archaic
French *Passio*. The second is, and no less important, that of establishing
the era when the first French *Planctus* were developed and of evaluating
the possibilities of couplings and influences, direct or indirect, between
the earliest French and Italian *Planctus*, given the metrical affinities which
have been determined.

The critic encounters the first problem again, in fact, with extreme
urgency but in new terms and a highly dramatic fashion, when he considers that the *Planctus* of the Virgin that appears in the *Passion provençale du
manuscrit Didot* of the middle of the fourteenth century[67] is simply an
incomplete reproduction of a more correct and complete form of the same
Planctus preserved in a manuscript belonging to the Church of Santa Maria
la Vella of Ager, in Catalonia, which certainly dates from the thirteenth
century, if not actually from the twelfth. Villanueva, who was the first to
provide information on it, held that it was earlier than the thirteenth century[68] and Chabaneau considered it "une pièce liturgique . . . qui se
chantait probablement au XIIIᵉ siècle, et déjà peut-être au XIIᵉ siècle, le

jeudi et le vendredi saint, dans nombre d'églises du midi de la France et de la Catalogne."[69]

The *Planctus* preserved in the Church of Santa Maria la Vella, which was originally dedicated to San Pedro,[70] allows us to complete the lacunae in the text of the *Planctus* in the *Passion provençale du manuscrit Didot*. For reasons of historical and linguistic character I consider it worthwhile to reproduce in its entirety the version of the *Planctus* of Ager and not the critical reconstruction of this text made by Chabaneau:[71]

Planctus Sanctae Mariae virginis metro vernaculo
scriptus ante sec. XIII

I. Augats, Seyos, qui credets Deu lo payere,
   Augats, sius plau, de Ihu lo salvayre,
   Per nos pres mort, et no lo preset gayre,
   Sus en la creu on lo preyget lo layre,
   Et lach merce axi com o det fayre.
      Oy bels fyls cars,
   Molt mes lo iorn doloros e amars.

II. Auyts, barons, qui passats per la via,
    Si es dolor tan gran com es la mia
    Del meu car fyl que Deus donat mavia,
    Quel vey morir a mort tan descausida.
    Mort, com nom prens? Volentera moria.
       Oy bels fyls cars,
    Molt mes lo iorn doloros e amars.

III. . . . m'apelavon Maria;
     Or me scamiats mos noms, lasa, esmarida
     Que mariment nauray, ay mays cascun dia
     Del meu fyl car mon conort que navia.
     Jueus lan pres sens tort que nols tenia:
     La un lo bat, e laltre vey quel lia.
        Oy bels fyls cars,
     Molt mes lo iorn doloros e amars.

IV. Tots temps jiray dolenta e smarida,
    Car aquel gaugs que eu aver solia,
    Or mes tornats en dolor e en ira
    Regardant fyl quel cors meu partoria.
      Oy bels fyls cars,
    Molt mes lo iorn doloros e amars.

V. Aras dublen les dolos a Maria,
    E diu ploran que sofrir nou poria
    Quel gladi . . . que Simeon deia
    Que de dolor lo cor meu partiria,
    Car be no say quem dia.
      Oy bels fyls cars,
    Molt mes lo iorn doloros e amars.

VI. Molt me pesa lo greu mal quel vey trayre.
    Ay! ques fara lavia la sa mayre.
    Tu vas morir, que es mon fyl e mon paire,
    De tot lo mon es apellat salvayre.
      Oy bels fyls cars,
    Molt mes lo iorn doloros e amars.

VII. Cascunes pens si sol un fyl avia,
    Si auria dol si penyar lo veya.
    Donc io lasa quel fyl de Deu noyria,
    Ben dey plorar, uy may la . . . el dia.
      Oy bels fyls cars,
    Molt mes lo iorn doloros e amars.

VIII. Mayre, dix Deus, nous donec maraveyla,
    Si eu vuyl morir ni sofrir tant gran pena;
    Quel mal queu hay, a vos gran gaug amena,
    De paradis sotç dona e regina.
      Oy bels fyls cars,
    Molt mes lo iorn doloros e amars.

IX. Cant ai Ihesus las dolos de sa mayre,
    Clemet Johuan axi com o pot fayre:

Cosin Johuan, a vos coman ma mayre,
Quel siats fyl, e ela a vos mayre,
Om paradis abduy ayats repayre.
  Oy bels fyls cars,
Molt mes lo iorn doloros et amars.[72]

The second problem, that of research into the early French *Planctus* and the relationship between French and Italian *Planctus*, acquires considerable significance, both historical and literary, when we take into account the recent discovery, in Germany, of a tenth-century chant or hymn in Old Romansh. The hymn, called the *Augsburger Passionslied*, contains one of the earliest brief *Planctus* extant:

> alespins batraunt sos caus
> et abes lan staudiraunt sos lad
> et en la crux lapenderaunt
>
> et oblaeid lopotaraunt
> si greu est a paerlaer
> et en la cruz lapendera[un]t.[73]

Before proceeding to a closer examination of this text, we shall provide the necessary translation:

> With thorns they will strike his head
> and with a lance pierce his side,
> and upon the cross they will hang him.
>
> And with vinegar they will give him to drink
> (so hard is it to speak of it)
> and upon the cross they will hang him.

In his magisterial study of the *Augsburger Passionslied*, Helmut Berschin offers a comparison between the text and the Gospel passages from which it is drawn.[74] The first verse, "alespins batraunt sos caus," recalls the scene of the crowning with thorns—"et plectentes coronam de spinis, posuerunt super caput eius" (Matthew 27:29)—even though the verb *batraunt-battuere* seems to suggest an echo of Matthew 27:30: "Et expuentes in eum, acceperunt arundinem, et percutiebant caput eius." The second verse, "et abes lan staudiraunt sos lad," refers to the passage in John 19:34: "sed unus militum lancea latus eius aperuit." The fourth verse, "et oblaeid lopotaraunt," retraces the account of Mark 15:36: "Currens autem unus, et implens spongiam aceto, circumponensque calamo, potum dabat ei." The refrain, "et en la crux lapenderaunt," appearing as both the third and sixth verse, is a clear echo of the Crucifixion: "et crucifixerunt eum," Matthew 27:35, Mark 15:25, Luke 23:33, John 19:17.

The indisputable Romance character of this Passion chant of six verses is demonstrated by its phonetical, morphological, and lexical aspects, even if the problem of the exact place of origin of the text remains unresolved. The same is true for other Gallo-Romance texts from the ninth to the eleventh century: the *Serments de Strasbourg*, the *Cantilène d'Eulalie*, the fragment of *Jonas*, the *Passion du Christ* and the *Vie de Saint Léger*.[75]

A literary phenomenon of considerable interest is furnished by the fifth verse of the *Augsburger Passionslied*, "si greu est a parlaer," which could certainly be considered an expression of grief and of lament in the tradition of the *Planctus*. In fact, it shows singular textual affinities with the *Planctus* of Mallorca, which we have already discussed, of the fourteenth century, "Ay ten greus son nostras dolors," which in turn is a translation of the Latin refrain of the Easter drama of Vich of the twelfth century, "Heu, quantus est noster dolor."

Walter Berschin, without offering a precise response to his question, asks whether it is permissible to consider the *Augsburger Passionslied* within the context of the tradition of the genre *Planctus Mariae*.[76] Heinrich Kuen, for his part, after initially observing that the *Augsburger Passionslied*, which according to him is in fact a *Planctus*, was probably inspired by the *Planctus Mariae*, declares in the end that even if we cannot say with certainty that this *Passionslied* is the earliest Romansh plaint of the Virgin, we can say that it represents the earliest Romance plaint on Christ crucified.[77]

From a linguistic analysis of the text, especially the use of the future tense (*batraunt, staudiraunt, lapenderaunt, lopotaraunt*), Kuen remarks that the *Augsburger Passionslied* refers to the approaching events of the Passion and, therefore, was quite probably chanted in the tenth century during the liturgy of Good Friday or during the ceremony of the *Adoratio crucis* or before the Passion, at the moment when a reference is made to the imminent realization of the sufferings and the death of Christ.[78] Given its lyrical quality, we believe that the *Augsburger Passionslied* was recited during the ceremony of the *Adoratio crucis* to intensify the pathos generated by the commemoration of Christ's crucifixion. The possibility of its insertion during the reading of the *Passio*, however, seems unlikely, especially because the ancient custom of chanting the *Passio*, with a distribution of the principal parts among cantors, had been instituted beginning in the tenth century precisely with the intention of dramatizing the tragic events of Christ's Passion.[79]

The problem of research into early French *Planctus* and the relationship between Italian and French *Planctus* fits naturally into the broader picture of research into the dissemination of medieval sacred drama in Europe. Although distinguished specialists in the history of theater have opened new vistas for the study of medieval theater by analyzing and explaining its literary and aesthetic aspects, we should deplore all the same the absence of ample historical studies which would show the intimate and complementary affinities that often exist between the dramatic productions of different nations of the Western Catholic world. If the investigations into medieval theater have furnished detailed and competent analyses of the dramatic development of individual nations, they have omitted entirely the problem of the influence exerted by one nation upon another.[80]

And yet the possibilities for original and fruitful research in the diverse relations and analogies among the religious dramas of different nations are numerous. In the study of medieval dramatic art it is still possible to achieve very important results through a rigorous philological investigation (not one of a summarizing or popularizing nature) which would examine the international spread of medieval drama; the interdependence of liturgical and cultural centers; the part played by historical events; the means of communication among the diverse monastic communities, especially the Benedictine, which were normally the places where the sacred dramas were composed or copied; and the scope of the dissemination of dramas in various nations.

Undoubtedly, with the passage of years, the problem has caught the attention of eager scholars; exploratory and incomplete attempts have been made to determine the relations and the interdependence of religious

drama among the various nations of Europe. As early as 1846, for instance, Mone, a tireless explorer of liturgical sources, theorized in his
Schauspiele des Mittelalters that the sacred dramas of Germany were the result of an imitation of the French.[81] Maurice Wilmotte, on the other side,
in *Les passions allemandes du Rhin dans leurs rapports avec l'ancien théâtre français*
(1898) asserted that the German dramas of the Passion derive from French
influences.[82]

Although not directly interested in such special researches, Wilhelm
Creizenach was keenly aware of the problem of transmission and of the
inherent affinities of medieval drama; he offered, in his *Geschichte des neueren
Dramas* (1911), suggestions that deserve even today to be seriously explored:

> Bei Bahandlung der lateinischen Dramen hatten wir es fast immer mit einer
> Uberlieferung zu tun, die einerseits zu spärlich, anderseits zu verworren war,
> um den Ursprung der einzelnen Denkmaler erkennen zu lassen. Es wäre nicht
> undenkbar, das hier noch manche Ergebnisse zu gewissen waren, wenn mann
> die literarischen Wechselbeziehungen zwischen der Klostern und Stiftern, aus
> denen die Texte stammen, genauer untersuchen vollte.[83]

Although Karl Young realized the impossibility of establishing a family
tree of the affinities of dramatic texts, he eagerly hoped that future scholars would be able to determine numerous points of contact which he had
not had the possibility of studying.[84] On the basis of research limited to
France alone, it was finally Edith Wright who provided the methodology
for a study of the interdependence of the great centers of medieval drama
in that nation.[85] In 1944 Hadassah Posey Goodman published a comparative study intended to determine the direct relations among the dramatic Passion plays of France and Germany.[86] Of fundamental value for
its perception of the international character of the liturgical theater and for
its re-evaluation of the traditional presuppositions concerning it was the
essay of Mary H. Marshall, "Aesthetic Values of the Liturgical Drama,"
(1951) which underscored the necessity of a study of the liturgical dramas
of the Middle Ages founded upon a critical method intended to "ap-
prehend the total emotional experience."[87]

In 1960 the eminent French musicologist Solange Corbin published one
of the principal studies that investigated the question of international in-

fluences, particularly in the field of the affinities of rite and drama. In her book *La Déposition liturgique du Christ au Vendredi Saint*, Corbin studied the history of the *Depositio* in France, Germany, Italy, and Portugal; its dissemination; and its position in the history of the religious theater of the Middle Ages. She concluded that, although the ceremony of the *Depositio*, even retaining its clearly symbolic and liturgical character, lacked some of the basic elements of the drama, the ceremony still could have suggested or inspired the desire of representing other episodes of the Gospels. Corbin summarized the comparative character of her methodology when she wrote in her preface to her readers, "J'ai voulu m'assurer de l'origine et de la diffusion passée et actuelle du rite."[88]

In 1967 Helmut De Boor offered for the first time, in his *Die Textegeschichte der Lateinischen Osterfeiern*, an attempt at reconstructing, on an international level, the archetype of the Easter trope *Quem quaeritis*. In 1981 there appeared the luminous essay by Johann Drumbl, *Quem quaeritis: Teatro sacro dell'alto medioevo*, which through a critical and comparative study of the earliest compositions of the *Quem quaeritis* in Europe, tried to reconstruct the double alienation that separates medieval sacred drama from the modern observer and from the religious culture of the High Middle Ages.[89] Also outstanding are the researches devoted to the *Quem quaeritis* in its European context by the illustrious English musicologist William Smoldon, who has contributed quite substantially to the enhancement of research on this subject by means of a comparative study of his vast and rich collection of photocopies of original manuscripts of the *Quem quaeritis*.[90]

In 1970 we had the opportunity of publishing a comparative study of the origin and development of the medieval Latin Passion play. More recently, Jörg O. Fichte, in his *Expository Voices in Medieval Drama: Essays on the Mode and Function of Dramatic Exposition*, has analyzed the expository methods of Latin, German, and English dramatic texts. John Arnold has offered, in a powerful work of research and interpretation, an analysis of the dramatic structure and the use of time in twelve dramas of the Passion, in Latin and the vernacular, which come from Italy, Germany, France and England.[91] Of incalculable benefit and value for the recovery of this fundamental period in the history of the European theater and for the evaluation of influences, affinities, and congruities on an international level are the researches in the medieval theater published in these last years by the Medieval Center of Kalamazoo,[92] the Centro Studio of Viterbo,[93] and the Association Internationale pour l'Etude du Théâtre Médiéval.[94]

The necessity of evaluating the possibilities of couplings and affinities between forms of Italian drama and similar forms of European drama is dictated by the existence of liturgical dramas of the Passion—the Passion of Montecassino and the fragment of the *Officium quarti militis* of Sulmona in Italy and the *Ludus breviter de Passione* and the *Ludus de Passione* of Benediktbeurn in Germany, for example—which reveal a continuity, in the realm of medieval Latin dramaturgy, between the twelfth and the fourteenth centuries. This continuity suggests the possibility of influences and affinities not only between the sacred drama in the vernacular of these two countries—the Passion of Montecassino with its lament in the vernacular and the *Ludus de Passione* with its ample and numerous passages in German—but between the religious theater of Italy and that of France.[95] These relationships have not yet been explored. As the illustrious Belgian medievalist Omer Jodogne remarked so aptly in 1964:

> Pour le XIIe comme pour le XIIIe siècle, est prouvée désormais l'existence d'une véritable tradition des drames liturgiques sur la Passion. Nous ne pouvons pas douter que ces drames ont circulé et, en l'occurrence, que les drames découverts en Italie ou en Germanie aient pénétré en France, d'autant plus qu'ils sont l'oeuvre d'un order religieux aussi international que celui de saint Benoît. On n'a jamais nié les caractères communes du repertoire dramatique de l'Eglise d'Occident.
>
> Cette tradition a dû influencer les dramaturges français du XIVe siècle et meme du XVe, car, on l'oublie vraiment, les drames liturgiques n'ont cessé d'être représentés dans l'église jusqu' au XVIe siècle.[96]

We have had the occasion, in this connection, to show elsewhere, in the light of an analysis of historical and religious conditions and of textual affinities, the influence exercised by the text of the *Officium quarti militis* of Sulmona, which is an integral part of the Passion of Montecassino, upon the *Ludus Paschalis* of Tours.[97] Other studies have shown affinities between the *Ludus de Passione* and the *Mystère de la Passion* of Jean Michel, with reference to the role of Mary Magdalene,[98] as well as general influences of the *Ludus de Passione* upon two German dramas of the Passion in the vernacular, *Das St. Galler Passionsspiel* and *Das Wiener Passionsspiel*, especially in the scenes that dramatize Magdalene *in gaudio* and her eventual conversion.[99] In the absence, however, of clear proof and of precise studies of a textual and comparative character, we share the opinion of Accarie that the Passion of Montecassino and the two dramas of the Passion of Benediktbeuern constitute only "l'aboutissement du drame liturgique, et n'inaugurent nullement le genre du Mystère de la Passion."[100]

In the area of medieval dramaturgy in the vernacular, studies and researches of a textual character into influences and relationships at both the national and the international level have provided us with partial results. Characteristic elements in the composition of the Passion of Clermont-Ferrand of the tenth century, for instance, and of the Lombard Passion of the thirteenth century have been traced back to similar narrative techniques.[101] Other researches have established the influence, within France, of the *Passion des jongleurs*, a narrative poem of the twelfth or the beginning of the thirteenth century, upon two French dramas of the Passion of the fourteenth century, the *Passion du Palatinus* and the *Passion d'Autun*.[102] These researches show that, despite the obvious evolution of the medieval French theater across the centuries, dramatic compositions such as the *Seinte Resurreccion* of the twelfth century, the *Passion du Palatinus*, the *Passion d'Autun*, the *Passion provençale*, and the fragment of the *Passion Sion* continue, as a whole, the forms and techniques of the old tradition of liturgical drama.[103]

But although we acknowledge, within well-defined limits and in specific dramas of the French Middle Ages, the survival of dramatic elements, of expressive forms, and of stylistic matrices and repertoires derived from the tradition of liturgical drama, we regard as totally unfounded and critically indefensible Regueiro's assertion that the *Visitatio sepulchri* of the Catalan monastery of Ripoll, of the twelfth century, represents "el primer drama litúrgico en toda Europa que contiene en su integridad todos los elementos esenciales que van a constituir más tarde los grandes ciclos medievales" and that "el *mystère* medieval no es más que una simple amplificación lineal del diseño dramático de la *Visitatio* del siglo XII."[104]

These assertions of Reguerio follow the example of the evolutionary theory of Gustave Cohen, who endowed the early *Quem quaeritis* with an excessive importance when he declared that "de cet embryon de drame sortira la colossale littérature des Passions du XVe siècle."[105] A theoretically sounder and more rational position on the evolution of medieval drama is that put forth by Konigson. Even while he holds that the definitive transformation of liturgical drama and consequently the birth of a new theater should be attributed to the passage of the medieval theater "de l'enceinte cléricale au milieu urbain," that is to the change of the theater's location, he still asserts that the figurative system of symbolic representation remains the same from liturgical drama to the great mysteries of the following centuries.[106]

The survival, in some later dramatic compositions, of theatrical procedures deriving from the liturgical tradition, generally reflects the quality of sensibility and of creative technique of the medieval author, who, in whatever literary genre he is working, normally assumes the guise of a *continuateur* or a *remanieur*.[107] In fact, far from seeking to free himself from the guardianship and authority of tradition, the medieval writer intends "agissant en continuateur ou en renouveleur" to exercise his own personal creative ability by staying ever tightly bound to the inheritance accumulated by tradition.

This is made especially evident, in France, by the imposing *mystères* of the fifteenth century, the Passion of Eustache Mercadé, the Passion of Arnould Greban, and the Passion of Jean Michel, all of whom take up again and rehandle a Passion whose elaboration, as we have seen, had begun in the thirteenth century.[108] But despite the obvious instances of dependence and of relationship that can be established and objectively specified between these dramas of the Passion and earlier dramatic sources, it remains unchallengeable, from the theatrical viewpoint, that such sources have not imposed any particular form of representation and that "il faut décidément chercher ailleurs de quoi expliquer comment toutes ces oeuvres ont été *jouées*."[109] As Jodogne has already quite properly pointed out, the dramatic texts which have come down to us offer only what was said on the stage and give only a summary account of what was done on it, but "le texte est loin d'être toute l'oeuvre dramatique."[110]

In their awareness of the notable development and the considerable transformations undergone by the scenic apparatus of the medieval sacred theater over the course of centuries, some scholars of medieval dramaturgy have recently devoted themselves to a thorough-going re-evaluation of the scenography of such dramas. They have done so not only to establish some fundamental criteria of distinction between the objective experience of representation in particular dramatic texts of the Middle Ages and the potential for theatrical execution present in other texts,[111] but to attempt to recover, in a contemporary production of some specimens of liturgical drama, the ritual immediacy and the symbolic character that make it distinctive.[112]

In Germany as in France, the outlook for fruitful results deriving from precise investigations and researches into the relations, derivations, and imitations among various dramatic compositions seems to be richer in sacred drama in the vernacular than in liturgical drama, especially with regard to the dramas of the Passion. In the light of recent studies, in fact, it is proper to hold the following theses with relative certainty. The Passion of Montecassino, the earliest Latin drama of the Passion, did not exercise any influence upon the development of the two Latin dramas of the Passion of Benediktbeurn.[113] And if there exists the possibility of a theory of the Italian origin of the German dramas of the Passion—on the basis provided by the chronological priority of the drama of Montecassino and by information we have on the representation of the Passion in Siena around 1200 and in Padua in 1243 or 1244—this theory has not yet been explored.[114] Finally, the Latin dramas of the Passion do not constitute the sources of the German dramas of the Passion in the vernacular, because the latter are considered novel and independent creations.[115] On the other hand, very real possibilities of authentic and effective relations and dependence can be established among some of these German dramas of the Passion in the vernacular, even if they are limited and restricted to single scenes or parts of these dramas.[116]

The dramatic production of the German Middle Ages offers, chronologically, the spectacle of an apparently gradual evolution of the drama of the Passion and of its passage from Latin to predominantly vernacular forms. Beginning with the Latin dramas of Benediktbeurn, the *Ludus breviter de*

Passione and the *Ludus de Passione*, composed in the first half of the thirteenth century, one proceeds to the *Frankfurter Dirigirolle* of the first years of the fourteenth century, a type of dramatic scenario composed predominantly of distichs in the vernacular with Latin phrases sprinkled throughout. Froning considers it the "Kernstück der ganzen westmitteldeutschen dramatischen Entwicklung."[117] *Das Wiener Passionsspiel*, which belongs to the same period, consists of 532 distichs, of which 137 are in Latin; and in *Das St. Galler Passionsspiel*, also of the fourteenth century, the transition from Latin to the vernacular is especially pronounced.[118] One finally comes, in the last years of the fourteenth century, to *Das Frankfurter Passionsspiel*, written almost entirely in the vernacular; and to later compositions, like *Das Alsfelder Passionsspiel, Das Luzerner Passionsspiel, Das Donaueschinger Passionsspiel*, and the several *Altdeutsche Passionsspiele aus Tirol*, along with others of less importance, which date between the end of the fourteenth century and the second half of the fifteenth.

The relations, influences, and derivations existing among some scenes of the early German dramas of the Passion have been exhaustively discussed by scholars like Hartl, Werner, Bergmann, Michael, Rudick, West, and Greisenegger.[119] Their researches into the structure and the development of these German dramas of the Passion have shown the importance of a comparative study of texts in establishing the existence of precious bonds, whether they be weak or strong, among these dramatic compositions. This is true even if the absence of precise evidence on the origin of the German dramas of the Passion in Latin and in the vernacular allows us only to suppose the passage from the Latin to the vernacular across the intermediate stage of those German dramas of the Passion in which Latin coexists with the vernacular.[120]

In England scholars have achieved notable results with a comparative critical methodology in their analysis of the mystery cycles or cycle plays, the extensive dramatic productions in the vernacular that flourished between 1350 and 1450 but that have come down to us in manuscripts of a later date. Studies of the constitutive elements of these dramas and of the cultural texture of the age have allowed a precise identification of dramatic and narrative components, national as well as international, which are present in the chain of creation and transmission of some of these dramas.

The old theory that considered the mystery plays simple translations of French originals has been abandoned[121] and replaced by the thesis that the origin of English sacred drama is the result, in general, of a gradual and indigenous process of creativity in which dramatic compositions in the vernacular were composed in strict conformity with, but not as literal translations of, models provided by liturgical drama.[122] Still, some of the mystery cycles are clearly the result of French influences. Precise parallels exist, for instance, between the dramatic cycle of Chester and *Le Mystère du Viel Testament*,[123] while the influence of the narrative poem *The Northern Passion*—which represents a translation of the French poem *La Passion des jongleurs* done in England in the first years of the fourteenth century—has already been illustrated upon the dramatic cycles of York, Towneley, and the *Ludus Coventriae*[124] (we must except the Chester cycle).

Possible discoveries of further French influences upon the English theater of this period should not be ruled out, given the European character of the medieval theater and the fact that until the middle of the fourteenth century, French remained the language of tradition, culture, and educated society in England. On the national level significant impulses upon the dramatic cycle of Chester were exercised by the fourteenth-century narrative poem *A Stanzaic Life of Christ*. It represents a compilation, done at Chester, of two famous Latin works, the *Legenda Aurea* of Iacopo da Voragine and the *Polychronicon* of Ralph Higden.[125] Although the dramatic activity represented by the mystery cycles constitutes a theatrical phenomenon that provides an intimate reflection of the character, cultural temperament, and poetic creativity of the English people, the dramatic affinities to which we have referred show clearly that the English sacred theater in the vernacular fits, even in the singularity and uniqueness of its language, into the traditional framework of medieval European theater. Further studies of a comparative character, such as that undertaken by Dunn to illustrate the French origin of the miracle play and its importance in the historical reconstruction of the medieval theater,[126] will be of inestimable value in determining the precise character of English sacred theater in the vernacular in the European context.

The development of a method of study and research of a comparative character is absolutely necessary to determine the origin of the medieval

Spanish theater, which remains, given the scarcity of documentation, the least-known area in the vast dramatic production of the Middle Ages. As early as 1883, in a historical preamble to his *Orígines del teatro español*, Fernández de Moratín asserted that "la escasez de documentos no permite de dar una idea más individual de aquel teatro."[127] The numerous publications that diverse scholars have devoted to this complex and thorny question over the course of years have been particularly unfruitful. They have been intended to rebut theories and theses of various predecessors rather than being directed to an elucidation of the dawn of the sacred theater of Spain, through a systematic research into new documents and new theses. The conclusions reached, many times, by the critics of the history of theater upon Spanish medieval dramaturgy have been based on utterly improbable hypotheses, on a priori schemes, and on historical assertions of doubtful standing. López Estrada, for instance, although he realizes that "el teatro castellano de la época de los orígines es pobre," declares all the same, with his customary deference to traditional positions and with an intentional bias, that "los presupuestos sobre los que se basa la exploración del teatro medieval se dieron en Castilla lo mismo que en otras partes de España y de la Europa occidental."[128]

But a study of the historical context of the Iberian peninsula in the Middle Ages shows that the *presupuestos* to which Estrada refers—that is, the creative process of the religious drama which took place in Europe through the diffusion of the Roman liturgical model and the evolution of Latin liturgical ceremonies from the forms and gestures of the liturgical chant toward ever more dramatic dimensions—did not have a chance to develop in Castile because of the special historical conditions which at that time isolated the region from the current of the Latin cultural tradition. In fact, we know that, under French influence, centers of Latin culture—the most important of which was the monastery of Santa Maria de Ripoll—existed in Navarre and Catalonia in the eleventh century. Castile, in contrast, remained tied to the orbit of the Islamic culture of the south, which was much superior to the Christian of the north.[129]

Humberto López Morales, in his essay *Tradición y creación en los orígines del teatro castellano*, has given us a lively incentive to explore this problem. After displaying the discernment of his judgment by reviewing the various theses expressed on the origin or even the existence of a sacred theater in Castile from the eighteenth century to our own day, he concludes with the assertion that an analysis of the evidence provided "nos lleva a concluir que el drama fue un elemento extraño en Castilla en los tiempos medios."[130]

The same conclusions were reached ten years earlier by Robert Donovan, one of the first of the rare scholars who have devoted themselves to offering a profile of the dramatic production in Spain during the Middle Ages through an analysis and an interpretation, both critical and historical, of the murky crucible of available documents. Donovan's attempt to achieve a greater appreciation of the sacred theater of Spain, to reduce it to both a historical and a literary homogeneity, to solve irreconcilable differences, and to illuminate the cultural background of this theater constitutes an enterprise of great critical devotion but modest results. In fact, given the scarcity of dramatic evidence and of precise documents and references, Donovan has to conclude that "the silence of the Castilian manuscripts in this regard is a strong argument that the Latin church plays were not very common in this part of the peninsula."[131]

Donovan directly connects the absence of a tradition of liturgical drama in Castile with the historical conditions that prevailed in Spain in the first centuries of the Middle Ages. In this period the development of liturgical drama in France, England, Italy, Germany, and Switzerland was facilitated by the obvious relations and interdependence of the various monastic communities and churches of these nations. The same considerations are also valid for Catalonia, the northern region of the peninsula, which from the reconquest of Charlemagne (768–814) until the twelfth century remained ecclesiastically and politically bound to France, while the rest of Spain lay subject to Arab domination until the middle of the eleventh century.[132] And it is in Catalonia, whose dioceses were dependent on the episcopal see of Narbonne, France, that the researches of Donovan have yielded abundant results through the discovery of new texts of liturgical drama. These may not constitute a collection of texts as considerable as that of the liturgical theater of France, Germany, England, and Italy, but they still offer a precise picture of the origin and evolution of medieval sacred drama in that region and of its relations with the dramatic tradition of France.[133] Recent research undertaken by Surtz has opened new vistas toward the understanding of the medieval theater of Castile and Catalonia.[134]

The existence in the thirteenth century of a liturgical theater and one in the vernacular in Castile was presupposed on the basis of evidence provided by one of the *Siete partidas* of Alfonso X (1221–84), called the Wise. Here is the pertinent passage from *Partida I:*

> Representacion ay que pueden los clericos fazer, asi como de la nascenzia de Nuestro Senor Jesu Christo, en que muestra como el angel vino a los pastores e como les dixo como era Jesu Christo nacido. E otrosi de su aparicion, como los tres Reyes Magos lo vinieron a adorar. E de su Resurreccion, que muestra que fue crucificado e resucitado al tercer dia: tales cosas como estas que muevan al ome a fazer bien e a aver devocion en la fe, pueden las fazer.[135]

The validity and the accuracy of the information provided by this *Partida*, as evidence of irrefutable authority for the survival at this time, in Castile, of a liturgical and vernacular theater has, however, been cast into doubt. The *Partida*, it is necessary to note, is a work of synthesis, one of those compositions of a collective character, like the *compendia* and the encyclopedias, which were compiled in the Middle Ages to preserve the knowledge and doctrine transmitted across the centuries but which often did not have any relation or connection with contemporary reality. The celebrated Spanish critic, Menéndez Pidal, was one of the first to recognize the recapitulative character of the *Partidas*. This is especially true of all that concerns the interdictions against *los juglares* and *las juglaresas*, which constitute a reflex of the condemnation of the jester or minstrel which is found, in the Middle Ages, at all levels of learned clerical culture—theologians, canonists, and preacher-confessors—and which is articulated and reiterated in the tradition of the medieval encyclopedia from the *Etymologiae* of Isidore of Seville (c. 560–636), through the *Didascalion* of Hugh of St. Victor (1096–1141), to the *Polycraticus* of John of Salisbury (1110–80).[136] It was taken up again in the thirteenth century, in the manuals of preaching, from Jacques de Vitry to Umberto of Romans to Gilbert de Tournai.[137] The interdictions against jesters contained in *Partida I* of Alfonso I, in particular, are translations of the decisions expressed in Roman or canon law and of those enunciated by Innocent III (1160–1216) in a decretal of 1207;[138] they therefore do not reflect the actual conditions in Castile.[139]

But if the total absence of documents and dramatic evidence does not allow us to establish the existence of a liturgical drama in Castile, the existence of a sacred theater in the vernacular is attested by a fragment from the end of the twelfth century,[140] known as the *Representación* or *Auto de los Reyes Magos*, deriving from the cathedral of Toledo and composed some years before the compilation of the *Siete partidas*. The *Auto de los Reyes Magos*, a fragment of 147 polimetric verses, is our unique testimonial to the medieval theater in Castile and is "como una flor exótica con la cual quedan alejadas las esperanzas de encontrar fundamentos textuales para un teatro litúrgico castellano."[141] In an essay of textual and comparative criticism of the *Auto de los Reyes Magos*, Sturdivant has shown, however, that the immediate sources of this *Auto* are found not in a liturgical Latin drama but very probably in a dramatic composition in the vernacular of French origin and provenance.[142] This thesis has recently been challenged by Regueiro, who has rejected the conclusions of Sturdivant and Lapesa. Both of the latter had written off the idea of a native dramatic tradition in Castile.[143] Regueiro refuses to accept the notion of an evolutionary process which supposes foreign models for the *Auto de los Reyes Magos*. Instead he proposes that the liturgical center of Ripoll could certainly be considered the focal point for the radiation of a Spanish liturgical and vernacular dramatic tradition: "El foco de irradiación del cual se desprendió, hacia el oeste castellano, no solamente la práctica del drama litúrgico sino tambien las representaciones religiosas en romance."[144]

Regueiro, however, does not offer any proof for his theory; Sturdivant, on the other hand, offers a very accurate and detailed comparison of the *Auto de los Reyes Magos* with other Latin dramatic versions of the Three Magi. This allows her to assert that this drama does not derive from Latin liturgical dramas: "The conclusion, then, to be drawn from a comparative study of the Latin Magi liturgical plays and the *Reyes Magos*, is that there is no evidence of any direct relation between them."[145]

But how would one justify the solution of continuity, in Castile, between the forms of liturgical theater and that of dramatic production in the vernacular? Donovan and Carreter comment that the cause of the problem is that, when the religious dramas were introduced for the first time into Castile, they were already written in the vernacular; as a consequence there was never any need to adopt the dramatic texts of the Latin liturgical tradition.[146]

But if the dramatic evidence for a study of the sacred theater of Castile is very slight, there are numerous texts of liturgical drama coming from Catalonia, one of the great centers of medieval liturgical theater: "The early liturgical drama is centered in Catalonia, and although it was carried from there to other places, or perhaps in individual instances may have been introduced directly from abroad, the Latin liturgical play is predominantly a Catalan rather than a Castilian form."[147] One of the principal influences toward the development of liturgical drama in Catalonia was the liturgical reform undertaken by Charlemagne. This resulted in the introduction into Catalonia, from the very time of the reconquest, of the Roman-Frankish rite, which replaced the traditional Mozarabic. The religious bonds between France and Catalonia began with the first years of the ninth century when Narbonne was set up as the metropolitan see for all the Catalan dioceses: Elna, Gerona, Barcelona, Vich, and Urgel. The archbishop of Narbonne presided at the Councils of Urgel in 799 and 892, at the Council of Barcelona in 991, and at the Council of Vich in 1027. At the beginning of the ninth century the French canonical system had been introduced into the cathedrals of Catalonia.[148] The introduction and adoption of the Roman-Frankish rite in Catalonia[149] contributed to the development of the liturgical drama in one of its greatest centers of cultural and liturgical activity: the Benedictine monastery of Ripoll.[150]

The modest dimensions of medieval sacred drama in Spain, outside Catalan territory, underscore the urgency as well as the necessity of a comparative study of dramatic sources. Such a study should compare the sources not only among the several territorial divisions of Spain but between Spain and other European countries, to determine the relations between the various texts and to trace the precise profile of the history of medieval sacred theater in Spain. Such a comparative methodology is especially necessary to ascertain the origin and the development of the drama of the Passion in Spain. Donovan, for instance, in his researches was not able to provide any dramatic text of the Passion in Latin or the vernacular. Vivian, without any evidence, presupposes its existence when she declares, "aun cuando carezcamos de pruebas escritas acerca de representaciones medievales españolas de la Pasión, la vida y la muerte de Jesucristo fue tema muy común en la poesía de finales del siglo XV."[151] Darbord offers some remarks on two Spanish poems of the Passion in the vernacular of the last years of the fifteenth century, but *ex vacuo* and *in medias res*, that is without any reference to the historical context or to a tradition of the Passion, native or foreign.[152]

The study of the embryonic development of the drama of the Passion in Spain is rendered singularly difficult because the first brief *Autos* on the Passion, still extant, date from the end of the fifteenth century to the first years of the sixteenth. They are the *Representación a la muy bendita pasión y muerte de nuestro precioso Redentor* of Juan del Encina, of 1496; the *Auto de la Pasión* of Lucas Fernández, of 1514; and the anonymous *Tres pasos de la Pasión y una égloga de la Resurrección* of 1520. Contrary to the opinion of Gillet, who considers the *Tres pasos de la Pasión* a drama of the Passion—a Passion play—an analysis of this narrative poem shows that its anonymous author does not deal with the principal events of the Passion of Christ. While the traditional dramas of the Passion emphasize the salient moments of the Passion and often begin chronologically with the betrayal of Judas, the narrative poem *Tres pasos de la Pasión* devotes its first 160 lines to the prophecies of David, Solomon, Isaiah, and Jeremiah. To the Passion, specifically its last events, are given only 67 lines: vv. 161–80, which present Christ as he says farewell to his Mother; vv. 181–210, which show Christ on the road to Calvary; vv. 211–30, which present the scene of Mary and John at the foot of the cross and include a brief appearance by Nicodemus accompanied by Joseph of Arimathea.[153] To these three compositions we must add the *Coplas de la Pasión* of Comendador Román, a work from between 1485 and 1490, which Pérez Gómez considers the earliest Spanish chant of the Passion, if we leave aside the *autos* and the *representaciones*,[154] and the *Passión trobada* of Diego de San Pedro, a narrative poem on the Passion, composed of 248 strophes in *quintillas dobles* (17 of these strophes are of a preliminary character), and printed in Salamanca in 1495.[155]

The lack of documents and dramatic texts on the Passion in Spain for the period that runs from the composition of the first sacred drama in the vernacular, the *Auto de los Reyes Magos* of the twelfth century, to the *Coplas de las Pasión* of Comendador Román, of the end of the fifteenth century, has led some scholars to chronological and literary deductions of dubious validity. Vivian, for instance, in her study of the *Pasión trobada* of 1495 tries to fit this narrative poem into the orbit of the dramatic tradition of the Middle Ages but in extremely general terms and without offering precise references to sources or possible relationships:

> Diego de San Pedro . . . se movía dentro de una amplia tradición europea y española que no le concedía mucho margen para la originalidad en la elección de detalles. Resulta imposible especular sobre las fuentes orales y escritas utilizadas por Diego de San Pedro. . . . Sin embargo, un estudio de los temas de la Pasión tal como se manifestan en *La passión trobada* . . . revela las tradiciones de la Pasión que circulaban por España en el período de la Edad Media, y demuestra que Diego de San Pedro se sirvió de ellas para lograr los efectos dramáticos de su poema.[156]

The declarations of Vivian are based on evidence provided *ex silentio;* this becomes obvious when she herself remarks a little before the passage cited that we lack "pruebas escritas acerca de representaciones medievales españolas de la Pasión." Even less sustainable are her assertions about the literary character of the *Pasión trobada.* Vivian considers this narrative poem a drama of the Passion, but it was clearly intended for private or public reading, as can be deduced from the paragraph in prose set before the poem itself. "Comienza la passión trobada por el dicho diego de san pedro en la qual van enxeridas algunas razones contemplatiuas puestas a fin de prouocar amás devotión alos que la leyeren y oyeren."[157]

This explains why Vivian, despite her effort to set *La Passión trobada* in the historical context of the medieval drama of the Passion, is forced to admit that this poem *could pass* as a theatrical work because of its *dramatic style:* "La originalidad de *La passión* no radica ni en su tradicional presentación de temas ni en sus formas literarias convencionales, sino en el estilo dramático del poema; de tal modo que podría pasar por obra religiosa teatral." And because of its adaptability to dramatic exigencies: *"La Passión trobada* resulta, pues muchísimo más adaptable a las exigencias del teatro religioso."[158]

But the *Passión trobada* is not a drama. The remarks of Pérez Gómez, therefore, are perfectly sound, when he considers this composition "el primer poema, genuinamente narrativo, de la Pasión de Cristo que se compuso en verso castellano" and when he places Diego de San Pedro, its author, in the vast catalog of Castilian poets who, from 1492 to 1694, dealt with the Passion of Christ "como tema poético."[159] In the light of these considerations, there remains the compelling necessity of solving the problem of the passage from the form of narrative poetry to that considered traditionally dramatic, the *Autos* on the Passion. In the wake of the hypothesis put forward by Vivian, who had attempted to reduce the temporal limits of this passage by trying to establish an analogy between the narrative poem *La Passión trobada* and the twelfth- and thirteenth-century French narrative poems of the Passion,[160] Iglesias goes beyond this hypothesis and suggests that the Castilian theme of the Passion, before it was a drama was narrative poetry: "El tema castellano de la Pasión, asunto literario, principia por ser antes que drama poesía narrativa."[161] Iglesias, eliminating the possibility of an embryonic stage in which the first Spanish dramas on the Passion had the opportunity of developing, sees the narrative poem as the immediate predecessor of the drama.[162]

After declaring that *La Passión trobada* is a dramatic narrative poem, Iglesias concludes that the Castilian theater of the Passion is the literary outlet of narrative poetry.[163] And in this way he explains the problem of the "ausencia," that is the absence of dramatic texts on the Passion at the inception of the dramatic tradition in medieval Spain. "Los autos y los poemas castellanos de la Pasión son la clave que nos franquea la comprensión de la ausencia."[164] The hypothesis of Vivian—scholars have never considered the French narrative poems on the Passion as dramatic works in the precise sense of that word—and the theory of Iglesias do not however solve the problem of why narrative poems on the Passion flowered late, at the end of the fifteenth century, in Castile; nor do they offer satisfying definitions of what constitutes, in their opinion, the dramatic essence of these narrative poems of the Passion.

Vivian, as we have seen, arrives at a hypothetical conclusion, that *La Passión trobada* "podía ser adaptada a la escena religiosa,"[165] while Iglesias justifies its dramatic character, along with that of the other narrative poems of the Passion, on the basis of weak and esoteric critical positions intended to show that, all things being taken into consideration, there is no clear difference between the *teatro* and the *poesía narrativa*. This is so because both the narrative poems and the dramas on the Passion "resemblan idénticos clichés, usan recursos estilísticos iguales y el instrumento expresivo de que se sirven es el mismo."[166] Since medieval languages did not have a word to express the concept of "theater,"—the technical language transmitted by medieval liturgical drama is *ordo*, *ludus*, and *officium*, and only later do theatrical terms such as *mistère*, *moralité*, and *sacre rappresentazioni* appear—the temptation is often irresistible, as Zumthor remarks, to read any text we have received as a clear communication of what at one time could have been the *representation*.[167]

Although the essay by Vivian and, in particular, the study of Iglesias constitute an important step toward a fundamental re-evaluation of medieval Castilian theater, narrative poems like *La Passión trobada* cannot be considered true dramas of the Passion,[168] nor can the hypothesis of the existence of a dramatic tradition in Spain between the twelfth and the fifteenth century be sustained, as Alborg and Ruiz Ramón do, by suggesting that the dramatic texts were probably transmitted orally.[169]

A new dramatic *Auto* of the Passion, composed by Alonso del Campo between 1496 and 1499, which reproduces in its text some verses taken from the *Passión trobada*,[170] was recently found among the holdings of the Archivo de Obra y Fábrica at the cathedral in Toledo. The discovery supports our opinion of the necessity of comparative research on the dramatic traditions of the various territorial regions of Spain; the archives of cathedrals and parish churches, which have not been completely explored, may yield important new sources.[171] The history of the drama of the Passion in Spain has not yet been written. Missing for Spain, as D'Amico lamented,[172] is a vast organic work comparable to those of Sepet, Magnin, D'Ancona, De Bartholomaeis, and, I would add, Young, Creizenach, and Wickham on the origins of French, Italian, German, and English theater in the Middle Ages.

It is also necessary to investigate the influence exercised by France in the development of the liturgical drama of Catalonia and in the flowering of the first evidence of sacred drama in the vernacular in Castile. The existence of a chronological hiatus of some three hundred years requires explanation. We must therefore reaffirm the necessity for a study and a review, on the vast horizon of medieval dramaturgy, of the principal points of its ramifications and connections, on both the national and the international level. Connections, relations, and influences have been shown and at times suggested in this brief investigation into the possibilities of original and fruitful research in the field of medieval Italian, French, German, English, and Spanish theater. These connections can be more profitably and more extensively observed as we begin to probe more deeply into the origins and the development of the *Planctus Mariae*.

CHAPTER IX

CONCLUSIONS

OUR systematic explorations of the *Planctus Mariae* are intended to offer a larger framework, at once theological and liturgical, for the *Planctus* and to determine its precise location in the area of medieval dramaturgy; they now impel us to formulate some conclusions that we consider substantially valid. One of the basic conclusions which emerges from our inquiries is that the *Planctus Mariae* does not constitute the original nucleus of the drama of the Passion.[1] It is a lyrical and emotive composition meant to intensify, at the very moment of the Son's Passion, the sorrowful torment and awful agony of his Mother. Passing beyond the limits of the sacred and ecstatic nature of the liturgical language, the *Planctus* makes it possible to explore, with a freer capacity for understanding and a richness of imagination, some of the deepest stirrings of the Mother's heart. It opens, within the gamut of the emotions, far-reaching vistas and a most deeply felt inner suffering. Upon the historical and literary background represented by the cultural tradition of medieval dramaturgy, a great variety of *Planctus* are projected. There is the poetically intimate, private and short grief of the *Planctus*—"si greu est a paerlaer"—of the *Augsburger Passionslied* of the tenth century. There is the touching and expressive suffering of the Mother, articulated in authentic and traditional *Planctus Mariae:* for example, the *Planctus ante nescia;* the *Planctus* of the Passion of Montecassino and the French *Planctus* preserved in the Laurentiana, both of the twelfth century; the *Planctus* of *Ager*, the *Duelo* of Berceo, and the Abruzzi *Lamentatio*, all of the thirteenth century; and the *Planctus* of Cividale, the *Planctus* of the Biblioteca Civica of Bergamo, and the *Planctus* of the *Ordinarium ecclesiae Patavinae* of the fourteenth century. In them all, the *Planctus Mariae*, as a lyrical form, is always characterized by an essential and constant aesthetic orientation and by a precise spiritual objective: the articulation of the Mother's grief and affection, motivated only in part by the need to illustrate the physical and spiritual travail of the God-Man.[2]

Uniquely illuminating and useful in the critical evaluation of the development of the *Planctus Mariae* is the profound propulsion given to its evolution by the patristic and medieval tradition in its exegesis of the metaphorical image in the prophecy of the aged Simeon, "et tuam ipsius animam pertransibit gladius." This image, in its symbolic and static character, almost abstract and dogmatic, still communicated both implicitly and explicitly the unplumbable depths of Mary's grief at the foot of the cross; it thus revealed itself to be a miraculous instrument in the exaltation and the deepening of the theme of compassion. Furthermore, from the first mention of the compassion of the Virgin, in *Homilia XVII* of Origen, to its liturgical expression in the *Officium de compassione Beatae Mariae Virginis* of Bonaventure, among other places,[3] the image will be elaborated with mounting frequency during the Middle Ages: it will occur in complex dramatic arrangements, in the liturgy, in monastic spirituality, in the drama, and in iconography.[4]

It is to the rich tradition of Greek theology, as we have had the opportunity to state, that the credit belongs for having supplied, both historically and spiritually, the thematic line for sounding the profound human and spiritual travail implicit in the prophecy of the aged Simeon. Joseph the Hymnographer (c. 816–886), born in Sicily, offers an outstanding instance of this emphatic evocation, in the Greek liturgical tradition, of the image of the Virgin, *gladio vulnerata*, in his *Mariale*, a collection of six hundred sacred hymns, "suavissimas melodias ab eo scriptas in Virginem ac Dei Matrem."[5] A poetic and melodic underscoring of the image of the *gladius Passionis* is found in the canon of Feria IV, at matins: "*Gladio vulnerata es*, o castissima, in passione Filii tui, ut illum vidisti lancea perfossum, atque removentem gladium illum qui fidelibus divinum ingressum in paradisum prohibebat."[6]

Of particular significance for our purposes is the discovery that the evocation of the image of the *gladius Passionis*, which pierces the maternal heart, is immediately illuminated by the consideration of her expressions of grief and anguish, which give meaning and a psychological character to the image: "Injustam aspiciens mortem Genitrix tua, o Christe, cum dolore ad te clamabat: O Fili, judex juste, quomodo injuste judicaris, cum ipse velis justo judicio absolvere eos qui ob pristinam transgressionem condemnati fuerant et in corruptionem ceciderunt?"[7]

The image of the *gladius Passionis*, evoked in a canon of Feria VI, at matins—"Venerabilis prophetae sermo impletus est: *gladius enim cor tuum pertransivit*, o Domina, quando in ligno Filium tuum lancea vulneratum suspexisti"[8]—is privileged with incisive realism in its direct repercussion in the heart of the Mother, in whom there burst forth emotional expressions of authentic grief: "Incarnatus est ex castis sanguinibus tuis Altissimus, o purissima; quem cum intuereris in ligno injuste exaltatum, suspirabas cum lacrymis, et misericordiae ejus viscera magnificabas."[9]

At times, between the image of the *gladius Passionis* and the expression of maternal grief there is established a compositional proportion, an essential harmony, which proceeds from the evocation of the stylized vision of the *gladius* toward a more empirical image of inwardness in order to objectify concretely the drama etched in the Mother's heart: "Clavis te populus iniquus confixit: et nunc *doloris gladius* dilacerat cor meum, o Creator meus. Ita cum lacrymis Virgo clamabat."[10]

This merging of the image and anguish is realized with balance and expressed with harmony in a melody of a canon of Feria VI, at matins, by means of the intimate relationship established between the *gladius Passionis* and the agony of the Virgin: "Pertransivit *gladius cor tuum*, quemadmodum praedixerat Simeon, o Domina; cum Christum crucifixum vidisti solum lancea perfodi; *quamobrem* dolores sustinens in gemitus erumpebas."[11]

And it is from the spontaneous conceptual convergence of the image of the *gladius Passionis* and the *compassio materna*, introduced for the first time, as we have seen, by Peter Damian and by the vein represented by the *preces compassionis*, that there will spring the fruitful and luminous current of lyrical and mystical emotionalism of the eleventh and twelfth century. This in turn will lead to the creation and composition of the *Planctus Mariae* and to their eventual incorporation in the dramas of the Passion.

The *Planctus Mariae*, the lyrical composition whose creative freedom offered the opportunity of plumbing, with wealth of invention, the recesses of the Mother's heart and of outlining all of the ineffable aspects of her suffering, will be elaborated in an extraordinary number of stylistic shadings, in both Latin and the vernacular, between the twelfth and the fifteenth century. But within this vast production, neither the composers of the *Planctus Mariae* nor the authors of the dramas of the Passion will hesitate to adopt earlier *Planctus* of exalted artistic worth or of original thematic richness and to incorporate them partially or wholly in their compositions, to imitate them, and at times to translate them.

An instance of this tendency is provided by the fourteenth-century *Planctus* of Cividale, some nine stanzas of which are also found in the *Planctus* "Flete, fideles animae" of the thirteenth century, and by the vernacular *Planctus* of the *Passion provençale* of the middle of the fourteenth century, whose opening verses,

> Aujhat, baros que passat per la via,
> S'en hes dolor tan gran com es la mia,
> Del mieu car filh, mon conort e ma vida,[12]

constitute a translation of the first verses of the Latin *Planctus* "Qui per viam pergitis," composed quite probably in the first years of that century:

> Qui per viam pergitis,
> hic mecum sedete,
> Si est dolor similis
> ut meus, videte;
> Meum dulcem filium
> pariter lugete.[13]

No less interesting for giving an idea of this phenomenon in the tradition of the *Planctus* in the vernacular are the clear relations between the *Planctus* of Ager, of the thirteenth century, and the *Planctus* of the above-mentioned *Passion provençale*, which is nothing but an incomplete reproduction of that of Ager.

The adoption of the themes of earlier *Planctus* that are distinctive for the richness of their content, their stylistic excellence, and the complexity of their emotions or their lyrical elaboration, is reflected in notable measure in the medieval production of *Planctus Mariae*. A clear instance of this type of imitation and relationship is offered by the thematic and stylistic parallels that can be established between the *Contrasto fra la croce e la Vergine*, a *lauda* in dialogue form in *decima rima*, of the first years of the fourteenth century,[14] and a *Pianto della Vergine*, also in *decima rima*, composed probably a few years later.[15] The obvious affinities between the *Contrasto* and the *Pianto della Vergine* extend not only to content but to the selection and disposition of expressive material.[16] Chiarini is of the opinion that, beyond the considerations of the possible use of common models, the direct relationship of imitation between the two texts seems to indicate that the imitator was the author of the *Pianto*. Our hypothesis is that the antecedents of the *Contrasto* are to be found, within the general frame of our subject, in the literary tradition of those *Planctus Mariae* which had explored, with a rigorous psychological analysis, the theme of the debate between the Virgin and the cross. A *Planctus Mariae* of the twelfth century, which we have already discussed, offers a singular expression of this theme.[17] Although true textual comparisons between the *Contrasto* and this *Planctus* cannot be established, the poetic context of the two compositions offers us the possibility of perceiving particular instances of a similar thematic repertory, which we should certainly attribute to the existence of a *Planctus* on the subject and not to the accidental correspondence of similar poetic devices. An example of such thematic comparisons is found in the first stanza of the *Planctus:*

> Ante crucem virgo stabat,
> Christi poenas cogitabat,
> totam se dilaniabat,
> vultum lavat lacrimis,

and by the first verses of the first stanza of the *Contrasto:*

> Ben vorrea plangere quando mi rimembro
> del pianto che facea Virgo Maria,
> stando fracasato omni membro
> a pie de la croce et forte languia.[18]

An identical thematic structure occurs in these verses of the eighth stanza of the *Contrasto,*

A questo offitio non te chiama el Padre,
ma'l tuo filiolo che per segno se pone.
La parte che t'e chesta tu l'ai data
em mano d'Eva che t'avea aspetata.
De Lui Adamo attende l'andata,
che redmisca sua ofensione[19]

and stanzas XX and XXI of the *Planctus*,

XX
Nichil convenientius
quam Christus Adae filius
patri succurrat penitus,
  ut secum ad coelum redeat:

XXI
Virgo tu Evae filia
morte damnata libera
solve serpentis vincula,
  mundus te laudet et serviat.

Poetic emulation, the use of earlier texts, and their integration in similar forms of contemporary literature, constitute a phenomenon extremely well known in the cultural tradition of the Middle Ages. But the integral reproduction of earlier or contemporary *Planctus Mariae* and their grafting onto or their irruption into dramas of the Passion represents a phenomenon that must be considered in the realm of its dramatic and emotional components and in its linguistic context: the problem of farcitura.

The insertion of the *Planctus Mariae* in liturgical drama was originally determined by the fact that the sorrowful expressions of the Virgin's compassion contained in them offered the opportunity to extend and increase the emotive and expressive level of the dramas in which the *Planctus* were inserted. This grafting constituted a decisive step toward a more intimate humanizing of these dramas at the moment of the Passion and the death of Christ.[20] The insertion, in fact, of the *Planctus ante nescia* and the plaint "Flete, fideles animae" in the narrative texture of the *Ludus de Passione* at the moment of the Crucifixion and death of Christ has no influence upon the development of the action, nor does it hamper it or interfere with it. These *Planctus* express a static condition, a psychological state which, without producing any consequence from which the dramatic action could develop, constitutes one of the principal components of the scene of the Crucifixion.[21]

The anonymous author of the Passion of Montecassino had aimed at this emotive and expressive intensification of the scene of the Crucifixion and the death of Christ a hundred years earlier, when he inserted at the culminating moment of the Son's death, the intensely pathetic image of his Mother. The Virgin, thoroughly penetrated by the bloody sufferings of her Son, offers, in anguished expressions of humanity, a deeply lyrical transfiguration of her Son's sorrow as reflected in her own soul. This profound illustration of the intense maternal pathos crystalized, in the Passion of Montecassino, in a vernacular *Planctus* of three lines, cannot be uprooted from its linguistic context and from the importance it assumes "as a document of the earliest Italian poetry, especially since it was still indissolubly linked to music and to drama."[22] And it is a liturgical drama in which the vernacular enters timidly, in Italy, for the first time.[23]

The transplanting of this vernacular *Planctus*, in the twelfth century, into the Passion of Montecassino—a transplanting that confirms in Italy the beginning of "an evolution of the Latin drama to a drama entirely in the vernacular, through the phase of the 'farcitura'"[24]—has to be placed and explored in the wider perspective of the flowering of the first documents of the tradition of literary hybridism and of poetic bilingualism in the Middle Ages. This is particularly true of the first dramatic compositions, especially in France, in a process documented in that nation from the beginning of the twelfth century and illustrated by works like the *Sponsus* and the *Jeu* or *Mystère d'Adam*.[25]

This process of *farcitura* or of poetic bilingualism, which in France as in Italy seems to have been used especially in liturgical and dramatic texts, does not imply that a man of letters of the eleventh or twelfth century might express himself indifferently in the vernacular or in Latin, but rather it implies the possibility of "l'usage libre et créateur de chacun de ces idiomes par rapport à l'objet et dans la fonction qui lui convient."[26]

This practice of poetic functionalism, which Roncaglia defines as an "instrument of realistic expression,"[27] is intended to produce a definite stylistic effect, that of surprise or of unique evocation. This method of producing a particular psychological or cathartic effect in a reader or the public, by way of the extraordinary characterization of a person, is a stylistic technique in keeping with the aesthetics of the drama where the author, to give emphasis to a person, has him pronounce a discourse in a language different from the one of the context. When this happens, "il en résulte un changement de ton, comparable . . . à un changement de style: du noble au mediocre, or de l'humble au superbe."[28]

This is precisely what happens in the Passion of Montecassino: the anonymous author inserts, at the high points of the drama of the Son, a *Planctus Mariae* in the vernacular not only to "confer an official investiture upon a genre particularly dear to the devotion of the people,"[29] but to establish at the most significant point of the *Passio* an indissoluble link between Son and Mother, between divine and human. The fusion between the *sermo gravis* or *sublimis* of the liturgical language and the *sermo remissus* or *humilis* of the vernacular is brilliantly illustrated by Auerbach in his analysis of the *Mystère d'Adam* and the *Pianto della Madonna* of Jacopone da Todi, which represents, in its stylistic expression, a re-elaboration of the traditional fusion between the two styles accentuated by Saint Augustine and which, in its own turn, represents a transposition at the artistic level of the fusion between *sublimitas* and *humilitas* realized theologically in the Incarnation and Passion of Christ. The same thing happens in the Passion of Montecassino, where the lament in the vernacular, expressed at the most pathetic moment of the divine drama, allows the Virgin, "totally involved in the Passion of Christ, even though unable to interfere in it," to share with the faithful her exemplary grief and to offer herself to them as a real and concrete model.[30]

It is naturally impossible for the literary critic to measure and to perceive, at the distance of several centuries, the fullness of the emotive and cathartic effect of this vernacular *Planctus* inserted in a liturgical drama which, as with all ritual and cultural ceremonies, remains for us "quelque chose de totalement insaisissable."[31] But beyond the obvious dimensions of the emotive intensification of the scene of the Crucifixion and of the death of Christ, this *Planctus Mariae*, the earliest Italian lament in the vernacular, constitutes a manifestation of that religious need which, in France as well as Italy, must be counted among the fundamental drives toward the creation of a literature in the vernacular.[32] This religious need—joined with the other need (more artistically profound and substantial) represented by the desire of contemporary writers, especially at the beginning of the thirteenth century, to achieve spontaneity of inspiration and immediacy of expression[33]—led the composer of the Passion of Montecassino to introduce into the liturgical complex of his drama the lament of the Virgin in the vernacular.

In the realm of medieval European dramaturgy between the twelfth and the end of the fourteenth century, the *Planctus Mariae*, both in its Latin elaborations and in its vernacular manifestations, constitutes a lyrical, emotive form of singular significance, not only as a literary genre, but especially as an essential and fruitful testimonial of the Mariological thought of the Middle Ages. The motif of the *Planctus Mariae* was born originally, like that of the *Pietà*,[34] in the bosom of the Greek spiritual tradition, and transfigured when it came in contact with the Western Latin spirituality of the eleventh and twelfth centuries. Together with the pictorial representation of the image of the *Pietà*, it constitutes one of the most splendid realizations and presentations of maternal pathos expressed by the creativity of medieval man. The theme of the sorrow and the compassion of the Virgin, so wondrously and lyrically illustrated by the vast repertory of *Planctus* transmitted to us, is indicative of the important role of the *Planctus* in providing to successive centuries one of the most original and fundamental themes of the spirituality of the eleventh and twelfth centuries but also of its trenchant efficacy in setting forth and in making more plausible, with rich expressiveness and profound humanity, the intensity of grief of the Mother's heart, utterly and entirely possessed by the absoluteness and the fullness of the bloody human drama of God incarnate.

NOTES

Chapter I · The Critical Context

1 · Wechssler, *Die romanischen Marienklagen*, p. 98: "In Italien ist das wulgarsprächliche Drama uberhaupt aus der Dichtungen der Laudesen und zwar speciell aus den Marienklagen erwachsen. Und in den Ländern, welche ander als Italien schon zuvor ein wulgarsprächliches geistliches Drama entwickelt haben, beruhen wenigsten die Passionsspiele auf unsere Literaturgattung. Im früheren Mittelalter gab es keine anderen Dramatisierung der Leidengeschichte als die Marienklagen."

2 · Craig, *English Religious Drama*, p. 46; Creizenach, *Geschichte des Neuren Dramas*, 1:248; de Julleville, *Les Mystères*, 2:57.

3 · Taylor, "The English Planctus Mariae," p. 633.

4 · Young, *The Drama of the Medieval Church*, 1:538.

5 · Chambers, *The Medieval Stage*, 2:39: "The *planctus* must be regarded as the starting-point of a drama of the Passion, which presently established itself beside the drama of the Resurrection." In our own days the same opinion has been maintained by W. L. Smoldon in his "Liturgical Drama," p. 193, when he asserts that "the core of the Passion Play would seem to be the various *planctus*—extra-liturgical composition represented as being sung by one or another of the mourners at the foot of the Cross."

6 · Sepet, *Origines catholiques du théâtre moderne*, p. 29.

7 · Young, *The Drama of the Medieval Church*, 1:495–98.

8 · Lipphardt, "Marienklagen und Liturgie," pp. 201–4. See, too, his "Studien zu den Marienklagen und Germanische Totenklagen," pp. 394–96.

9 · Kienast, "Die deutschsprachige Lyrik des Mittelalters," p. 890.

10 · Giovanni Cremaschi, "Planctus Mariae," p. 394. See also Vecchi, "Innodia e dramma sacro."

11 · Young, *The Drama of the Medieval Church*, pp. 507–12; de Bartolomaeis, *Origini della poesia drammatica italiana*, pp. 482–85.

12 · Young, *The Drama of the Medieval Church*, pp. 498–99. Giovanni Grano, in

"Planctus Mariae," pp. 48–51, notes the textual identity of some stanzas from the *Planctus* of Cividale and from the *Planctus* "Flete fideles animae," but he refers to the latter *Planctus* with the title of *Lamentum Beate Marie Virginis.*

13 · Cremaschi, "Planctus Mariae," pp. 393–468.

14 · For the text of the *Planctus* "Qui per viam pergitis," consult Young, *The Drama of the Medieval Church,* 1:500–502.

15 · Billanovich, "Uffizi drammatici della chiesa padovana," esp. pp. 84–86.

16 · See Young, *The Drama of the Medieval Church,* 1:700.

17 · Billanovich, "Uffizi drammatici della chiesa padovana," p. 95.

18 · Creizenach, *Geschichte des Neuren Dramas,* 1:248: "Es wäre möglich, dass die dialogischen Erweiterungen der Sequenz im karfreitagsgottesdienste schon zu einer Zeit verwendet wurden, wo es keine eigentlichen Passionsspiele gab und dass dann die Dichter der Passionsspiele . . . sie für ihre Zwecke benutzen. Aber es könnte auch amgekehrt vorgekommen sein, dass die Dichter der Karfreitagsspiele zus umfangreiche Passionstexten schöpften." See also Meier, *Die Gestalt Marias,* pp. 178–79.

19 · De Vito, *L'origine del dramma liturgico,* p. 164.

20 · Craig, *English Religious Drama,* p. 47; Grace Frank, too, in her *Medieval French Drama,* p. 29, holds that though they were "potentially dramatic," the *Planctus* "remained lyrical and static."

21 · Craig, "The Origin of the Passion Play."

22 · Inguanez, "Un dramma della Passione del secolo XII," pp. 41–42.

23 · Young, *The Drama of the Medieval Church,* 1:538.

24 · Grano, "Planctus Mariae," p. 19. In view of the numerous essays published on the *Planctus* in Italy, France, Germany, and the English-speaking world, it seems strange that, without knowing them, Walter Tortoreto can observe that "their origin is still mysterious." See his *Genesi di una sacra rappresentazione abruzzese,* p. 34.

25 · Mâle, *L'Art religieux du XIIIᵉ siècle en France,* p. 223.

26 · Preface to the Mass of Easter.

27 · Huglo, "L'Intensité dramatique," pp. 103–4; Grano, "Planctus Mariae," pp. 18–20. On the dramatic intensity of the liturgy of Holy Week see my essay "Italian Theater of the Middle Ages," pp. 279–86.

28 · *PL* 159:271–86.

29 · *PL* 182:1133–42.

30 · Saint Bonaventure, *Meditationes vitae Christi,* in *Opera omnia,* 12:509–630.

31 · For the text of the *Stabat Mater,* see Raby, *Christian Latin Poetry,* p. 440.

32 · Ubertinus de Casali, *Arbor vitae crucifixae.* On the fortune of the *Arbor*

vitae, composed in 1305, see Callaey, "L'Influence et la diffusion de l'*Arbor vitae* d'Ubertin de Casale."

33 · Bodenstedt, *The Vita Christi of Ludolphus the Carthusian.*

34 · Saint Bernardine of Siena. *Opera omnia*, 5:68–170.

35 · *PL* 182:1135.

36 · *PL* 184:742–67, 770–72; 954–66.

37 · *PL* 184:1319–24.

38 · *PL* 183, Saint Bernard, *Sermones in Cantica, Sermo XLIII*, 4, col. 995. Saint Bernard seems to be echoing the words of Saint Paul: "Non enim iudicavi me scire aliquid inter vos, nisi Iesum Christum, et hunc crucifixum" (1 Cor. 2:3). De Ghellinck, *L'Essor de la littérature latine au XIIᵉ siècle*, 1:183–84.

39 · Pourrat, *La Spiritualité chrétienne*, 2:481; Vernet, *La Spiritualité médiévale*, p. 18; Salmon, *L'Office divin*, p. 243, writes that "à partir surtout de la seconde moitié du siècle [XIIᵉ], la spiritualité devient plus individualiste, plus sensible et plus 'dévote,' plus portée à la méditation du Christ souffrant et crucifié qu'à celle de sa résurrection ou de sa Passion."

40 · Saint Bonaventure, *Opera omnia*, 8:120.

41 · Raby, *Christian Latin Poetry*, p. 418; the motto seems to be derived from the words of Saint Paul (Gal. 6:14), "Mihi autem absit gloriari, nisi in cruce Domini Jesu Christi."

42 · A learned and ample analysis of the Passion piety of Saint Francis is found in the study of von Rieden, "Das Leiden Christi im Leben des Hl. Franziskus von Assisi."

43 · Raby, *Christian Latin Poetry*, p. 423; Fortini, *La lauda in Assisi e le origini del teatro italiano*, p. 382; de Zedelgem, "Aperçu historique sur la dévotion au chemin de la Croix."

44 · Getto, *Letteratura religiosa dal Due al Novecento*, p. 18; Perry, *La Passion des jongleurs*, pp. 26–27.

45 · Jeffrey, *The Early English Lyric and Franciscan Spirituality*, pp. 53–55.

46 · Gilson, "Saint Bonaventure et l'iconographie de la Passion," p. 424.

47 · Marrow, *Passion Iconography in Northern European Art of the Late Middle Ages and Early Renaissance*, p. 25.

48 · Mincione, "Le sequenze abruzzesi," pp. 51–55.

49 · Auerbach, *Mimesis*, p. 148: "On the other hand, Franciscan power of expression led to a still more direct and intense representation of human events; it asserts itself in popular religious poetry, which, during the thirteenth century, under the influence of the Franciscan and other popular ecstatic movements, treated the Passion scene especially (Mary at the cross) as a livingly dramatic and human

episode." On the diffusion of Franciscan spirituality in Europe, see Fleming, *An Introduction to the Franciscan Literature of the Middle Ages*.

50 · Menestò, "Le laude drammatiche di Iacopone da Todi," pp. 109–10.

51 · Petrocchi, "La letteratura religiosa," p. 557.

52 · Menestò, "Le laude drammatiche di Iacopone da Todi," p. 109.

53 · Jeffrey, "Franciscan Spirituality and the Rise of Early English Drama," pp. 90–100; Pasch, "Trinitarian Symbolism and Medieval English Drama," pp. 75–84; Anderson, *Drama and Imagery in English Medieval Churches*, p. 53. On the influence of the Franciscans on English medieval art, see the several essays in Little, *Franciscan History and Legend in English Medieval Art*.

54 · Goad, *Greyfriars*, pp. 168ff.; Wickham, *Early English Stages 1300–1660*, 1:124–28.

55 · On the development of the medieval dramatic tradition in the vernacular, with reference to the *Jeu d'Adam*, instructive pages have been written by, among others, Maurice Accarie (*Le Théâtre sacré de la fin du Moyen Age*, pp. 41–49), by Jean-Charles Payen ("Idéologie et théâtralité dans l'Ordo Representationis Adae"), and by Rosanna Brusegan (in her excellent study "Verità e finzione nel *Jeu d'Adam*"). On the international level, the most profound studies of the medieval French theater in the vernacular are today being carried out by Jean-Charles Payen, Michel Rousse, Maurice Accarie, Jean-Claude Aubailly, G. A. Runnalls, A. E. Knight, W. Noomen, and Lynette Muir.

56 · Saint Bonaventure, in his *Legenda maior*, recalls the representation of the scene of the Nativity, after Saint Francis had received permission from Honorius III to represent it: "Contigit autem anno tertio ante obitum suum, ut memoriam nativitatis pueri Iesu ad devotionem excitandam apud castrum Graecii disponeret agere, cum quanta maiori solemnitate valeret. Ne vero hoc novitati posset ascribi, a Summo Pontifice petita et obtenta licentia, fecit praeparari praesepium, apportari foenum, bovem et asinum ad locum adduci. Advocantur Fratres, adveniunt populi, personat silva voces, et venerabilis illa nox luminibus copiosis et claris laudibusque sonoris et consonis et splendens efficitur et solennis. Stabat vir Dei coram proesepio pietate repletus." *Seraphici Doctoris S. Bonaventurae Legendae Duae de Vita S. Francisci Seraphici*, p. 111. Carmelo Musumarra, nevertheless, asserts in *La sacra rappresentazione della Natività nella tradizione italiana*, p. 7, that the famous creche of Greccio created by Saint Francis cannot be considered a true and proper work of the theater, inasmuch as it merely is an attempt to transform and adapt the liturgy to the comprehension of a public larger than the usual one, which was well educated and prepared to understand the divine mysteries.

57 · Owst, "Sermon and Drama."

58 · Jeffrey, "Franciscan Spirituality and the Rise of the Early English Drama," pp. 18–25. The Franciscan sermon, which in its oratorical completeness included, at times, song, music, dialogue, recitation, and changes in voice, was a true *rappresentazione*. Harry Caplan, in a valuable volume, *Of Eloquence*, offers an analysis of the development of classical oratory and of its influence upon the *artes praedicandi* of the Middle Ages. Of notable interest from a chronological and comparative point of view is the volume of Jean Longère, *La Prédication médiévale*, which examines the essential characteristics of the sermon in Europe from the patristic age to the sixteenth century. In an excellent essay, "Michel Menot et la téchnique du sermon médiévale," Etienne Gilson presents a detailed examination of the structure of the medieval sermon in the light of the *ars concionandi* of Franciscan origin. On the nature of the medieval English sermon in relation to the monastic orders, see Pfander, *The Popular Sermon of the Medieval Friar in England*. On instruction in general in the orbit of the spirituality of the twelfth century, see Bynum, *Docere Verbo et Exemplo*. On the sermons of Dominicans and Franciscans in medieval England, we refer the reader to the study of Owst, *Preaching in Medieval England*.

59 · Jeffrey, "Franciscan Spirituality and the Rise of Early English Drama," pp. 25–28; de Bartholomaeis, *Origini della poesia drammatica italiana*, pp. 325–32. See on this subject Toschi, *L'antico dramma sacro italiano*, 1:xxvi–xxviii. See, too, Lupinetti, *Canto popolare abruzzese*, 3:25.

60 · Craddock, "Franciscan Influence on Early English Drama," pp. 386–87; Jeffrey, "Franciscan Spirituality and the Rise of Early English Drama," p. 37.

61 · Jeffrey, "Franciscan Spirituality and the Rise of Early English Drama," pp. 39–44. Agostino Lombardo, in his introduction to *Teatro inglese del Medioevo e del Rinascimento*, p. xxix, agrees with those critics who consider the homily, which had risen to singular importance in the religious life of England "with the rebirth of preaching due to the work of the Franciscans and Dominicans in the twelfth and thirteenth centuries," one of the constitutive elements of the morality play. Robert Potter, in his *English Morality Play*, specifies the contribution of the Franciscans to this dramatic form when he says that "the mixture of doctrine and realism in the morality play has its origins in this tradition, and the immediate sources of allegory in the morality play are almost invariably found in medieval sermon literature" (p. 20).

62 · Craddock, "Franciscan Influences on Early English Drama," pp. 399–405.

63 · Ibid., p. 417; Jeffrey, "Franciscan Spirituality and the Rise of Early English Drama," p. 46.

64 · Blume and Dreves, *Analecta hymnica Medii Aevi*, 50:571–74.

65 · Longpré, "La Chapelle de la Passion des Cordeliers de Troyes," p. 322.

66 · Blume and Dreves, *Analecta hymnica Medii Aevi*, 50:571–74.

Chapter II · Mary as Co-Redemptrix

1 · John 19:25–26.

2 · *PL* 16:1271.

3 · *PL* 16:333.

4 · *PL* 16:1431. See the passage in the *Expositio Evangelii secundum Lucam*, *PL* 15:1930–31.

5 · Roschini, "De modo quo B. Virgo animi dolorem sustinuit," p. 210.

6 · *De sacrificio Abrahae et B. Mariae*, *PL* 196:1047.

7 · *Elucidatio in Cantica Canticorum*, *PL* 210:58–59.

8 · *PL* 16:1271.

9 · Roschini, "Corredemptio in S. Scriptura," p. 291.

10 · Ibid., p. 299.

11 · Roschini, "Corredemptio apud Patres," p. 304.

12 · Carol, *De corredemptione Beatae Virginis Mariae disquisitio positiva*, p. 138.

13 · Ibid., p. 150.

14 · Ibid., p. 152.

15 · *Mariale*, no. 99 in *PG* 105:1258.

16 · On this theme see the excellent essay of J. Galot, "La Plus Ancienne Affirmation de la corédemption mariale."

17 · Wenger, *L'Assomption de la T.S. Vierge dans la tradition byzantine du VIᵉ au Xᵉ siècle*, p. 404.

18 · Galot, "La Plus Ancienne Affirmation de la corédemption mariale," esp. pp. 194, 208.

19 · Wenger, *L'Assomption de la T.S. Vierge dans la tradition byzantine du VIᵉ au Xᵉ siècle*," pp. 397, 407.

20 · Carol, *De corredemptione Beatae Virginis Mariae disquisitio positiva*, p. 156.

21 · Arnauld comments on the last seven words of Christ in the following chronological order, which reflects the textual tradition of the Holy Scripture:

Primum Verbum. *Deus meus, Deus meus, quare me dereliquisti?*
Secundum. *Amen dico tibi, hodie mecum eris in paradiso.*
Tertium. *Mater, ecce filius tuus, ad matrem; et ad discipulum, Ecce mater tua.*

Quartum. *Sitio.*

Quintum. *Pater, ignosce illis, quia nesciunt quid faciunt.*

Sextum. *Consummatum est.*

Septimum. *Pater, in manus tuas commendo spiritum meum.*

22 · *PL* 189:1694–95.

23 · *PL* 189:1727.

24 · Carol, *De corredemptione Beatae Virginis Mariae disquisitio positiva,* p. 164.

25 · Desmarais, *S. Albert le Grand,* p. 70.

26 · Luke 2:35–36.

27 · Desmarais, *S. Albert le Grand,* p. 71.

28 · Ibid.

29 · Ibid., p. 72.

30 · Ibid., p. 73.

31 · Ibid., p. 74.

32 · Korošak, "De cooperatione B. Virginis ad salutem mundi," p. 522.

33 · Simbula, *La maternità spirituale di Maria in alcuni autori francescanai dei secoli XIII–XV,* pp. 101–2.

34 · Martínez, "La cooperación de María a la obra salvífica de Cristo según el pensamiento de P. J. Olivi," p. 348.

35 · Ramon Lull, *Obras,* 10:182.

36 · Ramon Lull, *Obras Literarias,* pp. 1084–86. The pages containing the *Plant de la Verge* are 1070–92. Although this plaint is generally known by the title of *Plant de la Verge,* it seems that it was initially known by the name of its *Incipit:* "De la passio e lo desconort que ac nostra Dona de son fil." The present title seems more logical in view of the last stanza, in which Lull writes, "Finit es aquest Plant, qui es tam doloros / de la Verge reina."

37 · Ibid., p. 1086.

38 · J. S. Pons, in his essay "Raymond Lulle et le 'Plant de Notre Dame Saint Marie,'" speaking of the dramatic ceremony of the *Quem quaeritis* represented in the fourteenth century, says that it was quite probably preceded by a lyrical poem similar to the Plant of Lull: "Comme le drame religieux se développe surtout autour de la scène liturgique des trois Maries au sépulchre, il se peut qu'il ait été precédé d'une représentation assez semblable au poème de Lulle. *Le livre de Cérémonies de la cathédrale Saint Jean de Perpignan* mentionne, pour une date plus récente, il est vrai, l'obligation qu'avaient les prêtres de la communauté de *faire la représentation de Marie Majeure et de Saint Jean Evangéliste et des autres Maries et de faire chanter* le plant" (p. 10).

39 · Ugolini, *Testi volgari abruzzesi del Duecento*, pp. 3–4; Chiaverini, *"Ore plangamo de lu Siniore" nel Codice del Papa Celestino V*, p. 36. Ugolini, in his discussion of the constitutive elements of the text of *Lamentatio* and of the genre of the *Lament*, asserts that "il tema del *Pianto della Madonna* precede nel tempo il *Lamento* a più personaggi che ne è una amplificazione" (p. 26).

40 · Ibid., pp. 43 and 45.

Chapter III · The "Planctus Mariae" and the Eastern Tradition

1 · Lipphardt, "Studien zu den Marienklagen und germanische Totenklagen," p. 395.

2 · Luis, "Evolutio historica doctrinae de Compassione B. Mariae Virginis," p. 261.

3 · Ibid., p. 262.

4 · Luke 2:35.

5 · *In Lucam homilia XVII, PG* 13:1845.

6 · Ibid.

7 · Vannutelli, *Actorum Pilati textus synoptici*, pp. 3–4.

8 · Ibid., p. 93. The *spasm (tramorticio)* experienced by the Virgin in the excess of her grief was originally venerated in the crypt of the Abbey of Santa Maria Latina, located next to Golgotha. From the beginning of the thirteenth century the site of the legend was located in a small church called Santa Maria dello Spasmo, which is the crypt of the present-day church of the Armenian Catholics. On this subject see Cothenet, "Marie dans les Apocryphes," p. 111; Abel, "Sanctuaires marials en Palestine," p. 861; and Folgorait, *La Vergine Bella in S. Bernardino da Siena*, pp. 324–45.

9 · Vannutelli, *Actorum Pilati textus synoptici*, p. 94.

10 · Ibid., p. 95.

11 · Ibid.

12 · Ibid., p. 100.

13 · Wright, *A Short History of Syriac Literature*, p. 34.

14 · Saint Ephraem Syrus, *Opera omnia in sex tomos distributa*, 6:574–75.

15 · Ibid., p. 574.

16 · Ibid.

17 · Ibid.

18 · Ibid., p. 575.

19 · Ibid.

20 · Castellino, "Letterature cuneiformi e cristiane orientali," p. 393.

21 · Assemani, *Bibliotheca orientalis*, 1:290–99.

22 · Martin, "Lettres de Jacques de Saroug aux moines du Couvent de Mar Bassus, et à Paul d'Edesse."

23 · Peeters, "Jacques de Saroug appartient-il à la secte monophysite?"

24 · Vona, *Omelie mariologiche di S. Giacomo di Sarug*, pp. 28–35.

25 · Vona, *Omelie mariologiche di S. Giacomo di Sarug*, p. 37.

26 · Baumstark, "Zwei syrische Dichtungen auf das Entschlafen der aller-selingsten Jungfrau," p. 92.

27 · Dahane, "La Passion dans la liturgie syrienne orientale"; Khouri-Sarkis, "La Passion dans la liturgie syrienne occidentale."

28 · Khouri-Sarkis, "La Passion dans la liturgie syrienne occidentale," p. 203.

29 · Pitra, *Analecta sacra*, 1:101–7. A fine edition of the *Canticum de Virgine juxta Crucem* and of other hymns of Romanos is that prepared by de Matons, *Romanos le Mélode*.

30 · Pitra, *Analecta sacra*, 1:102.

31 · Ibid., pp. 102–3.

32 · Ibid., p. 105.

33 · "Der grösste und fruchtbarste Vertreter dieser neuen Gattung der griechisten Literatur." This is how Karl Krumbacher considers him in his "Die Literatur von Konstantin bis Heraklios," in *Die Griechische und Lateinische Literatur und Sprache*, p. 259. The discovery of the hymns of Romanos was made originally by F. J. Mone in his *Lateinische Hymnen des Mittelalters*.

34 · On this subject see Emereau, *St. Ephrem le Syrien*.

35 · Marjorie Carpenter, "Romanos and the Mystery Play of the East," esp. pp. 32–39. We owe to Cammelli, *Romano il Melode*, the idea of rearranging the *kontakia* of Romanos in accordance with the sequence of the ecclesiastical calendar. Cammelli writes, "But since the hymns of Romanos and, in general, of all the hymnographers, were written to celebrate the various feasts of the year, we believe it more opportune to make the kontakia follow the order of the ecclesiastical calendar" (p. 389).

36 · On this whole question and on the Byzantine theater, see my essay "The *Christos Paschon* and the Byzantine Theater," pp. 13–14. Basic for our knowledge of the Byzantine theater are the studies of Giorgio La Piana, *Le rappresentazioni sacre nella letteratura bizantina dalle origini al secolo IX* and "The Byzantine Theater"; Cottas, *Le Théâtre à Byzance;* Trifoglio, "Il Christus Patiens."

37 · Vogt, "Études sur le théâtre byzantin."

38 · Mahr, *The Cyprus Passion Play.*

39 · Mingana, "The Lament of the Virgin and the Martyrdom of Pilate." The

section of the essay that concerns the *Lament of the Virgin* occupies pp. 178–210, while the study of the *Martyrdom of Pilate* is on pp. 241–82.

40 · Tischendorf, *Evangelia apocrypha*, declares: "Evangelium, quippe quod Nicodemi diceretur, sat recenti memoria i.e. sexto fere saeculo prodisse opinabantur" (p. lvii).

41 · Mingana, "The Lament of the Virgin and the Martyrdom of Pilate," p. 182.

42 · Ibid., p. 183.

43 · Ibid., pp. 187–88.

44 · Ibid., p. 190.

45 · John 19:25–26.

46 · Oratio VIII, *In SS. Mariam Assistentem Cruci*, PG 100:1462.

47 · Ibid.

48 · Oratio VIII, *In SS. Deiparae ingressum in templum*, PG 100, esp. 1447–50.

49 · Oratio VIII, *In SS. Mariam assistentem Cruci*, PG 100:1467.

50 · Ibid., 1471–74.

51 · *PG* 114:209–18.

52 · Ibid., 210.

53 · Ibid., 211.

54 · Ibid.

55 · Ibid., 211–14.

56 · Ibid., 215.

57 · Ibid., 218.

Chapter IV · Marian Exegesis: Mediation and Maternity

1 · Simbula, *La maternità spirituale di Maria*, p. 18.

2 · *Dialogus cum Tryphone Judaeo*, PG 6: 709–12.

3 · *Contra haereses*, 3.22, PG 7:958–60.

4 · Ibid., col. 959.

5 · *De carne Christi*, 7, PL 2:782.

6 · *Adversus haereses*, 3.2.78, PG 42:727–30.

7 · *Epistola LXIII*, 33, PL 16:1246–50.

8 · *Homilia in coemeterii appellationem et in crucem Domini et Dei et Salvatoris nostri Jesu Christi*, PG 49:396.

9 · *PG* 55:193.

10 · *PG* 50:687.

11 · *Epistola XXII, PL* 22:408.

12 · *De symbolo ad catechumenos, PL* 40:655–56.

13 · Vagaggini, *Maria nelle opere di Origene*, p. 119. For a historical and doctrinal study of the concept of the spiritual or divine motherhood of Mary see Philippe, "Le Mystère de la maternité divine de Marie"; Ragazzini, *La divina maternità di Maria nel suo concetto teologico integrale;* and Spedalieri, *Maternità spirituale della Vergine.*

14 · *PG* 82:888–909. The passage in which the term *Theotókos* occurs is found in col. 908: "Post haec agnoscimus resurrectionem mortuorum, cuius primitiae fuit Dominus noster Jesus Christus, qui corpus revera et non inani specie sumpsit ex Deipara Maria." *Deipara* is the Latin translation of *Theotókos.* Ambrose was the first to use the term *Theotókos* in the Western church, in his *De virginibus,* bk. 2, *PL* 16:222: "Quamvis *mater Domini,* discere tamen praecepta Domini desiderabat."

15 · Coathalem, *Le Parallélisme entre la Sainte Vierge et l'Eglise,* p. 53; Viller, *La Spiritualité des premiers siècles chrétiens,* p. 176.

16 · Spedalieri, *Maternità spirituale della Vergine,* pp. 251–73.

17 · Galot, "L'Intercession de Marie," p. 205. In his *Sermo in Dormitionem B. Mariae, PG* 98:366, Germanos refers to the mediation of Mary in these words: "Nam et nos in te abunde vitae aeternae altum pignus accepimus, atque ad Deum mediatricem humanis emigrantem nanciscimur." On the mediation of Mary read the essays of Bur, "La Médiation de Marie"; and of Druwé, "La Médiation universelle de Marie."

18 · Gripkey, *The Blessed Virgin Mary as Mediatrix,* p. 11.

19 · Wenger, *L'Assomption de la T.S. Vierge,* p. 404; see also Galot, "L'Intercession de Marie," pp. 522–26.

20 · Galot, "L'Intercession de Marie," p. 256.

21 · *Sermo CCVIII, PL* 39:2134.

22 · Ibid., col. 2107.

23 · Barré, *Prières anciennes de l'Occident à la Mère du Sauveur,* p. 125.

24 · Leclercq, "Dévotion et théologie mariales dans le monachisme bénédictin," p. 567.

25 · Anselm writes in his *Oratio ad Sanctam Mariam pro impetrando eius et Christi amore:* "Deus igitur est pater rerum creaturarum, et Maria mater rerum recreatarum. Deus est pater constitutionis omnium, et Maria mater restitutionis omnium" (Barré, *Prières anciennes de l'Occident à la Mère du Sauveur,* p. 304).

26 · Druwé, "La Médiation universelle de Marie," p. 503.

27 · Graef, *Mary: A History of Doctrine and Devotion,* 2:215.

28 · *Dominica infra octavam Assumptionis B.V. Mariae sermo, PL* 183:429–30.
29 · *Sermo in nativitate B.V. Mariae, PL* 183:439–40.
30 · Hogan, *Christ's Redemptive Sacrifice,* p. 101.
31 · Bur, *La Médiation de Marie,* pp. 484–85.
32 · *Libellus de laudibus B. Mariae Virginis, PL* 189:1726–27.

Chapter V · The Marian Cult and Devotion

1 · Ahsmann, *Le Culte de la sainte Vierge,* pp. 10–30.
2 · Vanderbrouke, Leclercq, and Bouyer, *La Spiritualité du Moyen Age,* p. 307.
3 · Druwé, "La Médiation universelle de Marie," p. 501.
4 · Davy, "La Présence de la Vierge au XIIᵉ siècle," p. 106. See also Delius, *Geschichte der Marienverehrung,* pp. 159–66. The illustrious art historian Emile Mâle expresses his opinion on this subject in this way: "C'est au XIIᵉ siècle que le culte de la Vierge, jusque-là si grave, commence à se nuancer de tendresse . . . au même moment, des ordres nouveaux apparaissent, qui commencent à parler de la Vierge avec un accent plus passionné, et l'on voit grandir des sentiments qui vont s'épanouir, avec une grâce poétique, au XIIIᵉ siècle" *L'Art religieux du XIIᵉ siècle en France,* p. 427. As we have already indicated, these sentiments of tenderness in describing the Virgin appear from the second half of the eleventh century, even if, in general, there exist earlier testimonials to the cult of the Virgin. Recently, for example, an American scholar, H. J. Turrin, in an interesting study, has claimed for the tenth century the honor of having been the century par excellence of the flowering of the fervent veneration of the Virgin Mary in the West. As evidence for this affirmation, Turrin cites the lyrical sequence of the tenth century, "Aureo flore," from the repertory of the Abbey of Saint-Martial of Limoges. According to him, it represents the highest point of a deeply rooted lyrical tradition in honor of the Virgin, the origins of which are found in the ninth century ("'Aureo flore' and the Question of Dating the Tradition of Marian Veneration in the Medieval West"). The ideas of Turrin are shared by Henri Barré, who already in 1960, in his "Prières mariales du Xᵉ siècle," p. 206, had maintained the existence of an uninterrupted and ever-expanding tradition of the Marian cult from the ninth to the tenth century. But the devotion to the Virgin in these centuries cannot in fact be compared with the intensity of the Marian cult of the eleventh and twelfth centuries, nor do we find in those centuries the concept of the compassion of the Virgin generally and sufficiently expressed. On the cult of the Virgin in the West from the

fifth to the twelfth century see Capelle, "La Liturgie mariale en Occident"; and Cecchin, "La concezione della Vergine."

5 · In the essay of Wilmart, "Cinq textes de prières composés par Anselme de Lucques," pp. 60–64, there appears an *Oratio ad Sanctam Mariam* in which Anselm, the bishop of Lucca, refers to the sorrows suffered by the Virgin when she saw the wounds of her Son: "Dignare, misericordissima domina, salutiferas manus tuas meis admouere doloribus et tue placationis medelam adhibere vulneribus, quia in te sola mihi fiducia est post salutare dei, Iesum christum, filium tuum. Tu, ut piissima mater, alliga uulnera, tu infunde uinum et oleum, tu appone malagma, tuis fomitibus dolorem immensum mitiga, et, si necesse est, cauterio apere ulcera. Cum securitate et fiducia leta sustineo, *cuius animam compassionis gladius penetrat et non minor dolor materna pertransit uiscera*" (p. 63).

6 · Druwé, "La Médiation universelle de Marie," pp. 501–2. On the order of the Servites, see G.-M. Roschini, "L'Ordre des Servites de Marie."

7 · On the Confrérie de Notre-Dame des Sept-Douleurs see Delehaye, "La Vierge aux Sept Glaives."

8 · Wilmart, *Auteurs spirituels et textes dévots du Moyen Age*, p. 513.

9 · Ibid., p. 514.

10 · Ibid. See also Mone, *Lateinischen Hymnen des Mittelalters*, 2:139.

11 · Wilmart, *Auteurs spirituels et textes dévots du Moyen Age*, pp. 522–26.

12 · Ibid., p. 524.

13 · Ibid., p. 525.

14 · Ibid., p. 535.

15 · Lutz and Perdrizet, *Speculum humanae salvationis*, 1:xviii–xix. See also Vanderbroucke, Leclercq, and Bouyer, *The Spirituality of the Middle Ages*, p. 347.

16 · Lutz and Pedrizet, *Speculum humanae salvationis*, 1:54.

17 · Ibid.

18 · Ibid., p. 56.

19 · Ibid., p. 62.

20 · *PL* 158:903–4.

21 · Du Manoir, "La Piété mariale de Saint Anselme de Cantorbery," p. 607.

22 · Blume and Dreves, *Analecta hymnica Medii Aevi*, 31:173.

23 · Ibid., pp. 174–75.

24 · Ibid., pp. 90–91.

25 · Blume and Dreves, *Analecta hymnica Medii Aevi*, 31:173–75, and 34:83, provide a general idea of this phenomenon.

26 · Ibid., 31:148–69, and 54:312–22, simply to offer examples.

Chapter VI · Planctus Mariae *and* Compassio Virginis

1 · For the text of the *Maestae parentis Christi* see Blume and Dreves, *Analecta hymnica Medii Aevi*, 54:318–20.

2 · Cremaschi, "Planctus Mariae," pp. 425–43 for the first lament, pp. 443–68 for the second.

3 · Mone, *Schauspiele des Mittelalters*, 1:41.

4 · Ibid., pp. 37–41.

5 · Blume and Dreves, *Analecta hymnica Medii Aevi*, 54:318–20.

6 · Daniel, *Thesaurus hymnologicum*, 5:187–89.

7 · Blume and Dreves, *Analecta hymnica Medii Aevi*, 54:320.

8 · Ibid.

9 · Ibid., 31:169–70.

10 · Mone, *Lateinischen Hymnen des Mittelalters*, no. 441, pp. 143–44, and no. 442, p. 144.

11 · Blume and Dreves, *Analecta hymnica Medii Aevi*, 48:510.

12 · Ibid., 31:148–49.

13 · Ibid., pp. 151–53.

14 · Ibid., p. 153.

15 · Ibid., pp. 155–68.

16 · Ibid., p. 156.

17 · Ibid., p. 158.

18 · Ibid., esp. pp. 159–62.

19 · Ibid., 53:178–79.

20 · Ibid., p. 178.

21 · Ibid.

22 · Ibid., p. 178. Basing his position upon the style of this *De compassione*, de Gourmont, *Le Latin mystique*, p. 367, erroneously attributes its composition to the tenth century.

23 · Lipphardt, "Studien zu den Marienklagen und germanische Totenklagen," p. 396.

24 · Mâle, *L'Art religieux de la fin du Moyen Age*, p. 122.

25 · Luis, "Evolutio historica doctrinae de Compassione B. Mariae Virginis," pp. 274–76; Machensen, "Mittelalterliche Tragödien," p. 99.

26 · Luis, "Evolutio historica doctrinae de Compassionis B. Mariae Virginis," p. 276; Wilmart, *Auteurs spirituels et textes dévots du Moyen Age*, pp. 505–9.

27 · Ermini, *Lo Stabat Mater*, especially for the arguments of attribution, pp. 5–9.

28 · Pacheu, *Jacopone da Todi*, p. 81.

29 · Misset, *Les Proses d'Adam de Saint-Victor*, p. 196.

30 · Wellner, *Adam von Sankt-Victor samtliche Sequenzen*, pp. 52–56, 58–62.

31 · D'Ancona, *Jacopone da Todi*, pp. 106–7.

32 · Sapegno, *Frate Jacopone*, p. 119.

33 · Ibid., pp. 60–61.

34 · Menestò, "Le laude drammatiche di Iacopone da Todi," p. 135.

35 · Toschi, *Il valore attuale ed eterno della poesia di Jacopone*, p. 38.

36 · Bernardi, *Fra Jacopone da Todi*, p. 17.

37 · Ermini, *Lo Stabat Mater*, p. 12. Capelle declares that "le *Stabat* témoigne clairement de l'évolution qui s'est opérée vers une piété plus dramatique, plus pénetrée de componction qu'épanouie, plus sensible à l'*abundavit peccatum* qu'au *superabundavit gratia*" ("La Liturgie mariale en occident," p. 242).

38 · Blume and Dreves, *Analecta hymnica Medii Aevi*, 54:312–13.

39 · Mone, *Lateinischen Hymnen des Mittelalters*, pp. 153–54.

Chapter VII · *The* Compassio *in Medieval Spirituality*

1 · *Sermo 45: In nativitatem Beatissimae Virginis Mariae, PL* 144:748.

2 · Druwé, "La Médiation universelle de Marie," p. 503.

3 · Leclercq, "Dévotion et théologie mariales," p. 557; Wilmart, *Auteurs spirituels*, pp. 506–7.

4 · *PL* 159:271–90.

5 · Ibid., 902–5. Du Manoir, referring to the *compassio* expressed in this *Oratio*, asserts that "Anselme nous introduit dans une nouvelle voie de la piété, qui n'a guère été explorée avant lui" ("La Piété mariale," p. 607).

6 · *PL* 182:1133–42.

7 · Barré, "Le 'Planctus Mariae' attribué à Saint Bernard." On this subject also see Chiari, "Il 'Planctus B. Mariae" operetta falsamente attribuita a San Bernardo."

8 · Barré, "Le 'Planctus Mariae' attribué à Saint Bernard," p. 253.

9 · Ibid., p. 251.

10 · Ibid., p. 258.

11 · *Beati Oglerii de Tridino opera quae supersunt.*

12 · Barré, "Le 'Planctus Mariae' attribué à Saint Bernard," p. 266.

13 · *PL* 182:1135.

14 · Ibid., col. 1138.

15 · Leclercq, "Jean de Fécamp et S. Bernard dans les florilèges anciens," p. 103.

16 · Barré, *Prières anciennes*, p. 229.

17 · Leclercq, *Dévotion et théologie mariales*, p. 561.

18 · *PL* 189, esp. cols. 1726–31.

19 · *PL* 159:567.

20 · *PL* 196:483–84.

21 · *PL* 183:437–38.

22 · De Dieu, "La Vierge et l'Ordre des Frères Mineurs," p. 785.

23 · Ibid., p. 791. Cattaneo, *Maria Santissima nella storia della spiritualità milanese*, p. 72. Da Milano, in his "La 'Summa contra haereticos' di Giacomo Capelli," p. 82, asserts that Giacomo composed the *Stimulus* "in the second half of the thirteenth century." The fathers of the College of Saint Bonaventure, however, say that "ex aetate codicum elucet, *Stimulum* iam saeculo XIII exeunte fuisse conscriptum" (*Stimulus amoris Fr. Jacobi Mediolanensis*, p. x).

24 · *Stimulus amoris Fr. Jacobi Mediolanensis*, pp. 77–81.

25 · Ubertinus de Casali, *Arbor vitae crucifixae*, p. 320.

26 · Ibid.

27 · Ibid., p. 321.

28 · Ibid., p. 324.

29 · Ibid.

30 · Livario Oliger, "Una nuova versione latina," p. 211.

31 · Künzle, *Heinrich Seuses Horologium sapientiae*, pp. 19–27.

32 · Künzle, however, declares that "die lateinische Fassung nicht einfach eine Ubersetzung darstellt" and that "das Hor ist allerdings mehr als eine frei Ubersetzung des Büchlein der ewigen Weisheit" (ibid., pp. 29, 42).

33 · Ibid., p. 513.

34 · Ibid., pp. 514–15.

35 · Ibid., p. 515.

36 · Ibid., p. 516.

37 · Marinageli, *Bernardino da Siena all'Aquila*, p. 15.

38 · Blume and Dreves, *Analecta hymnica Medii Aevi*, 36:216. We provide only some of the stanzas of this *Planctus* preserved in a Franciscan manuscript of the fifteenth century.

39 · Saint Bernardine of Siena, *Opera omnia*, 6:77–87.

40 · Ibid., p. 79.

41 · Ibid.

42 · In the *Liber de excellentia Virginis Mariae*, *PL* 159:566–67.

43 · Saint Bernardine of Siena, *Opera omnia*, 6: 79.

44 · Ibid., pp. 84–85.

45 · Ibid., 2:188–293.

46 · Ibid., p. 267.

47 · Ibid., pp. 268–69.

48 · On the thought of Bernardino de' Bustis on the compassion of the Virgin see Cucchi, *La mediazione universale della Santissima Vergine*, especially chap. 3.

49 · Grégoire, "Un lamento mariano," pp. 348–64.

50 · Wilmart, *Auteurs spirituels*, pp. 508–9, declares that "le XVᵉ [siècle], si l'on s'en rapporte aux textes jusqu'ici publiés, serait proprement l'âge où la Compassion a flori."

Chapter VIII · *The* Planctus Mariae *and the Theatrical Tradition.*

1 · Sticca, *The Latin Passion Play*, pp. 44–47.

2 · Barré, "Le 'Planctus Mariae' attribué à St. Bernard," pp. 245–46; Keppler, "Zur Passionspredigt des Mittelalters," esp. 4:179.

3 · Beissel, *Geschichte der Verehrung Marias in Deutschland*, pp. 379ff. Corbin, *La Déposition liturgique du Christ au Vendredi Saint*, pp. 210–13.

4 · Diller, *Redeformen des englischen Misterienspiels*, p. 74.

5 · Apollonio, *Storia del teatro italiano*, 1:192.

6 · A statute of the fourteenth century of the Compagnia del Crocifisso of Gubbio declares, for example, that on the evening of Good Friday, if the prior should wish it, the members of the confraternity should gather in a church "in qua ecclesia lacrimosas laudes et cantus dolorosos et amara Lamenta Virginis Mariae vidue proprio orbate Filio cum reverentia populo representent, magis ad lacrimas attendentes quam ad verba" (in Mazzatinti, "I disciplinati di Gubbio e i loro Uffizi drammatici," p. 96. Grano, in his "Planctus Mariae," pp. 48–51, shows, in his analysis of the *Planctus* of Cividale, that it is actually a cento of verses borrowed from other *Planctus* present in other liturgical dramas.

7 · Wolpers, "Englische Marienlyrik im Mittelalter," p. 21; Weber, *Theology and Poetry in the Middle English Lyric*, esp. pp. 94–121.

8 · Iglesias, *Las primeras representaciones castellanas de la Pasión de Cristo*, p. 163.

9 · Saugnieux, "La Tradition mariale et les 'Milagros' de Berceo," p. 63. Keller, *Gonzalo de Berceo*, p. 44, observes that the cult of the Virgin reached its apex, in Spain, in the thirteenth century: "In thirteenth-century Spain Mariolatry and Mariology reached a crest." On this subject see, too, Laurentino, "Cooperación de la Virgen María."

10 · Berceo, *El duelo de la Virgen*, p. 7. Hutton, the editor of this volume, reproduces on pp. 52–58 the edition of the *Liber de Passione* of Bernard taken from *PL* 182:1133–42; Oroz Reta, "Paralelismo literario," pp. 328–34.

11 · Saugnieux, "La Tradition mariale et les 'Milagros' de Berceo," p. 56.

12 · Berceo, *El duelo de la Virgen*, pp. 37–38.

13 · Today critics are unanimous in attributing the *Meditationes vitae Christi* to Joannes de Caulibus. Several studies followed in the wake of Oliger's essay "Le *Meditationes vitae Christi* del Pseudo-Bonaventura," which defended the originality of the work and attributed it to Joannes de Caulibus. Fisher, in his critical and philological study "Die *Meditationes vitae Christi*," asserted that the *Meditationes vitae Christi* are a compilation of two treatises: the *Meditationes de Passione Christi*, whose author is certainly Bonaventure, and the *Meditationes vitae Christi*, which should be attributed to an unknown Tuscan Franciscan. Stallings, in his thesis entitled *Meditaciones de Passione Christi olim Sancto Bonaventurae attributae*, asserts, after noting the structural and thematic correspondence of the two treatises, that the *Meditationes vitae Christi* is the work of an anonymous author. Then, too, there is the essay of Queirazza, "Intorno ad alcuni codici delle *Meditationes Vitae Christi*," which underscores the structural unity of the work. Finally, we have the comments of Levasti, *Mistici del duecento e del trecento*, p. 997, which contend that Giovanni de Caulibus is the probable author of the *Meditationes vitae Christi*. At present, the *communis opinio* seems to be that De Caulibus should be considered the author of the *Meditationes vitae Christi* and Bonaventure the author of the treatise contained within it, the *Meditationes de Passione Christi*.

14 · Mâle declares with reference to the *Meditationes vitae Christi* that while "les autres livres s'addressaient à l'intelligence, celui-là parle au coeur" (*L'Art religieux du XIIᵉ au XVIIᵉ siècles*, p. 92). Thomas, "Zur Rolle der 'Meditationes Vitae Christi' innerhalb der europaische Bild-Entwicklung der *Giotto-Zeit*," pp. 323–24.

15 · Saint Bonaventure, *Meditationes vitae Christi*, in *Opera omnia*, 12:609.

16 · Ibid.

17 · De Dieu, *La Vierge et l'Ordre des Frères Mineurs*, pp. 790–91.

18 · Saint Bonaventure, *Opera omnia*, 14:230–31.

19 · Mone, *Lateinischen Hymnen des Mittelalters*, 2:136: "Die Lieder von den Schmerzen Maria heissen bei den Griechen *Staurotheotokia*, weil es Ausrufe der Schmerzen Maria unter dem Kreuze sind. Sie entsprechen nicht des lautlosen Jammer derselben und sind daher mit Recht im Stabat mater vermieden. Dagegen haben die lateinischen und teutschen Marienklagen den Chrackter wie die griechischen, weil sie oft zu den Passionsspielen aus Monologue gebraucht wurden."

20 · Inguanez, "Un dramma della Passione del secolo XII," pp. 41–42.

21 · F. Mancini, "Temi e stilemi della 'Passio' umbra," p. 145. He finds the source for the parallel between the good thief and Mary in a passage from a letter

of Ambrose to the church of Vercelli: "Nam, si religiosum est quod latroni donatur venia, multo uberioris pietatis est quod a filio mater tanto affectu honoratur."

22 · Ibid., p. 146.

23 · Doglio, *Teatro in Europa*, p. 171.

24 · Sticca, *The Latin Passion Play*, pp. 84–87.

25 · Inguanez, "Un dramma della Passione del secolo XII," p. 52.

26 · Young, *The Drama of the Medieval Church*, 1:516.

27 · Ibid., p. 530.

28 · Ugolini, *Testi volgari abruzzesi del Duecento*, p. 23.

29 · Baldelli, "La lauda e i disciplinati," in his *Medioevo volgare da Montecassino all'Umbria*, p. 330; Ugolini, *Testi volgari abruzzesi del Duecento*, pp. 10–11. For the texts of the *Lamentatio Beate Marie de filio* and of the *Pianto delle Marie* we use Ugolini, pp. 42–46 and pp. 119–28.

30 · F. Mancini, "Temi e stilemi della 'Passio' umbra," p. 153.

31 · Ibid., p. 146. For the text of the Lombard Passion see Cotti, "Una 'Passione' lombarda del secolo XIII," 1:357–363, and Varanini, *Laude dugentesche*, pp. 109–20.

32 · F. Mancini, "Temi e stilemi della 'Passio' umbra," p. 146.

33 · Texts from Ugolini, *Testi volgari abruzzesi del Duecento: Lamentatio*, pp. 43–44, and *Pianto delle Marie*, pp. 122, 127.

34 · Ibid., p. 10.

35 · Baldelli, *Medioevo volgare da Montecassino all'Umbria*, p. ix.

36 · Frugoni, *Celestiniana*, p. 129; Ugolini, *Testi volgari abruzzesi del Duecento*, pp. 21–23; Baldelli, *Medioevo volgare da Montecassino all'Umbria*, pp. 331–32; Chiaverini, "Ore plangamo de lu Siniore," p. 34.

37 · Baldelli, "Dal 'Pianto' cassinese alla lauda umbra"; Menestò, "Le laude drammatiche di Iacopone da Todi," pp. 109–10; Toschi, *L'antico teatro religioso italiano*, pp. 47–48.

38 · For the text of the *Planctus* of Cividale see de Bartholomaeis, *Origini della poesia drammatica italiana*, pp. 482–84; Young, *The Drama of the Medieval Church*, 1:507–12; and Grano, "Planctus Mariae," pp. 41–43.

39 · De Bartholomaeis, *Origini della poesia drammatica italiana*, p. 133; Smoldon, *The Music of the Medieval Church Dramas*, p. 381.

40 · Donovan, *The Liturgical Drama in Medieval Spain*, p. 136.

41 · Ibid. For the text see pp. 78–81.

42 · Young, *The Drama of the Medieval Church*, 1:285.

43 · Ibid., pp. 439–40.

44 · Donovan, *The Liturgical Drama in Medieval Spain*, p. 137.

45 · Young, *The Drama of the Medieval Church*, 1:503–6.

46 · Mazzatinti, "I disciplinati di Gubbio e i loro Uffizi drammatici," p. 96; Ugolini, *Testi volgari abruzzesi del Duecento*, p. 23.

47 · Young, *The Drama of the Medieval Church*, 1:698.

48 · Maggiani, "La liturgia e la lauda drammatica espressione di liminalità."

49 · Blume and Dreves, *Analecta hymnica Medii Aevi*, 31:171.

50 · Cattin, "Testi melici e organizzazione rituale."

51 · Ibid., pp. 249–50. On the use of the cross in the early ceremonies of the *depositio* we refer the reader to Sheinghorn's splendid essay "The *Sepulchrum Domini*," p. 50.

52 · Cattin, "Testi melici e organizzazione rituale," p. 265.

53 · Ibid., pp. 250–54.

54 · Ibid., p. 260.

55 · Corbin, *La Déposition liturgique du Christ au Vendredi Saint*, p. 243.

56 · Coletti and Sheinghorn, "The Carmina Burana *Greater Passion Play* at the Cloisters," p. 141. For an analysis of the dramatic function of music in the medieval drama of Germany, both liturgical and in the vernacular, see Boletta, "The Role of Music in Medieval German Drama."

57 · Battisti, "Interstizi profani nell'arte figurativa," p. 85. For Edwards, however, in his *The Montecassino Passion and the Poetics of Medieval Drama*, pp. 54–55, the presence of the *Planctus* in the vernacular at the end of the Montecassino *Passio*, written entirely in Latin, is emblematic not so much of detachment from the mimetic context of the drama as of a more intimate participation of the laity in the liturgy, of a shared ritual experience, because "when the Virgin makes her lament in Italian, the effect is to join the witness of ordinary speech to that of the Biblical language."

58 · Magli and Piazza, "Lo sviluppo delle laudi drammatiche, p. 210.

59 · Heyse, *Romanische inedita auf italiänischen Bibliotheken*, p. 60. The text is reproduced by Bartsch and Wiese, *Chréstomathie de l'ancien français*, p. 106.

60 · Perry, *La Passion des jongleurs*, pages not numbered in the transcription of the text.

61 · Frank, *La Passion du Palatinus*, p. 48.

62 · Runnalls, *Le Mystère de la Passion Nostre Seigneur*, p. 206.

63 · Runnalls, "The French Passion Play Fragment of the University of Leyden," p. 104.

64 · Ugolini, *Testi volgari abruzzesi del Duecento*, pp. 18–19.

65 · Ugolini uses, in defense of his hypothesis, the discussions of D'Ovidio ("Studi sulla più antica versificazione francese," pp. 88–100) who had supposed the

possibility of an extra, unstressed syllable in an *octasyllabe*, which would make it correspond, in some instances, to the decasyllable of two quinaries. See Avalle, *Cultura e lingua francese*, pp. 86–87.

66 · Avalle, *Cultura e lingua francese*, p. 86. See, too, Norberg, *Introduction à l'étude de la versification latine médiévale*, p. 106; and Diez, "Die *Passion Christi*" in his *Zwei altromanische Gedichte*, pp. 5–6. On the problem of the versification in the Passion of Clermont-Ferrand, see Spenz, *Die syntaktische Bildung des Achtsilbigen Verses*.

67 · Shepard, *La Passion provençale du manuscrit Didot*, p. xxxiii. The *Planctus* occupies pp. 63–64.

68 · Villanueva, *Viaje a Solzona*, pp. 148, 281–83.

69 · Chabaneau, "Marius Sepet," p. 302.

70 · Villanueva, *Viaje a Solzona*, pp. 132–34.

71 · Chabaneau, "Sainte Marie Madeleine dans la littérature provençale," pp. 59–60.

72 · Villanueva, *Viaje a Solzona*, pp. 281–83. For the discussion of the language of the early text of this *Planctus*, that is, whether it was written in Provençal or Catalan, we refer the reader to the observations of Chabaneau, "Marius Sepet," pp. 302–4. It is interesting to observe that the first two verses of the second stanza of this *Planctus*—"Auyts, barons, qui passats per la via, / Si es dolor tan gran com es la mia"—are a translation of the first stanza of a Latin *Planctus* which begins in this fashion:

> Qui per viam pergitis,
> hic mecum sedete,
> Si est dolor similis
> ut meus, videte;
> Meum dulcem filium
> pariter lugete.

The beginning of this stanza was inspired in turn by the Lamentations of Jeremiah 1:2: "O vos omnes, qui transitis per viam, attendite, et videte si est dolor sicut dolor meus." For the complete text of the *Planctus*, "Qui per viam pergitis," which is preserved in a missal printed at Venice in 1523, but which certainly goes back to the thirteenth century, see Blume and Dreves, *Analecta hymnica Medii Aevi*, 10:79–81, and Young, *The Drama of the Medieval Church*, 1:500–502.

73 · Berschin, Berschin, and Schmidt, "'Augsburger Passionlied,'" p. 252.

74 · Ibid., pp. 262–63.

75 · Ibid., p. 268. Avalle, in *La letteratura medievale in lingua d'oc*, pp. 23–24, indicates that *La Passion du Christ* and *La Vie de Saint Léger* go back to Provençal originals of the tenth century and that the *Cantilène d'Eulalie* and *Le Fragment de Jonas* are illustrated by models in the north of France.

76 · Ibid., p. 271.

77 · Kuen, "Das Futurum im Augsburger Passionslied," p. 289: "So kann dieses nicht mit Sicherheit als älteste romanische Marienklage aufgefasst werden, wohl aber als älteste romanische Klage um den Gekreuzigten."

78 · Ibid.

79 · Ferretti, "Il canto della Passione nella Settimana Santa"; Coosemans, "Il canto del Passio"; Römer, "Die Liturgie des Karfreitags."

80 · Flanigan ("The Liturgical Drama and Its Tradition," p. 115) observes that "the studies on medieval drama that have an international character are practically non-existent." The need for a comparative study of the history of the theater has been advanced recently by Erbe ("Spirit and Necessity of Comparative Theatre History") and Batušić ("Esprit et nécessité de l'histoire comparative du théâtre").

81 · Mone, *Schauspiele des Mittelalters*, 2:164–68.

82 · Wilmotte, *Les Passions allemandes du Rhin*, esp. pp. 49, 50.

83 · Creizenach, *Geschichte des Neuren Dramas*, 1:101.

84 · Young, *The Drama of the Medieval Church*, 1:100.

85 · Wright, *The Dissemination of the Liturgical Drama in France*.

86 · Hadassah Posey Goodman, *Original Elements in the French and German Passion Plays*.

87 · Of a comparative character is Marshall's doctoral dissertation, her first study of the medieval theater: "The Relation of the Vernacular Religious Plays of the Middle Ages to the Liturgical Drama" (its principal reader was Karl Young).

88 · Corbin, *La Déposition liturgique du Christ au Vendredi Saint*, p. iii.

89 · Drumbl, *Quem quaeritis*, p. 14.

90 · Smoldon, *The Music of the Medieval Church Drama*. Smoldon wrote numerous essays on this subject; here we shall cite only two of them: "The Easter Sepulchre Music-Drama" and "The Origins of the *Quem Quaeritis* Trope."

91 · Arnold, "Time and the Religious Drama."

92 · Under the direction of Clifford Davidson, the Center of the University of Western Michigan has published, for example, studies of an international character such as *Studies in Medieval Drama*, *Drama and Art*, and *Drama in the Middle Ages: Comparative and Critical Essays*.

93 · Under the guidance of Federico Doglio, these volumes have so far appeared: *Dimensioni drammatiche della liturgia medievale*, *Il contributo dei giullari alla*

drammaturgia italiana delle origini, L'eredità classica nel Medioevo: Il linguaggio comico, Le laudi drammatiche umbre delle origini, Spectacoli conviviali dall'antichità classica alle corti del '400.

94 · Muller, *Le Théâtre au Moyen Age.* Muller is the editor of the review *Treteau,* the bulletin of the *Société* dedicated to the study of the medieval theater.

95 · Brinkmann, "Das religiöse Drama in Mittelalter," p. 271, attributes the development of the first German dramas in Latin on the Passion to the direct influence of the Christocentric piety of the Flagellants' movement. See also Kindermann, *Theatergeschichte Europas I. Antike und Mittelalter,* pp. 326–28, and more recently Hennig, "Der Abschluss des Grossen Passionsspiele in den 'Carmina Burana,'" esp. pp. 126–27.

96 · Jodogne, "Le plus ancien Mystère de la Passion," pp. 292–93.

97 · Sticca, "The Dramatic Context of the Tours *Ludus paschalis.*" On this subject see also Toschi, *Le origini del teatro italiano,* pp. 668–69.

98 · Jodogne, "Le plus ancien Mystère de la Passion," p. 293.

99 · West, *The Saint Gall Passion Play,* p. 39; and Boletta, "The Role of Music in Medieval German Drama," pp. 109–11.

100 · Accarie, *Le Théâtre sacré de la fin du Moyen Age,* p. 75.

101 · Varanini, *Laude dugentesche,* pp. 107–8.

102 · Frank, *La Passion du Palatinus,* p. v, and in her essays "The Palatine Passion and the Development of the Passion Play" and "Vernacular Sources and an Old French Passion Play."

103 · Noomen, "Passages narratifs dans les drames médiévaux français," p. 785.

104 · Regueiro, "Rito y popularismo en el teatro antiguo español," p. 13.

105 · Cohen, *Histoire de la mise en scène,* p. 20.

106 Konigson, *L'Espace théâtral médiéval,* pp. 8–9. Greisenegger, *Die Realität im religiösen Theater des Mittelalters,* pp. 35–36, considers the passage from the sacred place to the open air, the initial move outside the church, "der Schritt aus der Kirche," as one of the decisive actions, beginning with the middle of the twelfth century, in the evolution of the medieval religious theater.

107 · Le Gentil, "Réflexions sur la création littéraire au Moyen Age," p. 140. The continuity and the force of tradition in the Middle Ages are discussed by Curtius, *European Literature and the Latin Middle Ages,* pp. 391–97.

108 · Le Gentil, "Réflexions sur la création littéraire au Moyen Age," pp. 138–39.

109 · Accarie, *Le Théâtre sacré de la fin du Moyen Age,* p. 72.

110 · Jodogne, "Le théâtre français du Moyen Age," p. 20.

111 · Hult, "The Limits of Mime(sis)."

112 · Bourgeault, "Liturgical Dramaturgy."

113 · Sticca, *The Latin Passion Play,* pp. 134–44. Michael says, "Die beiden lateinischen Passionsspiele aus Italien: aus Montecassino und Sulmona—das letztere nur eine Fragment—sind fur die Deutsche Entwicklung ohne Bedeutung" ("Deutsche Literatur bis 1500,"2:582). Alluding to my studies on the subject, Michael will repeat his opinion later, in "Das deutsche Drama und Theater von der Reformation: "Leider lassen sich, soweit ich sehe, keinerlei Verbindunglinien von *Montecassino* nach *Benediktbeuren* ziehen" (p. 30).

114 · Bergmann, *Studien zu Entstehung und Geschichte,* p. 172.

115 · Ibid., pp. 172–73: "Im ganzen kann aus den chronologisch in Frage kommenden italienischen Zeugnissen wegen der inhaltlichen Undeutlichkeit der Nachrichten und wegen der formalen Eigenständigkeit der uberlieferten Texte eine Tradition lateinischer Passionsspiel, die den deutschen Passionsspiele zeitlich deutlich vorausginge und ihnen inhaltlich und formal als Vorbild gedient haben könnte, offenbar nicht erschlossen werden; eine solche Theorie italienischer Herkunft der deutschen Passionsspiele ist bisher auch nicht erwogen worden. . . . Die deutschen Passionsspiele mit ihrem lateinischen Bestandteilen haben offenbar kein direktes Vorbild in lateinischen Spielen gehabt und mussen daher als Ganzes selbständige Neuschöpfungen sein."

116 · Ibid., p. 173.

117 · Froning, *Das Drama des Mittelalters,* pp. 330–31.

118 · Werner, *Studien zu den Passions und Osterspielen,* p. 55.

119 · Hartl, "Die Entwicklung des Benediktbeurer Passionsspiels," and his "Untersuchungen zum St. Galler Passionsspiel"; Werner, *Studien zu den Passions und Osterspielen,* pp. 30–64; Bergmann, *Studien zu Entstehung und Geschichte,* pp. 84–174; Michael, *Das deutsche Drama des Mittelalters,* pp. 139–77, and in his essays "Deutsche Literatur bis 1500," pp. 582–84, and "Das deutsche Drama und Theater," pp. 35–38; Rudick, "Theme, Structure, and Sacred Context"; West, *The Saint Gall Passion Play,* pp. 17–49; Greisenegger, *Die Realität im religiösen Theater des Mittelalters,* pp. 226–80.

120 · Bergmann, *Studien zu Entstehung und Geschichte,* p. 257.

121 · Chambers, *The Mediaeval Stage,* 2:108, 146–47; Davidson, *Studies in the English Mystery Cycles,* p. 171.

122 · Wickham, *Early English Stages 1300–1660,* 2:145.

123 · Baugh, "The Chester Plays and French Influence"; Craig, *English Religious Drama,* p. 139; Woolf, *The English Mystery Cycles,* p. 306.

124 · Foster, *The Northern Passion,* 2:81–101; Robinson, "The Art of the York

Realist"; Davidson, "Civic Concern and Iconography in the York Passion," pp. 135–36; Axton, *European Drama of the Early Middle Ages*, p. 170.

125 · Foster, *A Stanzaic Life of Christ*, pp. xxviii–xliii; Wilson, "The Stanzaic Life of Christ and the Chester Plays"; Fichte, *Expository Voices in Medieval Drama*, pp. 101–7; Travis, *Dramatic Design in the Chester Cycle*, pp. 48–56.

126 · Dunn, "French Medievalists and the Saint's Play."

127 · Fernández de Moratín, *Orígines del teatro español*, p. 21.

128 · López Estrada, *Introducción a la literatura medieval española*, p. 474; Aubrun declares that "au Moyen Age, le 'théâtre' castillan n'offre point la diversité ni l'abondance souvent prolixe du 'théâtre' français" (*Histoire du théâtre espagnol*, p. 15).

129 · *Historia y crítica de la literatura española*, under the direction of Francisco Rico, vol. 1, *Edad Media*, ed. Deyermond, pp. 21–22.

130 · López Morales, *Tradición y creación en los orígines del teatro castellano*, p. 74. Crawford had declared in his *Spanish Drama Before Lope de Vega* that "the material is almost lacking for a study of the liturgical drama in Spain" (p. 9).

131 · Donovan, *The Liturgical Drama in Medieval Spain*, p. 171.

132 · Ibid., p. 168.

133 · Lázaro Carreter observes with reference to the texts discovered by Donovan that "todos los textos representan fórmulas muy primitivas, arcaicas para su tiempo, y todos, aun los más tardívos, proceden de centros de difusión situados en Francia o en el area catalana" (*Teatro medieval*, p. 26). Claramunt, in "En torno al Movimiento de los Disciplinantes en Cataluña," writes: "Las corrientes espirituales y políticas que repercutieron al sur de los Pirineos, fueron únicamente las surgidas en Francia, y sólo tendrán un terreno propicio en el principado de Cataluña, tan vinculado, por la política de los condes de Barcelona, a los acontecimientos y la Historia de Occitania y el Sur de Francia" (p. 328).

134 · Surtz, "El teatro en la Edad Media," pp. 63–154.

135 · Carreter, *Teatro medieval*, p. 37.

136 · One of the best studies on this subject is that of Casagrande and Vecchio, "L'interdizione del giullare nel vocabolario clericale."

137 · Ibid., p. 215.

138 · Fernández de Moratín, *Origines del teatro español*, p. 21; for the relevant part of the decretal of Innocent III, consult Young, *The Drama of the Medieval Church*, 2:416–17.

139 · Menéndez Pidal, *Poesía juglaresca y juglares*, p. 62.

140 · Valbuena Prat, *Historia del teatro español*, p. 13.

141 · López Morales, *Tradición y creación en los orígines del teatro castellano*, p. 66.

142 · Sturdivant, *The Misterio de los Reyes Magos*. Carreter writes that the whole of the *Auto de los Reyes Magos* "revela un origen galo. Pensamos que la clerecía francesa, numerosísima e influyente en aquella época, importó apresuradamente la práctica, nacida en su país, de dramatizar determinadas escenas evangélicas" (*Teatro Medieval*, p. 87).

143 · Lapesa, "Sobre el *Auto de los Reyes Magos*."

144 · Jose M. Regueiro, "El *Auto de los Reyes Magos* y el teatro litúrgico medieval," p. 153.

145 · Sturdivant, *The Misterio de los Reyes Magos*, pp. 55–56.

146 · Donovan, *The Liturgical Drama in Medieval Spain*, p. 73; Carreter, *Teatro medieval*: "La adopción de los tropos en latín fue frenada por la práctica de componer obras religiosas en lengua vulgar" (p. 36), and "Castilla se pasó sin ellos [tropos] porque importó una fase dramática—el texto externo en lengua vulgar—perfectamenta evolucionada" (p. 87).

147 · Shergold, *A History of the Spanish Stage*, p. 24.

148 · Donovan, *The Liturgical Drama in Medieval Spain*, pp. 26–27.

149 · David: "Les Eglises de ces régions qui dependaient de l'archévêque de Narbonne suiviaient le rite romain comme le reste de l'Empire des le IXᵉ siècle" (*Etudes historiques*, p. 395).

150 · Donovan writes that Catalonia was one of the most flourishing centers of medieval European liturgical drama and that "the abbey of Santa Maria de Ripoll has been accredited with being the focal point of its early development in this region" ("Two Celebrated Centers of Medieval Liturgical Drama," p. 41).

151 · Vivian, " 'La Passión Trobada' de Diego de San Pedro," p. 458.

152 · Darbord, "Premières Passions."

153 · For the text of this Auto see Gillet, "Tres pasos de las Pasión y una égloga de la Resurrección."

154 · Pérez Gómez, " 'La Pasión trobada' de Diego de San Pedro": "el más antiguo canto pasionario, dejando aparte los autos y representaciones" (p. 149). At the end of his essay, pp. 163–82, Pérez Gómez offers a reproduction in facsimile of the *Pasión trobada*.

155 · Ibid., p. 148; Vivian, " 'La Passión trobada' de Diego de San Pedro," p. 453.

156 · Vivian, " 'La Passión trobada' de Diego de San Pedro," p. 458.

157 · Pérez Gómez, " 'La Pasión trobada' de Diego de San Pedro," p. 165; López Morales declares that the *Passión trobada* "no era drama, sino un poema escrito para leer en voz alta" (*Tradición y creación en los orígines del teatro castellano*, p. 77).

158 · Vivian, "'La Passión trobada' de Diego de San Pedro," pp. 456, 466.

159 · Pérez Gómez, "'La Pasión trobada' de Diego de San Pedro," pp. 148–50.

160 · Vivian, "'La Passión trobada' de Diego de San Pedro," pp. 469–70.

161 · Iglesias, "Las primeras representaciones castellanas de la Pasión de Cristo," 1:233.

162 · Ibid., p. 238: "El teatro castellano vino por línea literaria de la poesía litúrgica narrativa."

163 · Ibid., 2:468. Keith Whinnom, for his part, has shown the influence of the *Meditationes vitae Christi* of the pseudo-Bonaventure upon Diego de San Pedro; see his "The Supposed Sources of Inspiration of Spanish Fifteenth-Century Narrative Religious Verse," pp. 275–80.

164 · Iglesias, "Las primeras representaciones castellanas de la Pasión de Cristo," 2:468.

165 · Vivian, "'La Pasión trobada' de Diego de San Pedro," p. 469.

166 · Iglesias, "Las primeras representaciones castellanas de la Pasión de Cristo," 2:233–35.

167 · Zumthor, *Essai de poétique médiévale*, p. 433.

168 · Torroja Menéndez and Rivas Palá, in an excellent study, *Teatro en Toledo en el siglo XV*, distinguish clearly between dramatic and nondramatic works on the Passion. Among these latter they include *La Passión trobada*, the *Coplas de la Pasión* and others: "Entre los autores de obras no dramáticas que trataron el tema de la Pasión y coinciden de alguna manera con Alonso del Campo hay que citar a Diego de San Pedro, el Comendador Román, Fray Ambrosio Montesino, Juan de Padilla" (p. 118).

169 · Alborg, *Historia de la literatura española*, 1:177–221, 484–515; Ruiz Ramón, *Historia del teatro español*, 1:13–25.

170 · Torroja Menéndez and Rivas Palá, *Teatro en Toledo en el siglo XV*, pp. 103–9.

171 · Ibid., p. 140: "La aparición del manuscrito del *Auto de la Pasión* indica que nuestros archivos catedralicios y parroquiales pueden no estar todavía tan explorados como se piensa . . . y que aún es posible el hallazgo de textos semejantes en los archivos españoles."

172 · D'Amico, *Storia del teatro drammatico*, 1:242.

Chapter IX · Conclusions

1 · Referring to a study of mine (among others), Bergmann writes, "Die szenischen Marienklagen sind in ganzen erst später uberliefert als die ältesten Pas-

sionsspiele und vermogen daher auch aus diesem Grunde die Entstehung der Passionsspiele nicht zu erklaren" (*Studien zu Entstehung und Geschichte*, p. 250). Grünberg, for his part, observes that the sequence *Planctus ante nescia* represents "das Kernstuck der späteren Passionen" (*Das religiöse Drama des Mittelalters*, 3:155).

2 · Bordier declares that "la fonction de ces complaintes est d'extérioriser une douleur pour susciter chez le spectateur une émotion semblable à celle du personnage; formules exclamatives et interrogatives, épithètes affectives, apostrophes, figures de rhétorique . . . tout cela relève d'une rhétorique de l'émotion" ("Lectures du *Palatinus*," pp. 459–60).

3 · Saint Bonaventure, *Opera omnia*, 14:227: "Prolem in cruce pendentem moesta Mater aspiciens, lacrymatur incessanter: pectus sacrum percutiens, plures movit ad moerorem suo ploratu querulo, natum videns cruentatum, crucis tensum patibulo. Animam moestae Parentis tunc pertransivit acrius, juxta verbum Simeonis, heu! passionis gladius."

4 · Labande-Mailfert, "La Douleur et la mort," pp. 314–15.

5 · These are the words of John the Deacon in his *In vitam S.P.N. Josephi Hymnographi*, PG 105:966. Impellizzeri, *La letteratura bizantina da Constantino agli iconoclasti*, p. 311, refers to Joseph the Hymnographer as "the most famous of the Sicilian hymnographers."

6 · *PG* 105:1282.

7 · Ibid.

8 · *PG* 105:1295.

9 · Ibid.

10 · *PG* 105:1311.

11 · *PG* 105:1314. Of particular assistance, in the discussion of the theme of the *gladius Passionis*, is the essay by Salaville, "Christus in orientalium pietate." For observations on the dramatic character of oriental rites, see Jungmann, *Die Stellung Christi im liturgischen Gebet*, p. 214; and Dumoutet, *Le Christ selon la chair*, p. 3. The image of the *gladius* as equivalent for the term *passio* figures prominently in Christocentric mysticism, from Saint Francis onward. (See Auerbach, *Literary Language and Its Public*, pp. 74–77.)

12 · Shepard, *La Passion provençale du manuscrit Didot*, p. 63.

13 · For the text of this *Planctus* see Young, *The Drama of the Medieval Church*, 1:500–2.

14 · Chiarini, "Il 'Contrasto fra la Croce e la Vergine.'"

15 · Mazzoni attributes it "to the last years of the thirteenth century or the first of the fourteenth" ("Un *Pianto della Vergine* in decima rima," p. 404), while Chiarini

conjectures that the composition of the *Contrasto* occurred earlier than that of the *Pianto della Vergine* ("Il 'Contrasto fra la Croce e la Vergine,' " p. 294).

16 · Chiarini, "Il 'Contrasto fra la Croce e la Vergine,' " p. 291.

17 · For this *Planctus*, preserved in a Latin manuscript of the twelfth century in the Biblioteca Civica of Turin (*Laudes* 749, 91), we use the version of 1439, written in Florence and preserved in Karlsruhe, Germany. (See Mone, *Schauspiele des Mittelalters*, 1:37–41).

18 · Chiarini, "Il 'Contrasto fra la Croce e la Vergine,' " p. 303.

19 · Ibid., p. 307.

20 · Diller, *Redeformen des englischen Mysterienspiels*, p. 74: "Als die lyrischen Planctus des 12. Jhs., in denen Maria selbst auftrat und ihren eigenen Schmerz kundtat, in die Liturgie und das liturgische Drama aufgenommen wurden, war ein bedeutender Schritt zur Humanisierung diese Feiern vollzogen." See, too, Fichte, *Expository Voices in Medieval Drama*, p. 72; and Schönbach, *Die Marienklagen*, pp. 56–62.

21 · Diller, *Redeformen des englischen Mysterienspiels*, p. 76. Meier observes that the *Planctus Mariae* contained in the *Ludus de Passione* fulfill a function of expressive and emotional power: "In . . . *Ludus de Passione* aus Benediktbeuren haben die Klagen Marias eine beträchtliche Vermehrung erfahren. Sie bilden den Hauptinhalt der Kreuzigungsszene" (*Die Gestalt Marias im geistlichen Schauspiel des deutschen Mittelalters*, p. 179).

22 · Toschi, *L'antico teatro religioso*, p. 135.

23 · Ibid., p. 124. Ruggieri, *Romanità e cristianesimo nell'europa medievale*, p. 213.

24 · De Bartholomaeis, *Origini della poesia drammatica italiana*, p. 135.

25 · Avalle indicates that "the *Sponsus* is the earliest liturgical drama in which there appear vernacular glosses in addition to the Latin text" (*Sponsus*, p. 9). Thomas, *Le "Sponsus,"* pp. 14–15; Fox, *The Middle Ages*, p. 243; Frank, *The Medieval French Drama*, pp. 58–64; Avalle, *La letteratura medievale in lingua d'oc*, pp. 22–29; Roncaglia, "I primi passi del volgare," p. 220; Knight, "Bilingualism in Medieval French Drama," pp. 248–49; Auerbach, *Literary Language*, pp. 284–86; De Ghellinck, *L'Essor de la littérature latine au XIIe siècle*, 2:265.

26 · Zumthor, "Un Problème d'esthétique médiévale," p. 303.

27 · Roncaglia, "I primi passi del volgare," p. 219.

28 · Zumthor, "Un Problème d'esthétique médiévale," p. 585.

29 · F. Mancini, "Temi e stilemi della 'Passio' umbra," p. 146; Vecchi, *Pietro Abelardo: I "Planctus,"* pp. 28–29. In Italy the earliest liturgical dramas were often presented in front of the public. This is confirmed by the presentation of the

Passion and the Resurrection of Christ at Padua in 1244 and at Cividale in 1298 and
1303. See on this subject: Ebert, "Die ältesten italienischen Mysterien"; D'Ancona, *Origini del teatro italiano*, 1:91; Kindermann, *Das Theaterpublikum des Mittelalters*, p. 202.

30 · Magli and Storoni Piazza, "Lo sviluppo delle laude drammatiche," p. 210;
Fichte, *Expository Voices in Medieval Drama*, p. 73.

31 · Jonsson, "Quels sont les rapports," p. 171.

32 · Monteverdi, "Lingue volgari e impulsi religiosi," p. 13. Auerbach, *Mimesis*,
p. 150: "Its popular character is apparent in the first place in matters of language. . . . It is further shown in the freedom with which the Biblical episode is
rendered, giving Mary a much more important and active part than even the Gospel according to Saint John does, so that the opportunity arises for dramatic development of her anxiety, her pain, and her mourning."

33 · Cellucci, "Il latino di fronte al volgare," p. 28.

34 · Panofsky, "Imago pietatis," p. 262; Denny, "Notes on the *Avignon Pietà*,"
p. 218; Millet, *Recherches sur l'iconographie de l'évangile*, pp. 489–516; Weitzmann,
"The Origin of the Threnos."

BIBLIOGRAPHY

Abel, F. M. "Sanctuaires marials en Palestine." *Maria* 4 (1956): 855–66.

Accarie, Maurice. *Le Théâtre sacré de la fin du Moyen Age: Etude sur le sens moral de la Passion de Jean Michel*. Geneva, 1979.

Ahsmann, Hubertus, Petrus, Johannes, Maria. *Le Culte de la sainte Vierge et la littérature française du Moyen Age*. Utrecht, 1930.

Alborg, Juan Luis. *Historia de la literatura española. Vol. 1, Edad Media y Renacimiento*. 2d ed. Madrid, 1972.

Anderson, M. D. *Drama and Imagery in English Medieval Churches*. Cambridge, 1963.

Andresen, Carl, and Gunter Klein, eds. *Theologia Crucis–Signum Crucis: Festschrift für Erich Dinkler zum 70. Geburtstag*. Tubingen, 1979.

Apollonio, Mario. *Storia del teatro italiano*. 2 vols. Florence, 1958.

Arasse, Daniel. "Fervebat Pietate Populus: Art, dévotion et société autour de la glorification de Saint Bernardin de Sienne." *Mélanges de l'Ecole française de Rome, Moyen Age–Temps Modernes* 89 (1977): 189–263.

Arnold, John Willis. "Time and the Religious Drama: An Investigation into the Formal Dramatic Structure of Twelve Passion Plays of the Middle Ages." 2 vols. Ph.D. diss., Michigan State University, 1977.

Assemani, J. S. *Bibliotheca orientalis*. Vol. 1. Rome, 1719.

Aubrun, Charles V. *Histoire du théâtre espagnol*. Paris, 1979.

Auerbach, Erich. *La letteratura medievale in lingua d'oc nella sua tradizione manoscritta*. Turin, 1961.

———. *Literary Language and Its Public in Late Latin Antiquity and in the Middle Ages*. Translated by Ralph Manheim. New York, 1965.

———. *Mimesis*. Translated by Willard Trask. New York, 1957.

Avalle, D'Arco Silvio. *Cultura e lingua francese delle origini nella "Passion" di Clermont-Ferrand*. Milan, 1962.

———. *Sponsus: Dramma delle vergini prudenti e delle vergini stolte*. Milan, 1965.

Axton, Richard. *European Drama of the Early Middle Ages*. Pittsburgh, 1975.

Baldelli, Ignazio. "Dal 'Pianto' cassinese alla lauda umbra." In *Le laudi drammatiche umbre delle origini*, pp. 47–63. Atti del V Convegno di Studio, Viterbo, 22–25 May 1980. Viterbo, 1981.

———. *Medioevo volgare da Montecassino all'Umbria*. Bari, 1971.

Barr, Cyrilla M. "The Popular Hymnody of Medieval Italy and Its Relationship to the Pious and Penitential Confraternities." *Studies in Medieval Culture* 3 (1970): 151–58.

Barré, H. "Le 'Planctus Mariae' attribué a S. Bernard." *Revue d'ascétique et de mystique* 28 (1952): 243–66.

———. *Prières anciennes de l'Occident à la Mère du Sauveur*. Paris, 1963.

———. "Prières mariales du Xᵉ siècle." *Ephemerides Mariologicae* 10 (1960): 196–206.

Bartsch, Karl, and Leo Wiese. *Chréstomathie de l'ancien français*. 12th ed. New York, 1958.

Battaglia, Salvatore. *La coscienza letteraria del medioevo*. Naples, 1965.

Battisti, Eugenio. "Interstizi profani nell'arte figurativa." *Il Contributo dei Giullari alla drammaturgia italiana delle origini*, pp. 69–112. Atti del II Convegno di Studio, Viterbo, 17–19 June 1977. Rome, 1978.

Batušić, Nicola. "Esprit et nécessité de l'histoire comparative du théâtre dans les études théâtrales comme discipline universitaire." *Maske und Kothurn* 25 (1979): 110–14.

Baugh, A. C. "The Chester Plays and French Influence." In *Schelling Anniversary Studies*, pp. 35–63. New York, 1923.

Baumstark, Anton. "Zwei syrische Dichtungen auf das Entschlafen der allerseligsten Jungfrau." *Oriens christianus* 5 (1905): 82–125.

Beati Oglerii de Tridino, abbatis monasterii Locediensis, ordinis cistercensium, in diocesi vercellensis, opera quae supersunt . . . nunc primum descripta ac notis declarata, cura et studio Ioannis Baptistae Adriani, cum proemio Joseph Raviola. Turin, 1873.

Beissel, Stephen. *Geschichte der Verehrung Marias in Deutschland*. Freiburg, 1909.

Berceo, Gonzalo de. *El duelo de la Virgen, los himnos, los loores de Nuestra Senora, los signos del juicio final*. Vol. 3 of *Obras Completas*, edited by Brian Hutton. London, 1975.

Bergmann, Rolf. *Studien zu Entstehung und Geschichte der deutschen Passionsspiele des 13. und 14. Jahrhunderts*. Munich, 1972.

Bernardi, Lina. *Fra Jacopone da Todi: Un revisionismo di una singolarissima figura*. Res Tudertinae, no. 16. Todi, 1978.

Bernardine of Siena, Saint. *Opera omnia*. Edited by the priests of the College of Saint Bonaventure. Quaracchi, 1956.

Berschin, Helmut, Walter Berschin, and Rolf Schmidt. "*Augsburger Passionslied:*

Ein neuer romanischer Text des X. Jahrhunderts." In *Lateinische Dichtungen des X. und XI. Jahrhunderts: Festgabe für Walther Bulst zum 80*. Geburtstag, edited by Walter Berschin and Reinhard Düchting, pp. 251–79. Heidelberg, 1971.

Bigongiari, Dino. "Were There Theaters in the Twelfth and Thirteenth Centuries?" *Romanic Review* 37 (1946): 201–24.

Billanovich, Giuseppe. "Uffizi drammatici della Chiesa padovana." *Rivista italiana del dramma* 4 (1940): 72–100.

Blasucci, Antonio. "La spiritualità in S. Bonaventura." In *S. Bonaventura 1274–1974: Volumen Commemorativum*, 4:567–606. Grottaferrata, 1974.

Blume, C., and G. M. Dreves. *Analecta hymnica Medii Aevi*. New York, 1961.

Bodenstedt, M. I. *The Vita Christi of Ludolphus the Carthusian*. Catholic University of America, Studies in Medieval and Renaissance Latin Language and Literature, vol. 16. Washington, 1944.

Boletta, W. "The Role of Music in Medieval German Drama: Easter Plays and Passion Plays." Ph.D. diss., Vanderbilt University, 1967.

Bonaventure, Saint. *Opera omnia*. Edited by A. C. Peltier. Paris, 1868.

————. *Seraphici Doctoris S. Bonaventurae Legendae duae de vita S. Francisci Seraphici*. Edited by the priests of the College of St. Bonaventure. Quaracchi, 1898.

Bonetti, Ignazio. *Le Stimmate della Passione: Dottrina e storia della devozione alle Cinque Piaghe*. Rovigo, 1952.

Borchers, Hans Heinrich. "Geschichte des deutschen Theaters." In *Deutsche Philologie im Aufriss*, edited by Wolfgang Stammler, 3: 417–588. Berlin, 1957.

Bordier, Jean-Pierre. "Lectures du Palatinus." *Le Moyen Age* 80 (1974): 429–82.

Bourgeault, Cynthia. "The Aesthetic Dimension in the Liturgy: A Theological Perspective for Literary Historians." *University of Toronto Quarterly* 52 (1982): 9–19.

————. "Liturgical Dramaturgy." *Comparative Drama* 17 (1983): 124–40.

Brinkmann, Hennig. "Das religiöse Drama in Mittelalter: Arten und Stufen." *Wirkendes Wort* 9 (1959): 257–74.

Bronzini, Giovanni. "Le origini del teatro italiano." *Cultura neolatina* 16–17 (1956–57): 201–39.

Brusegan, Rosanna. "Verità e finzione nel *Jeu d'Adam*." *Cultura neolatina* 40 (1980): 79–102.

Buckbee, Edward J. "The 'Jeu d'Adam' as 'Ordo Representacionis Evae': Truth and Dramatic Consequences." *Medioevo romanzo* 4, no. 3 (1977): 19–34.

Bur, Jacques. "La Médiation de Marie: Essai de synthèse spéculative." *Maria* 6 (1961): 473–512.

Bynum, Caroline Walker. *Docere Verbo et Exemplo: An Aspect of Twelfth-Century Spirituality.* Harvard Theological Studies, no. 31. Missoula, Mont., 1979.

Callaey, Frédégand, O.F.M. Cap. "L'Influence et la diffusion de l'*Arbor vitae* d'Ubertin de Casale." *Revue d'histoire ecclésiastique* 17 (1921): 533–46.

Callewaert, C. "L'Etude et l'esprit de la liturgie" and "La Méthode dans l'étude de la liturgie." In *Sacris Erudiri,* pp. 1–23, 25–40. The Hague, 1940.

Cammelli, G. *Romano il Melode.* Florence, 1930.

Capelle, B. "La Liturgie mariale en Occident." *Maria* 1 (1949): 217–45.

Caplan, Harry. *Of Eloquence: Studies in Ancient and Medieval Rhetoric.* Ithaca, N.Y.: 1970.

Carbonara, Giovanni. *Iussu Desiderii: Montecassino e l'architettura campano-abruzzese nell'undicesimo secolo.* Rome, 1979.

Cargnoni, Costanzo. "Storia della spiritualità italiana e letteratura spirituale francescana." *Collectanea francescana* 51 (1981): 293–324.

Carol, Junipero B. *De corredemptione Beatae Mariae disquisitio positiva.* Vatican City, 1950.

Carpenter, Marjorie. "Romanos and the Mystery Play of the East." *University of Missouri Studies* 11, no. 3 (1936): 21–51.

Carreter, Fernando Lázaro. *Teatro medieval.* Madrid, 1965.

Casagrande, Carla, and Silvana Vecchio. "L'interdizione del giullare nel vocabolario clericale del XII e del XIII secolo." In *Il contributo dei giullari alla drammaturgia italiana delle origini.* Atti del II Convegno di Studio, Viterbo, 17–19 June 1977, pp. 207–58. Rome, 1978.

Castellino, Giorgio R. "Letterature cuneiformi e cristiane orientali." In *Storia delle letterature d'Oriente,* pp. 93–461. Milan, 1969.

Cattaneo, Enrico. "Il dramma liturgico della Settimana Santa nel rito ambrosiano." *Ambrosius* 32 (1956): 65–91.

———. *Maria Santissima nella storia della spiritualità milanese.* Milan, 1955.

Cattin, Giulio. "Testi melici e organizzazione rituale nella processione fiorentina di 'Depositio' secondo il manoscritto 21 dell'Opera di S. Maria del Fiore." In *Dimensioni drammatiche della liturgia medioevale.* Atti del I Convegno di Studio, Viterbo, 31 May–2 June 1976, pp. 243–65. Rome, 1977.

Cecchin, A. "La concezione della Vergine nella liturgia della Chiesa occidentale anteriore al secolo XIII." *Marianum* 5 (1949): 51–114.

Cellucci, Luigi. "Il latino di fronte al volgare in Italia nei secoli XIII e XIV." *Cultura neolatina* 1 (1941): 211–39.

———. "Le 'Meditationes Vitae Christi' e i poemetti che ne furono ispirati." *Archivum romanicum* 22 (1938): 30–98.

Cercone, Franco. *La Madonna che scappa in piazza a Sulmona*. Sulmona, 1982.

Chabaneau, C. "Marius Sepet, la *Passion du Sauveur* Mystère provençal du XIIIe siècle." *Revue des langues romanes* 3 (1880): 301–5.

————. "Sainte Marie Madeleine dans la littérature provençale." *Revue des langues romanes* 28 (1885): 5–23, 53–71.

Chambers, E. K. *The Mediaeval Stage*. 2 vols. Oxford, 1903.

Chiari, A. "Il 'Planctus B. Mariae' operetta falsamente attribuita a San Bernardo." *Rivista storica benedettina* 17 (1926): 56–111.

Chiarini, Giorgio. "Il 'Contrasto fra la Croce e la Vergine' del Codice V.E. 477 alla luce della Testimonianza Senese." In *Testi e interpretazioni: Studi del seminario di filologia romanza dell'università di Firenze*, pp. 289–325. Milan-Naples, 1978.

Chiaverini, Antonio. *"Ore plangamo de lu Siniore" nel codice del Papa Celestino V.* Sulmona, 1971.

Claramunt, Salvador. "En torno al Movimiento de los Disciplinantes en Cataluña." In *Risultati e prospettive della ricerca sul movimento dei Disciplinati*. Convegno Internazionale di Studio, Perugia, 5–7 December 1969, pp. 328–30. Perugia, 1972.

Coathalem, H. *Le Parallélisme entre la Sainte Vierge et l'Eglise dans la tradition latine jusqu'à la fin du XIIe siècle*. Analecta gregoriana, vol. 74. Rome, 1954.

Cohen, Gustave. "Le Drame liturgique en France." *Rivista di Studi Teatrali* 9–12 (1954): 13–31.

————. *Histoire de la mise en scène dans le théâtre religieux français du Moyen Age*. Paris, 1926.

————. "Un Terme de scénologie médiévale: 'Lieu' ou 'mansion'?" In *Mélanges de philologie et d'histoire littéraire offerts à Edmond Huguet*, pp. 52–58. Paris, n.d.

————. *Le Théâtre religieux*. Vol. 1 of *Le Théâtre en France au Moyen Age*. Paris, 1931.

Coletti, Theresa, and Pamela Sheinghorn. "The Carmina Burana *Greater Passion Play* at the Cloisters." *Research Opportunities in Renaissance Drama* 25 (1982): 139–44.

Contini, G. *Teatro religioso del Medio Evo fuori d'Italia*. Milan, 1949.

Coosemans, Vincenzo. "Il canto del *Passio*." *Rivista liturgica* 6 (1919): 49–55.

Corbin, Solange. *La Déposition liturgique du Christ au Vendredi Saint: Sa place dans l'histoire des rites et du théâtre religieux*. Paris, 1960.

————. "Teatro religioso." In *La Musica: enciclopedia storica*, ed. Guido M. Gatti and A. Basso, 4: 619–27. Turin, 1966.

Cothenet, E. "Marie dans les Apocryphes." *Maria* 6 (1961): 73–156.

Cottas, Vénétia. *Le Théâtre à Byzance*. Paris, 1931.

Cotti, Maria. "Una 'Passione' lombarda del secolo XIII." In *Studi in onore di Alfredo*

Schiaffini. 2 vols. *Rivista di cultura classica e medioevale* 7 (1965): vol. 1, pp. 347–56, commentary; pp. 357–63, text.

Craddock, Lawrence G., O.F.M. "Franciscan Influences on Early English Drama." *Franciscan Studies* 10 (1950): 383–417.

Craig, Hardin. *English Religious Drama.* Oxford, 1955.

———. "The Origin of the Passion Play: Matters of Theory as Well as Fact." *University of Missouri Studies* 21 (1946): 83–90.

Craik, T. W. "Violence in the English Miracle Plays." In *Medieval Drama,* edited by Neville Denny, pp. 173–95. London, 1973.

Crawford, J. P. Wickersham. *Spanish Drama Before Lope de Vega.* Philadelphia, 1922.

Creizenach, Wilhelm. *Geschichte des Neuren Dramas.* Vol. 1. 2d ed. Halle, 1911.

Cremaschi, Giovanni. "Planctus Mariae: Nuovi testi inediti." *Aevum* 29 (1955): 193–468.

Cucchi, Francesco. *La mediazione universale della Santissima Vergine.* Milan, 1942.

Curtius, Ernst Robert. *European Literature and the Latin Middle Ages.* Translated by Willard Trask. New York, 1963.

Dahan, Gilbert. "Les Lamentations dans le drame religieux (XIe–XIIIe siècles)." *Treteaux* 3 (1981): 1–18. There is no discussion of the *Planctus Mariae.*

Dahane, Dominique. "La Passion dans la liturgie syrienne orientale." *L'Orient syrien* 2 (1957): 185–92.

D'Alverny, Marie-Thérèse. "Comment les théologiens et les philosophes voient la femme." *Cahiers de civilisation médiévale* 20, nos. 2–3 (1977): 105–29.

D'Amico, Silvio. *Storia del teatro drammatico.* Vol. 1. Rome, 1982.

Da Milano, Ilarino. "La 'Summa contra haereticos' di Giacomo Capelli e un suo quaresimale inedito." *Collectanea francescana* 10 (1940): 66–82.

D'Ancona, Alessandro. *Jacopone da Todi: Il Giullare di Dio del secolo XIII.* Todi, 1914.

———. *Origini del teatro italiano.* 2 vols. Turin, 1891.

Daniel, Herm. Aldalbert. *Thesaurus hymnologicum.* 5 vols. Halle, 1841–46.

Darbord, Michel. "Premières Passions: La Passion et la Résurrection chez le Comendador Román et Diego de San Pedro." In *La Poésie religieuse espagnole des rois catholiques à Philippe II,* pp. 79–106. Paris, 1965.

David, Pierre. *Etudes historiques sur la Galice et le Portugal du VIe au XIIe siècle.* Paris, 1947.

Davidson, Charles. *Studies in the English Mystery Cycles.* New Haven, Conn., 1892.

Davidson, Clifford. "Civic Concern and Iconography in the York Passion." *Annuale mediaevale* 15 (1947): 125–49.

———. *Drama and Art.* Kalamazoo, 1977.

_____, C. J. Gianakaris, and John H. Stroupe, eds. *Drama in the Middle Ages: Comparative and Critical Essays.* New York, 1982.

Davy, M. M. "La Présence de la Vierge Marie au XIIᵉ siècle." *La Table ronde* 129 (September 1958): 106–13.

De Bartholomaeis, Vincenzo. *Laude drammatiche e rappresentazioni sacre.* 3 vols. Florence, 1943.

_____. *Origini della poesia drammatica italiana.* 2d ed. Turin, 1952.

_____. "Ricerche Abruzzesi." *Bullettino dell'Istituto Storico Italiano* 8 (1889): 77–173.

_____. *Il teatro abruzzese del Medio Evo.* Bologna, 1924.

De Boor, Helmut. *Die Textgeschichte der Lateinischen Osterfeiern.* Tubingen, 1967.

De Dieu, Jean. "La Vierge et l'Ordre des Frères Mineurs." *Maria* 2 (1952): 785–831.

De Ghellinck, J. *L'Essor de la littérature latine au XIIᵉ siècle.* 2 vols. Paris, 1946.

De Gourmont, Remy. *Le Latin mystique.* Paris, 1930.

De Julleville, Petit. *Les Mystères.* 2 vols. Paris, 1880.

Delaruelle, Etienne. "Saint François d'Assise et la piété populaire." *San Francesco nella ricerca storica degli ultimi ottanta anni.* Convegni del Centro di Studi sulla Spiritualità Medievale, Todi, 13–16 October 1968, pp. 127–54. Todi, 1971.

Delehaye, H. "La Vierge aux Sept Glaives." *Analecta bollandiana* 12 (1893): 332–52.

Delius, Walter. *Geschichte der Marienverehrung.* Munich, 1963.

De Matons, Jose Grosdidier. *Romanos le Mélode.* Vol. 4 of *Hymnes.* Sources Chrétiennes, no. 128. Paris, 1967.

Denny, Don. "Notes on the *Avignon Pietà.*" *Speculum* 44 (1969): 213–33.

De Ros, Fidèle. "Le Planctus Mariae du pseudo-Anselme." *Revue d'ascétique et de mystique* 25 (1949): 270–83.

De Saint-Damien, Marie. "L'associée du Christ sauveur." *Etudes Franciscaines* 11 (1961): 17–31; 12 (1962): 185–202.

Desmarais, M. M. S. *Albert le Grand: Docteur de la médiation mariale.* Paris and Ottawa, 1935.

De Vito, Maria Sofia. *Le origini del dramma liturgico.* Milan, 1938.

Deyermond, Alan, ed. *Edad Media.* Vol. 1 of *Historia y crítica de la literatura española,* edited by Francisco Rico. Barcelona, 1980.

De Zedelgem, P. Amédée. "Aperçu historique sur la dévotion au chemin de la Croix." *Collectanea franciscana* 18–19 (1948–49): 45–142.

Diez, Friedrich. *Zwei altromanische Gedichte.* Bonn, 1876.

Diller, Hans-Jürgen. *Redeformen des englischen Mysterienspiels*. Munich, 1973.

Doglio, Federico. *Teatro in Europa*. Vol. 1. Milan, 1982.

Donovan, Richard B. *The Liturgical Drama in Medieval Spain*. Toronto, 1958.

———. "Two Celebrated Centers of Medieval Liturgical Drama: Fleury and Ripoll." In *The Medieval Drama and Its Claudelian Revival*, edited by E. Catherine Dunn, pp. 41–51. Washington, 1970.

D'Ovidio, Francesco. "Studi sulla più antica versificazione francese." In *Versificazione romanza: Poetica e poesia medioevale*, vol. 2, pp. 9–136. Naples, 1932.

Drumbl, Johann. *Quem quaeritis: Teatro sacro dell'alto medioevo*. Rome, 1981.

Druwé, E. "La Médiation universelle de Marie." *Maria* 1 (1949): 419–572.

Du Manoir, Hubert. "La Piété mariale de Saint Anselme de Cantorbery." In *De cultu mariano saeculis VI–XI*, vol. 3, pp. 597–611. Rome, 1972.

Dumoutet, Edouard. *Le Christ selon la chair et la vie liturgique au Moyen Age*. Paris, 1932.

Dunn, Catherine E. "French Medievalists and the Saint's Play: A Problem for American Scholarship." *Medievalia et humanistica* 6 (1975): 51–62.

Ebert, Adolf. "Die ältesten italienischen Mysterien." *Jahrbuch für romanische und englische Literatur* 5 (1864): 51–74.

Edwards, Robert. *The Montecassino Passion and the Poetics of Medieval Drama*. Berkeley, 1977.

Emereau, C. *St. Ephrem le Syrien*. Paris, 1918.

Ephraim the Syrian, Saint. *Opera omnia*. 6 vols. Rome, 1947.

Erbe, Von Berit. "Spirit and Necessity of Comparative Theatre History as an Academic Subject." *Maske und Kothurn* 25 (1979): 103–9.

Ermini, Filippo. *Lo Stabat Mater e i Pianti della Vergine nella lirica del Medio Evo*. Rome, 1899.

———. *Storia della letteratura latina medievale*. Spoleto, 1960.

Faccioli, Emilio, ed. *Il teatro italiano: Dalle origini al Quattrocento*. 2 vols. Turin, 1975.

Falvey, Kathleen. "The First Perugian Passion Play: Aspects of Structure." *Comparative Drama* 11 (1977): 127–38.

Fernandez de Moratín, Leandro. *Orígines del teatro español*. Paris, 1883.

Ferretti, Paolo. "Il canto della Passione nella Settimana Santa." *Rivista liturgica* 5 (1918): 69–75.

Fichte, Jörg O. *Expository Voices in Medieval Drama: Essays on the Mode and Function of Dramatic Exposition*. Nuremberg, 1975.

Fiocco, A. *Teatro universale dalle origini ai nostri giorni*. 3 vols. Bologna, 1967.

Fisher, C. "Die *Meditationes vitae Christi*: Ihre handschriftliche Ueberlieferung und die Verfasserfrage." *Archivum franciscanum historicum* 25 (1932): 3–35, 175–348, 449–83.

Flanigan, C. Clifford. "The Liturgical Drama and Its Tradition: A Review of Scholarship 1965–1975." *Research Opportunities in Renaissance Drama* 18 (1975): 81–102; 19 (1976): 109–36.

Fleming, John V. *An Introduction to the Franciscan Literature of the Middle Ages.* Chicago, 1977.

Folgorait, G., O.S.M. *La Vergine Bella in S. Bernardino da Siena.* Milan, 1939.

Fortini, Arnaldo. *La lauda in Assisi e le origini del teatro italiano.* Assisi, 1961.

Foster, Frances A., ed. *The Northern Passion.* Early English Text Society. 2 vols. London, 1913–16.

————. *A Stanzaic Life of Christ.* Early English Text Society, no. 166. London, 1926.

Fox, John. *The Middle Ages.* In *The Literary History of France,* edited by P. E. Charvet. New York, 1974.

Franceschini, Ezio. *Teatro latino medievale.* Milan, 1960.

————. "Il teatro post-carolingio." In *I problemi comuni dell'Europa post-carolingia,* vol. 2, pp. 295–312. Spoleto, 1955.

Frank, Grace. *The Medieval French Drama.* Oxford, 1954.

————. *La Passion du Palatinus.* Paris, 1922.

————. "The Palatine Passion and the Development of the Passion Play." *PMLA* 35 (1920): 464–83.

————. "Vernacular Sources and an Old French Passion Play." *Modern Language Notes* 35 (1920): 257–69.

Frohlich, Walter. *De Lamentacione Sancte Marie.* Leipzig, 1902.

Fronig, Richard. *Das Drama des Mittelalters.* Darmstadt, 1964.

Frugoni. A. *Celestiniana.* Rome, 1954.

Frugoni, Chiara. "L'Iconographie de la femme au cours des Xe–XIIe siècles." *Cahiers de civilisation médiévale* 20, nos. 2–3 (1977): 177–88.

Galot, Jean. "L'Intercession de Marie." *Maria* 6 (1961): 515–50.

————. "La Plus Ancienne Affirmation de la corédemption mariale." *Recherches de science religieuse* 45 (1957): 187–208.

Gamer, Helena M. "Mimes, Musicians, and the Origin of the Medieval Religious Play." *Deutsche Beiträge zur geistigen Uberlieferung* 5 (1956): 9–28.

Garrone, Virginia Galante. *L'apparato scenico del dramma sacro in Italia.* Turin, 1935.

Gasca Queirazza, G. "Intorno ad alcuni codici delle *Meditationes vitae Christi.*" *Archivum franciscanum historicum* 55 (1962): 252–58; 56 (1963): 162–74; 57 (1964): 538–51.

Génicot, L. *La spiritualité médiévale*. Paris, 1958.

Getto, Giovanni. *Letteratura religiosa dal Due al Novecento*. Florence, 1967.

Ghéon, Henri. *The Art of the Theatre*. New York, 1961.

Ghilardi, Fernando. "Le origini del teatro italiano e San Francesco." *L'Italia francescana* 30 (1955): 341–51; 31 (1956): 81–87.

———. *Storia del teatro*. Vol. 1. Milan, 1961.

Giammarco, E. *Storia della cultura e della letteratura abruzzese*. Rome, 1969.

Gillet, Joseph E. "Tres pasos de la Pasión y una égloga de la Resurrección." *PMLA* 47 (1932): 949–80.

Gilson, Etienne. "Michel Menot et la téchnique du sermon médiéval." In *Les Idées et les lettres*, pp. 93–154. Paris, 1955.

———. "Saint Bonaventure et l'iconographie de la Passion." *Revue d'histoire franciscaine* 1 (1924): 405–24.

Glenmes, H. "Der hl. Bonaventura und die Imitatio Christi." *Franziskanische Studien* 15 (1928): 294–315.

Goad, Harold. *Greyfriars*. London, 1947.

Goodman, Hadassah Posey. *Original Elements in the French and German Passion Plays*. Bryn Mawr, 1944.

Gougaud, D. L. *Dévotions et pratiques ascétiques du moyen age*. Maredsous, 1925.

Graef, Hilda. *Mary: A History of Doctrine and Devotion*. 2 vols. New York, 1963–65.

Grano, Giovanni. "Planctus Mariae: Analisi e sviluppo di una forma prototeatrale." *Rivista italiana di drammaturgia* 18 (1980): 7–63.

Grégoire, Réginald. "Un lamento mariano ed altri testi inediti di Paracleto Malvezzi (+ 1487)." *Marianum* 39 (1977): 348–64.

Greisenegger, Wolfgang. *Die Realität im religiösen Theater des Mittelalters*. Vienna, 1978.

Gripkey, Mary Vincentine. *The Blessed Virgin as Mediatrix in the Latin and Old French Legend Prior to the Fourteenth Century*. Washington, 1938.

Grünberg, Alexander. *Das religiöse Drama des Mittelalters*. 3 vols. Vienna, 1965.

Guardini, Romano. *The Spirit of the Liturgy*. Translated by Ada Lane. New York, 1935.

Guéranger, Prosper. *L'Année liturgique: La Passion et la Semaine Sainte*. Paris, 1909.

Hardison, O. B., Jr. *Christian Rite and Christian Drama in the Middle Ages*. Baltimore, 1965.

Hartl, Eduard. *Das Benediktbeurer Passionsspiel: Das St. Galler Passionsspiel*. Halle, 1952.

———. *Das Drama des Mittelalters*. Vol. 1. Leipzig, 1937.

———. "Die Entwicklung des Benediktbeuerer Passionsspiels in den 'Carmina Burana.'" *Euphorion* 46 (1952): 113–37.

———. "Untersuchungen zum St. Galler Passionsspiel." In *Festschrift für Wolfgang Stammler*, pp. 109–29. Berlin, 1953.

Hennig, Ursula. "Der Abschluss des Grossen Passionsspiels in den 'Carmina Burana.'" *Mittellateinisches Jahrbuch* 15 (1980): 121–27.

Heyse, Paul. *Romanische inedita auf italiänischen Bibliotheken*. Berlin, 1856.

Hirn, Yrjo. *The Sacred Shrine*. Boston, 1957.

Hogan, William F. *Christ's Redemptive Sacrifice*. Englewood Cliffs, N.J., 1965.

Huglo, Michel. "L'Intensité dramatique de la liturgie de la Semaine Sainte." In *Dimensioni drammatiche della liturgia medioevale*. Atti del I Convegno di Studio, Viterbo, 31 May–2 June 1976, pp. 93–105. Rome, 1977.

Hult, David F. "The Limits of Mime(sis): Notes Toward a Generic Revision of Medieval Theater." *L'Esprit créateur* 23 (1983): 49–63.

Iglesias, Luis G. "Las primeras representaciones castellanas de la Pasión de Cristo, Estudio Interpretativo." 2 vols. Ph.D. diss., Tulane University, 1977.

Impellizzeri, Salvatore. *La letteratura bizantina da Costantino agli iconoclasti*. Bari, 1965.

Inguanez, D. M. "Un dramma della Passione del secolo XII." *Miscellanea cassinese* 12 (1936): 7–36.

———. "Un dramma della Passione del secolo XII." With a foreword by Giulio Bertoni. *Miscellanea cassinese* 18 (1939): 7–55.

Jeffrey, David L. *The Early English Lyric and Franciscan Spirituality*. Lincoln, 1975.

———. "Franciscan Spirituality and the Rise of Early English Drama." *Mosaic* 8, no. 4 (1975): 17–46.

Jodogne, Omer. "Le plus ancien mystère de la Passion." *Académie Royale de Belgique, Classe des lettres et des sciences morales et politiques: Bulletin*, 5th ser., vol. 50 (1964): 282–94.

———. "Recherches sur les débuts du théâtre religieux en France." *Cahiers de civilisation médiévale* 8 (1965): 1–24, 179–89.

———. "Le Théâtre français du Moyen Age: Recherches sur l'aspect dramatique des textes. In *The Medieval Drama*, edited by Sandro Sticca, pp. 1–21. Albany, N.Y., 1972.

Jonsson, Ritva. "Quels sont les rapports entre Amalaire de Metz et les tropes liturgiques?" In *Culto cristiano: Politica imperiale Carolingia*. Convegni di Studi sulla Spiritualità Medievale, Todi, 9–12 October 1977, pp. 171–220. Todi, 1978.

Jungmann, Joseph. *The Mass of the Roman Rite: Its Origin and Development*. 2 vols. New York, 1950.

————. *Die Stellung Christi im liturgischen Gebet*. Münster, 1925.

Keller, John Esten. *Gonzalo de Berceo*. New York, 1972.

Keppler, P. "Zur Passionspredigt des Mittelalters." *Historisches Jahrbuch* 3 (1882): 285–315; 4 (1883): 161–88.

Khouri-Sarkis, Gabriel. "La Passion dans la liturgie syrienne occidentale." *L'Orient syrien* 2 (1957): 193–204.

Kienast, Richard. "Die deutschsprachige Lyrik des Mittelalters." In *Deutsche Philologie im Aufriss*, edited by Wolfgang Stammler, 2:772–902. Berlin, 1954.

Kindermann, Heinz. *Theatergeschichte Europas I. Antike und Mittelalter*. Salzburg, 1967.

————. *Das Theaterpublikum des Mittelalters*. Salzburg, 1980.

Knight, Alan E. "Bilingualism in Medieval French Drama." In *Jean Misrahi Memorial Volume: Studies in Medieval Literature*, edited by Hans R. Runte, pp. 247–64. Columbia, S.C., 1977.

Koehler, Theodore P. "Les Origines d'un thème dévotionnel: La Maternité spirituelle de Marie dans la piété occidentale entre 750–1100. Etude historique et culturelle." In *De culto mariano saeculis VI–XI*, 4:347–79. Rome, 1972.

Konigson, Elie. *L'Espace théâtral médiéval*. Paris, 1957.

Korošak, Bruno, O.F.M. "De cooperatione B. Virginis ad salutem mundi." In *Mariologia S. Alberti Magni eiusque coaequalium*, pp. 491–587. Rome, 1954.

Krumbacker, Karl. "Die Literatur von Konstantin bis Heraklios." In *Die Griechische und Lateinische Literatur und Sprache: Die Kultur der Gegenwart*, vol. 1, pt. 8, ed. Paul Hinneberg, pp. 254–67. Berlin and Leipzig, 1905.

Kuen, Heinrich. "Das Futurum im Augsburger Passionslied." *Zeitschrift für romanische Philologie* 95 (1979): 283–89.

Künzle, Pius. *Heinrich Seuses Horologium sapientiae*. Freiburg, 1977.

Labande-Mailfert, Yvonne. "La Douleur et la mort dans l'art des XIIe et XIIIe siècles." *Il dolore e la morte nella spiritualità dei secoli XII e XIII*. Convegni del Centro di Studi sulla Spiritualità Medievale, Todi, 7–10 October 1962, 5:295–332. Todi, 1967.

Langfors, Artur. "Contributions à la bibliographie des plaintes de la Vierge." *Revue des languages romanes* 53 (1910): 58–69.

Lapesa, Rafael. "Sobre el *Auto de los Reyes Magos:* Sus rimas anómalas y el posible origen de su autor." In *Homenaje a Fritz Krüger*, 2:591–99. Mendoza, 1954. Reprinted in Lapesa's *De la Edad Media a nuestros días: Estudios de historia literaria*, pp. 37–47. Madrid, 1967.

La Piana, Giorgio. "The Byzantine Theater." *Speculum* 11 (1936) 171–211.

———. *Le rappresentazioni sacre nella letteratura bizantina dalle origini al secolo IV.* Grottaferrata, 1912.

Laurentino, P. "Cooperación de la Virgen María en la obra redentora de Cristo según los poetas españoles." *Ephemerides mariologicae* 16 (1966): 393–478.

Laurion, Gaston. "Essai de groupement des hymnes médiévales à la Croix." *Cahiers de civilisation médiévale* 6 (1963): 327–31.

Lazzeri, Gerolamo. *Antologia dei primi secoli della letteratura italiana.* Milan, 1954.

Leclercq, Jean. "Dévotion et théologie mariales dans le monachisme bénédictin." *Maria* 2 (1952): 549–78.

———. "Dévotion privée, piété populaire et liturgie au Moyen Age." In *Etudes de pastorale liturgique*, pp. 148–73. Paris, 1944.

———. "Jean de Fécamp et S. Bernard dans les florilèges anciens." *Analecta Monastica* 20 (1948): 94–108.

Le Gentil, Pierre. "Réflexions sur la création littéraire au Moyen Age." *Cultura neolatina* 20 (1960): 129–40.

Leuterman, Teodoro. *Ordo casinensis Hebdomadae maioris* (saec. XII). *Miscellanea cassinese* 20 (1941).

Levasti, Arrigo. *Mistici del duecento e del trecento.* Milan, 1960.

Lipphardt, Walther. "Marienklagen und Liturgie." *Jahrbuch für Liturgiewissenschaft* 12 (1932): 198–205.

———. "Studien zu den Marienklagen und germanische Totenklagen." *Beiträge zur Geschichte der deutschen Sprache und Literatur* 58 (1934): 390–444.

Little, A. G. *Franciscan History and Legend in English Medieval Art.* Manchester, 1937.

Liuzzi, Ferdinando. *La lauda e i primordi della melodia italiana.* 2 vols. Rome, 1934.

Lombardo, Agostino. *Teatro inglese del Medioevo e del Rinascimento.* Florence, 1963.

Longère, Jean. *La Prédication médiévale.* Paris, 1963.

Longpré, Ephrem P., O.F.M. "La Chapelle de la Passion des Cordeliers de Troyes." *Archivum franciscanum historicum* 27 (1934): 321–52.

Loomis, R. S., and G. Cohen. "Were There Theatres in the Twelfth and Thirteenth Centuries?" *Speculum* 20 (1945): 92–98.

López Estrada, Francisco. *Introducción a la literatura medieval española.* Madrid, 1979.

López Morales, Humberto. *Tradición y creación en los orígines del teatro castellano.* Madrid, 1968.

Luis, Angelus. "Evolutio historica doctrinae de Compassione B. Mariae Virginis." *Marianum* 5 (1943): 261–85.

Lupinetti, Donatangelo. *Canto popolare abruzzese.* Centro Studi Abruzzesi, vol. 3. Pescara, 1973.

Lutz, J., and P. Pedrizet, eds. *Speculum humanae salvationis.* 2 vols. Paris, 1907–9.

Machensen, Lutz. "Mittelalterlichen Tragödien: Gedanken über Wesen und Grenzen des Mittelalters." In *Festschrift für Wolfgang Stammler*, pp. 92–108. Berlin, 1955.

Maggiani, Silvano. "La liturgia e la lauda espressione di liminalità." In *Le laude drammatiche umbre delle origini.* Atti del V Convegno di Studio, Viterbo, 22–25 May 1980, pp. 65–79. Viterbo, 1981.

Magli, Adriano, and Anna Maria Storoni Piazza. "Lo sviluppo delle laudi drammatiche in rapporto al concetto di spazio e di tempo." In *Le laudi drammatiche umbre delle origini.* Atti del V Convegno di Studio, Viterbo, 22–25 May 1980, pp. 201–15. Viterbo, 1981.

Mahr, Augustus C. *The Cyprus Passion Cycle.* Notre Dame, Ind., 1947.

Mâle, Emile. *L'Art religieux de la fin du Moyen Age.* Paris, 1946.

———. *L'Art religieux du XIIᵉ siècle en France.* 2d ed. Paris, 1924.

———. *L'Art religieux du XIIIᵉ au XVIIIᵉ siècle.* Paris, 1948.

———. *L'Art religieux du XIIIᵉ siècle en France.* Paris, 1958.

Mancini, Franco. "Temi e stilemi della 'Passio' umbra." In *Le laude drammatiche umbre delle origini.* Atti del V Convegno di Studio, Viterbo, 22–25 May 1980, pp. 141–64. Viterbo, 1981.

Mancini, Valentino. "Public et espace scénique dans le théâtre du Moyen Age." *Revue d'histoire du théâtre* 17 (1965): 307–403.

Manitius, Max. *Geschichte der lateinischen Literatur des Mittelalters.* 3 vols. Munich, 1911–31.

Maranini, Lorenza. *Teatro francese I: Dalle origini alla fondazione della Comédie Française.* Pavia, 1969.

Marcel, Gabriel. *Théâtre et religion.* Lyons, 1958.

Marinageli, Giacinto. *Bernardino da Siena all'Aquila.* Aquila, 1979.

Marrow, James H. *Passion Iconography in Northern European Art of the Late Middle Ages and Early Renaissance.* Brussels, 1979.

Marshall, Mary. "Aesthetic Values of the Liturgical Drama." *English Institute Essays* (1950): 89–115. Reprinted in *Medieval English Drama*, edited by Jerome Taylor and Alan H. Nelson, pp. 28–43. Chicago, 1972.

———. "The Relation of the Vernacular Religious Plays of the Middle Ages to the Liturgical Drama." Ph.D. diss., Yale University, 1932.

———. "Theatre in the Middle Ages: Evidence from Dictionaries and Glosses." *Symposium* 4 (1950): 1–39, 366–89.

Marshall, Robert D. "The Development of Medieval Drama: A New Theology." *Studies in Medieval Culture* 4 (1974): 407–17.

Martin, P. "Lettres de Jacques de Saroug aux moines du Couvent de Mar Bassus et à Paul d'Edesse." *Zeitschrift der deutschen morgenlandischen Gesellschaft* 30 (1876): 217–75.

Martínez, Pedro de Alcántara, O.F.M. "La cooperación de María a la obra salvífica de Cristo según el pensamiento de P. J. Olivi." In *Studies Honoring Ignatius Charles Brady,* edited by Romano Stephen Almagno and Conrad L. Harkins, O.F.M. Franciscan Institute Publications, Theology Series, no. 6, pp. 341–55. St. Bonaventure, N.Y., 1976.

Mathieu, Michel. "Distanciation et émotion dans le théâtre liturgique au Moyen Age." *Revue d'histoire du théâtre* 21 (1969): 95–117.

Mazzatinti, G. "I disciplinati di Gubbio e i loro Uffizi drammatici." *Giornale di filologia romanza* 3 (1880): 85–102.

Mazzoni, Guido. "Un *Pianto della Vergine* in decima rima." In *Atti del Reale Istituto Veneto,* ser. 7, 2:403–24. Venice, 1890–91.

Meier, Theo. *Die Gestalt Marias im geistlichen Schauspiel des deutschen Mittelalters.* Berlin, 1959.

Menéndez Pidal, Ramón. *Poesía juglaresca y juglares.* 5th ed. Madrid, 1962.

Menestò, Enrico. "Le laude drammatiche di Iacopone da Todi: Fonti e struttura." In *Le laudi drammatiche umbre delle origini.* Atti del V Convegno di Studio Viterbo, 22–25 May 1980, pp. 105–40. Viterbo, 1981.

Michael, Wolfgang. *Das deutsche Drama des Mittelalters.* Berlin, 1971.

———. "Das deutsche Drama und Theater von der Reformation: Ein Forschungsbericht." *Deutsche Viertljarhrsschrift für Literaturwissenschaft und Geistesgeschichte* 47 (1973): 1–47.

———. "Deutsche Literatur bis 1500: Drama." In *Kurzer Grundriss der germanischen Philologie bis 1500,* edited by Ludwig E. Schmitt, pp. 573–607. Berlin, 1970.

Millet, G. *Recherches sur l'iconographie de l'évangile.* Paris, 1916.

Mincione, Giuseppino. "Le sequenze abruzzesi." *Bullettino della deputazione abruzzese di storia patria* 66–68 (1976–78): 39–67.

Mingana, A. "The Lament of the Virgin and the Martyrdom of Pilate." *Woodbrooke Studies* 2 (1928): 163–282.

Misset, E. *Les Proses d'Adam de Saint-Victor.* Paris, 1900.

Möbius, Helga. *Passion und Auferstehung in Kultur und Kunst des Mittelalters.* Berlin, 1978; Vienna, 1979.

Mohrmann, Christine. "Pascha, Passio, Transitus." *Etudes sur le latin des chrétiens,* pp. 205–22. Rome, 1961.

Monaci, Ernesto. "Appunti per la storia del teatro italiano: Uffizi drammatici dei disciplinati dell'Umbria." *Rivista di Filologia Romanza* 1 (1872): 235–71; 2 (1875): 29–42.

Mone, F. J. *Lateinische Hymnen des Mittelalters.* 3 vols. Freiburg, 1853–55.

———. *Schauspiele des Mittelalters.* 2 vols. Karlsruhe, 1846.

Monteverdi, Angelo. "Lingue volgari e impulsi religiosi." *Cultura neolatina* 6–7 (1946–47): 7–21.

Moran, Sue E. "An Umbrian *Lauda* of the First Sunday of Advent." *Comitatus* 7 (1976): 1–14.

Morini, A. M. *Origini del culto alla Addolorata.* Rome, 1893.

Muller, Gari R. *Le Théâtre au Moyen Age.* Montreal, 1981. This is a collection of essays by several authors.

Mushacke, W. "Tractatus Beati Bernhardi de planctu Beatae Mariae." *Romanische Bibliothek* 3 (1890): 41–50.

Musumarra, Carmelo. *La sacra rappresentazione della Natività nella tradizione italiana.* Florence, 1957.

Noomen, W. "Le *Jeu d'Adam*: Etude descriptive et analytique." *Romania* 89 (1968): 145–93.

———. "Passages narratifs dans les drames médiévaux français: Essai d'interprétation." *Revue belge de philologie et d'histoire* 36 (1958): 761–85.

———. "Remarques sur la versification du plus ancien théâtre français: L'Enchainement des répliques et la rime mnémonique." *Neophilologus* 40 (1956): 179–93, 249–58.

Norberg, Dag. *Introduction à l'étude de la versification latine médiévale.* Stockholm, 1958.

Oliger, Livario. "Le *Meditationes vitae Christi* del Pseudo-Bonaventura." *Studi francescani* 7 (1921): 143–83; 8 (1922): 18–47.

———. "Una nuova versione latina delle Cento Meditazioni sulla Passione del B. Enrico Susone O.P." *Archivio italiano per la storia della pietà* 2 (1959): 209–30.

Oroz Reta, José. "Paralelismo literario entre el *Duelo* de Berceo y el *De Lamentatione* y *Los Evangelios.*" *Helmántica* 2 (1951): 324–40.

Otto, R. "Der Planctus Mariae." *Modern Language Notes* 14 (1899): 210–15.

Owst, G. R. *Preaching in Medieval England.* Cambridge, 1926.

———. "Sermon and Drama." In *Literature and Pulpit in Medieval England,* pp. 471–547. New York, 1961.

Pacheau, J. *Jacopone da Todi.* Paris, 1914.

Pächt, Otto. *The Rise of Pictorial Narrative in Twelfth-Century England.* Oxford, 1966.

Panofsky, Erwin. "Imago pietatis." *Festschrift für Max J. Friedlander zum 60. Geburtstag*, pp. 262–308. Leipzig, 1927.

Paris, Gaston. "Origines du théâtre italien." *Journal des savants* (1892): 670–85.

Pascal, R. "On the Origins of the Liturgical Drama of the Middle Ages." *Modern Language Review* 36 (1941): 369–87.

Pasch, William Allen. "Trinitarian Symbolism and Medieval English Drama." Ph.D. diss., University of Michigan, 1977.

Pasquini, Emilio. *Le origini e la scuola siciliana*. Bari, 1971.

Payen, Jean-Charles. "Idéologie et théâtralité dans l'Ordo Representationis Adae." *Etudes anglaises* 25 (1972): 19–29.

Peeters, P. "Jacques de Saroug appartient-il à la secte monophysite?" *Analecta bollandiana* 56 (1948): 134–98.

Pérez Gómez, Antonio. "La 'Passión trobada' de Diego de San Pedro." *Revista de literatura* 1 (1952): 147–82.

Perry, Anne Joubert Amari. *La Passion des jongleurs*. Paris, 1981.

Petrocchi, G. *Ascesi e mistica trecentesca*. Florence, 1957.

―――. "La letteratura religiosa." In *Storia della letteratura italiana: Le origini e il Duecento*, 1: 627–81. Milan, 1965.

―――. "Sulla composizione e data delle *Meditationes vitae Christi*." *Convivium* 20 (1952): 757–78.

Pfander, Homer G. *The Popular Sermon of the Medieval Friar in England*. New York, 1937.

Philippe, Marie-Dominique. "Le Mystère de la maternité divine de Marie." *Maria* 6 (1961): 369–416.

Pickering, F. P. *Literature and Art in the Middle Ages*. Coral Gables, Fla., 1970.

Pickering, Jerry V. *Theatre: A History of the Art*. New York, 1978.

Pietresson de Saint-Aubain, P. "La Passion de notre Seigneur Jésus Christ." *Bibliothèque de l'Ecole de Chartres* 85 (1924): 310–22.

Pignarre, Robert. *Histoire du théâtre*. Paris, 1957.

Pitra, Joannes Baptista. *Analecta sacra*. Vol. 1. Paris, 1876.

Pons, Joseph S. "Raymond Lulle et le Plant de Notre Dame Saint Marie." *Estudis universitaris Catalans* 12 (1936): 109–13.

Potter, Robert. *The English Morality Play*. Boston, 1975.

Pourrat, P. *La Spiritualité chrétienne*. 2 vols. Paris, 1947–51.

Predelli, Maria. "Notes sur la littérature populaire italienne du XIVe siècle." In *La Culture populaire au Moyen Age*, edited by Pierre Boglioni, pp. 185–200. Montreal, 1979.

Queirizza Gasca, G. "Intorno ad alcuni codici delle *Meditationes vitae Christi*." *Ar-*

chivum franciscanum historicum 55 (1962): 252–58; 56 (1963): 162–74; 57 (1964): 538–51.

Raby, F. J. E. *Christian Latin Poetry.* Oxford, 1953.

Ragazzini, S.-M. *La divina maternità di Maria nel suo concetto teologico integrale.* Roma-Longiano, 1948.

Ramon Lull. *Obras.* Edited by Salvador Galmés. Vol. 10. Madrid, 1915.

————. *Obras literarias.* Edited by Miguel Batllori and Miguel Caldentey. Madrid, 1948.

Regueiro, José M. "El *Auto de los Reyes Magos* y el teatro litúrgico medieval." *Hispanic Review* 45 (1977): 149–64.

————. "Rito y popularismo en el teatro antiguo español." *Romanische Forschungen* 89 (1977): 1–17.

Rey-Flaud, Henri. *Le Cercle magique: Essai sur le théâtre en rond à la fin du Moyen Age.* Paris, 1973.

Richstater, P. C., S.J. *Christusfrömmigkeit in ihrer historischen Entfaltung: Ein quellenmassiger Beitrag zur Geschichte des Gebets und des mystichen Innenleben der Kirche.* Cologne, 1949.

Robinson, J. W. "The Art of the York Realist." In *Medieval English Drama: Essays Critical and Contextual*, edited by Jerome Taylor and Alan H. Nelson, pp. 230–44. Chicago, 1972.

————. "The Late Medieval Cult of Jesus and the Mystery Plays." *PMLA* 80 (1965): 508–14.

Römer, G. "Die Liturgie der Karfreitags." *Zeitschrift für Katholische Theologie* 77 (1955): 208–13.

Roncaglia, Aurelio. "I primi passi del volgare." In *Storia della letteratura italiana: Le origini e il Duecento*, 1:180–241. Milan, 1965.

Roschini, G. M. "L'Ordre des Servites de Marie." *Maria* 2 (1952): 885–907.

Roschini, Gabriel P. "Corredemptio in S. Scriptura." In *Mariologia*, vol. 2, pt. 1, pp. 283–99. Rome, 1947.

————. "De modo quo B. Virgo animi dolorem sustinuit." In *Mariologia*, vol. 2, pt. 2, pp. 208–13. Rome, 1948.

Rudick, Michael. "Theme, Structure, and Sacred Context in the Benediktbeuern 'Passion' Play." *Speculum* 49 (1974): 267–86.

Ruggieri, Ruggero M. *Romanità e cristianesimo nell'europa medievale.* Rome, 1975.

Ruiz Ramón, Francisco. *Historia del teatro español.* Vol. 1. Madrid, 1948.

Runnalls, Graham A. "The French Passion Play Fragment of the University of Leiden." *Romania* 105 (1984): 88–110.

BIBLIOGRAPHY

————. *Le Mystère de la Passion Nostre Seigneur du manuscrit 1131 de la Bibliothèque Sainte-Geneviève.* Geneva, 1974.

Salaville, Severianus. "Christus in orientalium pietate: De pietate erga Christi humanitatem apud orientales liturgias et liturgicos commentatores." *Ephemerides liturgicae* 53, nos. 1–2 (1939): 13–59; 53, nos. 3–4 (1939): 350–85.

Salmon, Pierre. *L'Office divin.* Paris, 1959.

Sammaciccia, Bruno. *Trattato sulla passiologia: Storia esegetica della Passione di Gesù Cristo.* Pescara, 1978. This book is entirely without any scientific worth; it does not contain a single note or a single bibliographical reference.

Sandberg-Vavalà, Evelyn. *La croce dipinta italiana e l'iconografia della Passione.* Verona, 1929.

Sapegno, Natalino. *Frate Jacopone.* Naples, 1969.

Saugnieux, Joel. "La Tradition mariale et les 'Milagros' de Berceo." *Les Lettres romanes* 31 (1977): 32–65.

Schiller, Gertrude. *Iconography of Christian Art.* 2 vols. Translated by Janet Seligman. New York, 1972.

Schönbach, Anton. *Die Marienklagen.* Graz, 1874.

Schreiber, Cécil. "L'Univers compartimenté du théâtre médiéval." *French Review* 41 (1968): 468–78.

Schröder, A. "Die älteste Urkunde für St. Peter in Augsburg." *Zeitschrift des historischen Vereins für Schwaben und Neuburg* 50 (1932): 9–28.

Sepet, Marius. *Origines catholiques du théâtre moderne.* Paris, 1901.

Severin, Dorothy Sherman. "The Earliest Version of Diego de San Pedro's *La Passión Trobada.*" *Romanische Forschungen* 81 (1969): 176–92.

Sheinghorn, Pamela. "The *Sepulchrum Domini:* A Study in Art and Liturgy." *Studies in Iconography* 4 (1978): 37–60.

Shepard, William P. *La Passion provençale du manuscrit Didot.* Paris, 1928.

Shergold, N. D. *A History of the Spanish Stage from Medieval Times Until the End of the Seventeenth Century.* Oxford, 1967.

Simbula, Giuseppe. *La maternità spirituale di Maria in alcuni autori francescani dei secoli XIII–XIV.* Rome, 1967.

Sletjoe, Leif. "Quelques réflexions sur la naissance du théâtre religieux." In *Actes du Xe Congrès International de Linguistique et Philologie Romanes,* 2:667–75. Paris, 1965.

Smoldon, William L. "The Easter Sepulchre Music-Drama." *Music and Letters* 27 (1946): 1–17.

————. "Liturgical Drama." In *Early Medieval Music up to 1300,* edited by Dom

Anselm Hughes. New Oxford History of Music, 2: 176–219. New York, 1954.

———. *The Music of the Medieval Church Dramas.* Edited by Cynthia Bourgeault. London, 1980.

———. "The Origins of the Quem Queritis Trope and Easter Sepulchre Music-Dramas, as Demonstrated by Their Musical Settings." In *The Medieval Drama,* edited by Sandro Sticca, pp. 121–154. Albany, N.Y., 1972.

Spedalieri, Francesco P. *Maternità spirituale della Vergine.* Rome, 1968.

Spenz, Friedrich. *Die syntaktische Bildung des Achtsilbigen Verses in der Passion Christi und im Leodogar-Liede.* Marburg, 1887.

Spreckelmeyer, Goswin. *Das Kreuzzugslied des lateinischen Mittelalters.* Munich, 1974.

Stadlhuber, Josef. "Das Laienstundengebet vom Leiden Christi in seinem mittelalterlichen Fortleben." *Zeitschrift für katholische Theologie* 81–82 (1950): 282–325.

Stallings, Jordan M. *Meditaciones de Passione Christi olim Sancto Bonaventurae attributae.* Washington, D.C., 1965.

Stammler, Wolfgang. *Deutsche Philologie im Aufriss.* 3 vols. Berlin, 1954–59.

Sticca, Sandro. "Christian Drama and Christian Liturgy." *Latomus: Revue d'études latines* 26 (1967): 1025–34.

———. "The *Christos Paschon* and the Byzantine Theater." *Comparative Drama* 8 (1974): 13–44.

———. "Drama and Spirituality in the Middle Ages." *Mediaevalia et humanistica* 4 (1973): 69–87.

———. "The Dramatic Context of the Tours *Ludus paschalis* and the Sulmona Passion Fragment: A Study of Literary Influences." In *Le théâtre au Moyen Age,* edited by Gari R. Muller, pp. 85–115. Montreal, 1981.

———. "Dramma sacro e realismo comico nel teatro medioevale tedesco e francese (X–XII secoli): Da Hrotswitha di Ganderscheim al *Mystère d'Adam.*" In *L'eredità classica nel medioevo: Il linguaggio comico.* Atti del III Convegno di Studio, Viterbo, 26–28 May 1978, pp. 43–62. Viterbo, 1979.

———. "Italian Theater of the Middle Ages: From the *Quem quaeritis* to the *Lauda.*" *Forum italicum* 14 (1980): 275–310.

———. *The Latin Passion Play.* Albany, N.Y., 1970.

———. "The Literary Genesis of the Latin Passion Play and the Planctus Mariae: A New Christocentric and Marian Theology." In *The Medieval Drama,* pp. 49–63. Albany, 1972.

———. *Sulmona ed il teatro medievale abruzzese.* Sulmona, 1980.

Stimulus amoris Fr. Jacobi Mediolanensis. Bibliotheca franciscana ascetica Medii Aevi, vol. 4. Quaracchi, 1905.

Sturdivant, Winifred. *The Misterio de los Reyes Magos: Its Position in the Development of the Medieval Legend of the Three Kings*. Baltimore, 1927; rpt. ed, New York, 1973.

Surtz, Ronald E. "El teatro en la Edad Media." In *Historia del teatro en España*, edited by José María Díez Borque, pp. 63–174. Madrid, 1983.

Szövérffy, Joseph. "L'Hymnologie médiévale: Recherches et méthodes." *Cahiers de civilisation medievale* 4 (1961): 389–422.

————. "Kreislauf von Ideen und Bildern: Randbemerkungen zum mittelalterlichen Drama, zur Hymnendichtung und Ikonographie." *Zeitschrift für romanische Philologie* 77 (1961): 289–98.

Taylor, George C. "The English Planctus Mariae." *Modern Philology* 4 (1906–7): 605–37.

Terracini, Benvenuto. "Un dramma della Passione del secolo XII." *Archivio glottologico italiano* 29 (1937): 92–94.

Terruggia, Angela. "Lo sviluppo del dramma sacro visto attraverso i codici di Assisi." In *Atti del Centro Studi Origini del Teatro Italiano*, from *Annuario XI*, *Accademia Etrusca di Cortona*, pp. 171–98. Cortona, 1960.

Thien, H. *Ueber die englischen Marienklagen*. Kiel, 1906.

Thiry, Claude. *La Plainte funèbre*. Typologie des Sources du Moyen Age Occidental, no. 30. Brepols, 1978.

Thiry, Paul. *Le théâtre français au Moyen Age*. Brussels, 1944.

Thomas, Michael. "Zur Rolle der '*Meditationes vitae Christi*' innerhalb der europäische Bild-Entwicklung der *Giotto-Zeit*." In *Miscellanea codicologica F. Masai Dicata*, edited by Pierre Cockshaw, Monique-Cécile Garand, and Pierre Jodogne, 2:319–30. Ghent, 1979.

Thomas, Paul Lucien. *Le "Sponsus": Mystère des vierges sages et des vierges folles suivi des trois poèmes limousins et farcis*. Paris, 1951.

Tischendorf, Constantinus. *Evangelia apocrypha*. Leipzig, 1876.

Torroja Menéndez, Carmen, and Maria Rivas Palá. *Teatro en Toledo en el siglo XV: 'Auto de la Pasión' de Alonso del Campo*. Anejos del Boletin de la Real Academia Española, no. 35. Madrid, 1977.

Tortoreto, Walter. *Genesi di una sacra rappresentazione abruzzese: Deputazione abruzzese di storia patria, studi e testi*. Vol. 3. Aquila, 1983.

Toschi, Paolo. *L'antico dramma sacro italiano*. 2 vols. Florence, 1955.

————. *L'antico teatro religioso italiano*. Matera, 1966.

————. *Dal dramma liturgico alla rappresentazione sacra*. Florence, 1940.

————. "Narrazione e dramma nel nostro antico teatro religioso." *Rivista italiana del dramma* 2 (1937): 159–80.

————. *Le origini del teatro italiano.* Turin, 1955.

————. "L'origine romana del dramma liturgico." *Rivista italiana del dramma* 3 (1938): 257–68.

————. *Il valore attuale ed eterno della poesia di Jacopone.* Res Tudertinae, no. 4. Todi, 1964.

Toubert, Hélène. "Iconographie et histoire de la spiritualité médiévale." *Revue d'histoire de la spiritualité* 50 (1947): 265–84.

Travis, Peter W. *Dramatic Design in the Chester Cycle.* Chicago, 1982.

Trens, Manuel. *El arte en la Pasión de nuestro Señor.* Barcelona, 1945.

Trifoglio, Francesco. "Il Christus Patiens: Rassegna delle attribuzioni." *Rivista di Studi Classici* 22 (1974): 351–423.

Turrin, H. J. "'Aureo flore' and the Question of Dating the Tradition of Marian Veneration in the Medieval West." *Mittellateinisches Jahrbuch* 14 (1979): 76–88.

Tydeman, William. *The Theatre in the Middle Ages.* Cambridge, 1978.

Ubertinus de Casali. *Arbor vitae crucifixae.* Edited by Charles T. Davis. Turin, 1961.

Ugolini, Francesco. *Testi volgari abruzzesi del Duecento.* Turin, 1959.

Ulbert-Schede, Ute. *Das Andachtsbild des kreuztragenden Christus in der deutschen Kunst.* Munich, 1968.

Vagaggini, C. *Maria nelle opere di Origene.* Rome, 1942.

Valbuena Prat, Angel. *Historia del teatro español.* Barcelona, 1956.

Vandenbroucke, François, Jean Leclercq, and Louis Bouyer. *La Spiritualité du Moyen Age.* Paris, 1961.

Vannutelli, Primus. *Actorum Pilati textus synoptici.* Rome, 1938.

Varanini, Giorgio. *Lamenti storici pisani.* Pisa, 1968.

————. *Laude dugentesche.* Padua, 1972.

Vattaso, Marco. *Per la storia del dramma sacro in Italia.* Rome, 1959.

Vauchez, A. *La spiritualité du Moyen Age occidental (VIIIe–XIIe siècles).* Paris, 1975.

Vecchi, Giuseppe. *Due studi sui ritmi latini del Medio Evo.* Bologna, 1967.

————. "Innodia e dramma sacro." *Studi mediolatini e volgari* 1 (1953): 225–37.

————. *Pietro Abelardo: I "Planctus."* Modena, 1951.

————. *Uffici drammatici padovani.* Florence, 1954.

Vernet, Felix. *La Spiritualité médiévale.* Paris, 1929.

Vignaux, Paul. "Le Christocentrisme de saint Bonaventure et le problème d'une philosophie de la religion." *Contributi di spiritualità bonaventuriana.* Atti del

Simposio Internazionale, Padua, 15–18 September 1974. 3 vols., edited by Giorgio Zoppetti and Davide Maria Montagna, 1: 29–53. Padua, 1974–75.

Villanueva, Jaime. *Viaje a Solsona, Ager y Urgel, 1806 y 1807.* Vol. 9 of *Viaje literario a las iglesias de España.* Valencia, 1821.

Viller, R. P. *La Spiritualité des premiers siècles chrétiens.* Paris, 1930.

Visani, Oriana. "Pubblico e tempi del Quaresimale Padovano del 1455 di Roberto Caracciolo da Lecce." *Giornale storico della letteratura italiana* 157 (1980): 541–56.

Vivian, Dorothy Sherman. " 'La Passión trobada' de Diego de San Pedro, y sus relaciones con el drama medieval de la Pasión." *Anuario de estudios medievales* 1 (1964): 451–70.

Vogel, C. "Introduction aux sources de l'histoire du culte chrétien au Moyen Age." *Studi medievali,* ser. 3, vol. 3 (1962): 1–92.

Vogt, Albert. "Etudes sur le théâtre byzantin." *Byzantion* 6 (1931): 35–75.

Vona, Costantino. *Omelie mariologiche di S. Giacomo di Sarug.* Rome, 1953.

Von Rieden, Oktavian P. "Das Leiden Christi im Leben des Hl. Franziskus von Assisi: Eine quellenvergleichende Untersuchung im Lichte der zeitgenossischen Passionsfrömmigkeit." *Collectanea franciscana* 30 (1960): 5–30, 129–45, 241–63, 353–97.

Von Simon, Otto. "*Compassio* and *Co-redemptio* in Roger van der Weyden's *Descent from the Cross.*" *Art Bulletin* 35 (1953): 9–16.

Wagenaar-Nolthenius, Hélène. "Sur la construction musicale du drame liturgique." *Cahiers de civilisation médiévale* 3 (1960): 449–56.

Weber, Sarah Appleton. *Theology and Poetry in the Middle English Lyric.* Columbus, Ohio, 1969.

Wechssler, Eduard. *Die romanischen Marienklagen.* Halle, 1893.

Weitzmann, K. "The Origin of the Threnos." In *De artibus opuscula XL: Essays in Honor of Erwin Panofsky,* edited by M. Meiss, 1:476–90. New York, 1961.

Wellner, Franz. *Adam von Sankt-Victor samtliche Sequenzen.* Vienna, 1937.

Wenger, Antoine. *L'Assomption de la T.S. Vierge dans la tradition byzantine du VIe au Xe siècle.* Institut Français d'Etudes Byzantines. Paris, 1955.

Werner, Wilfred. *Studien zu den Passions und Osterspielen des deutschen Mittelalters in ihrem Ubergang vom Latein zur Volkssprache.* Berlin, 1963.

West, Larry E. *The Saint Gall Passion Play.* Brookline, Mass., 1976.

Whinnom, Keith. "The Supposed Sources of Inspiration of Spanish Fifteenth-Century Narrative Religious Verse." *Symposium* 17 (1963): 268–91.

Wickham, Glynne. *Early English Stages 1300–1660.* 2 vols. London, 1959–72.

Wilmart, A. *Auteurs spirituels et textes dévots du Moyen Age*. Paris, 1932.

———. "Cinq textes de prière composés par Anselme de Lucques pour la comtesse Mathilde." *Revue d'ascétique et de mystique* 19 (1938): 23–72.

Wilmotte, M. *Les Passions allemandes du Rhin dans leur rapport avec l'ancien théâtre français*. Paris, 1898.

Wilson, Robert. "The Stanzaic Life of Christ and the Chester Plays." *Studies in Philology* 27 (1931): 413–432.

Wolff, Edwin, "Die Terminologie des mittelalterlichen Dramas in bedeutungsgeschichtlicher Sicht." *Anglia* 78 (1960): 1–27.

Wolpers, Theodor. "Englische Marienlyrik im Mittelalter." *Anglia* 69 (1950): 3–88.

Woolf, Rosemary. *The English Mystery Plays*. Berkeley, 1972.

Wright, Edith A. *The Dissemination of the Liturgical Drama in France*. Bryn Mawr, 1936.

Wright, William. *A Short History of Syriac Literature*. 2d ed. Amsterdam, 1966.

Yearley, Janthia. "A Bibliography of Planctus in Latin, Provencal, French, German, English, Italian, Catalan, and Gallician-Portuguese from the Time of Bede to the Early Fifteenth Century." *Journal of the Plainsong and Medieval Music Society* 4 (1981): 12-52. This is an incomplete bibliography. The author does not differentiate among liturgical Planctus, funeral Planctus and Planctus of other types. This list does, however, represent a good beginning for the complete classification of the genre.

Young, Karl. *The Drama of the Medieval Church*. 2 vols. Oxford, 1933.

——— "Observations on the Origin of the Medieval Passion Play." *PMLA* 25 (1910): 309-54.

Zafarana, Zelina. "Pietà e devozione in San Bonaventura." In *S. Bonaventura francescano*. Convegni del Centro di Studi sulla Spiritualità Medievale, Todi, 14–17 October 1973, pp. 129-57. Todi, 1974.

Zumthor, Paul. *Essai de poétique médiévale*. Paris, 1972.

———. *Langue et téchnique poétiques à l'époque romane (XIe–XIIe siècles)*. Paris, 1963.

———. "Un Problème d'esthétique médiévale: L'Utilisation poétique du bilinguisme." *Le Moyen Age* 66 (1960): 301–36, 561–94.

INDEX

Abruzzi: *Lamentatio Beate Marie de Filio*, 29–30, 130–32, 145–46, 170, 186 (n. 39), 197 (n. 29)

Accarie, Maurice, 153

Acta Pilati B, 33, 34, 42

Adam of St. Victor: *Maestae parentis Christi* (*planctus*), 71, 77–78; *De trinitate, Heri mundus exultavit*, and *Gratulemur ad festivum*, 96; *versus tripartitus caudatus*, 96

Adoratio Crucis, 126, 133, 150, 151

Adriani, Ioannis Baptistae, 104

Aelred of Rievaulx, 55

Ager, *Planctus Sanctae Mariae Virginis*, 147, 148, 149, 170, 173

Alan de Lille, 20, 55

Alberic of Montecassino, 55

Albert the Great, 24, 25, 26, 27; Mary as *co-adiutrix et socia passionis*, 24, 25

Alborg, Juan Luis, 168

Alexander, bishop of Alexandria: *theotókos* in his *Epistola ad Alexandrum episcopum Constantinopolitanum*, 53

Alfonso X, the Wise: *Siete Partidas*, 162, 163

Alonso del Campo, *Auto de la Pasión*, 168

Alsfelder Passionsspiel, 121, 158

Alt Passional, 121

Ambrogio Autperto, 54; *Sermo CXXIV*, 55

Ambrose, Saint: *Epistola LXIII* and *De institutione Virginis*, 19; *De obitu Valentiniani*, 20; *Expositio in Psalmum XLIV* and *Homilia in sanctam Drosiden*, 53; Eva-Ave contrast, 52, 53

Anselm, Saint: *Dialogus de Passione Domini*, 7, 55, 103, 104; Mary as *mater restitutionis omnium*, 55, 189 (n. 25); *compassio*, 64, 65, 102, 103; *Oratio XX*, 65, 103

Anselm of Lucca, Saint, 55, 106

Arnauld of Bonnevalle, 23, 57; *De septem verbis Domini in cruce*, 23, 184–85 (n. 21); *De laudis Beatae Mariae Virginis*, 24, 106, 107

Arnold, John, 153

A Stanzaic Life of Christ, 120, 159

Auerbach, Erich, 177, 181 (n. 49), 208 (n. 32)

Augsburger Passionslied, 149, 150, 151; *planctus* in, 149, 150, 170

Augustine, Saint, 53

Auto de los Reyes Magos, 163, 166